Volume TWO

THE FORGOTTEN WAR

A PICTORIAL HISTORY OF WORLD WAR II IN ALASKA AND NORTHWESTERN CANADA

Volume TWO

THE FORGOTTEN WAR

A PICTORIAL HISTORY OF WORLD WAR II IN ALASKA AND NORTHWESTERN CANADA

BY STAN COHEN

PICTORIAL HISTORIES PUBLISHING COMPANY
MISSOULA, MONTANA

LIBRARY OF CONGRESS
CATALOG CARD NUMBER 81-80570

ISBN 0-933126-70-0

First Printing: December 1988
Second Printing: June 1989

Typography: Arrow Graphics, Missoula, Montana
Cover Design: Kirk Johnson, Missoula, Montana

PRINTED IN CANADA

PICTORIAL HISTORIES PUBLISHING COMPANY
713 South Third West, Missoula, Montana 59801

INTRODUCTION

Since the publication of *The Forgotten War*, seven years ago, this subject has been of expanding interest. I have been fortunate enough to visit the Aleutian Islands three times, while still making my yearly summer visit to Alaska and Northwestern Canada, mostly by the Alaska Highway. I have talked to and have corresponded with hundreds of veterans of the war in the North Country and have received many photos, stories, advice and corrections from these contacts. I have also attended several reunions of groups that participated in some phase of the "Forgotten War."

The interest in this out of the way theater of war has been amazing. My book has gone through nine printings and has been shipped throughout the world. Several other books which I have written or published on the subject have also sold throughout the world.

A movie was commissioned in 1985 by the Alaska Legislature to portray the state's role in World War II. Several first person accounts by participants have been published and many newspaper articles have been written. In March 1985, the Aleutian Campaign was featured on a CBS evening news report. The 40th anniversary of the opening of the Alaska Highway produced several seminars, celebrations and the publication of a book. Monuments have been erected by both Japanese and American veterans at various sites in the Aleutians.

Interest in this subject is still expanding as we approach the 50th anniversary of the 1942 Japanese invasion and the subsequent repulsion of the enemy troops in 1943. I would hope that some of this interest has been spurred on by my first book and also by my subsequent publications.

Since publication of my first volume, hundreds of new photos have come to light, along with volumes of additional information. Much of it is presented in this second volume. A third volume is in production, concentrating on subjects not covered in the first two volumes.

I did not deem it necessary to restate the narrative of cer-

tain events from the first volume except where it was critical to explain the photos in this volume. In many of these chapters, I use little or no narrative at all and have let the photos tell the story. One should refer to the first volume for needed information.

I have re-used photos from the first volume in only a few instances where I thought it was important for the photo essay, i.e., the downed zero on Akutan Island. There are literally thousands of photos available of most of the events that occurred in this battle zone from 1940-1945, and as I previously stated, a third volume is in the works.

It is very gratifying to me that this little-known theater of World War II is finally getting its due place in history. It has always amazed me—and even more so now that I have been able to visit some of the sites—how much actually went on in this theater once the military was forced to go into action after the Pearl Harbor attack.

Just driving the Alaska Highway today gives one a feel of what the troops had to endure in the 1942-43 construction days. The massive construction remains that I have visited at Dutch Harbor, Adak, Atka, Amchita and Cold Bay still amaze me. I regret that I have not had the opportunity to visit remains at Umnak Island, Kiska, Attu (I landed there for 15 minutes), and other places, but I'd like to someday. Although there are only a few quonset hut sites left on St. Paul Island in the Pribilofs, I was fortunate enough to spend five days there in the summer of 1987.

I hope this book will again give the reader, whether a veteran of the conflict or just an interested party, a more in-depth view of our "Forgotten War." Since I know this volume will eventually get into the hands of many veterans, I welcome letters or calls concerning the different articles in this book.

May this be the last book that I or any other author can write that brings the horrors of war so close to America's shores.

Stan Cohen

Acknowledgments

The second volume of the *Forgotten War* would not have been possible without the help and support of a number of people throughout the United States and Canada. First, I would like to thank John Cloe, historian for the Alaskan Air Command and Lyman Woodman, Lt. Col. retired, USAF, both in Anchorage who have helped me for many years and reviewed this manuscript. The staffs of the Yukon Archives in Whitehorse, Alaska State Library in Juneau, University of Alaska Archives, Anchorage Museum of History & Art, National Archives, Library of Congress, U.S. Army, Navy, Air Force and Marine Corps archives, Public Archives of Canada, Provincial Archives of British Columbia, Glenbow Archives in Calgary and the U.S. Army Corps of Engineers office in Anchorage, who were very helpful with photo research and information. Also helpful in my Alaska research were the Alaskan Air Command and Reeve Aleutian Airways.

The following people have provided photos or information for this book: Peter Ornawka, Hollywood, Fla.; Lawrence White, Minneapolis, Minn.; Bob Yeiter, Pasadena, Texas; Earl Brown, Fort Nelson, B.C.; Marwood Siverts, Fresno, Calif.; Gladys Anderson Nakkan, Minneapolis, Minn.; J. Penelepe Goforth, Unalaska, Alaska; Mike Bouchette, Appleton, Wis.; George Estes, Sioux City, Iowa; Ted Spencer, Anchorage, Alaska; James Mullen, Valentine, Nev.; Harold Womble, Stockton, Calif.; Russell Gettleman, Green Bay, Wis.; Mrs. Ingrid Curtin, Menaska, Wis.; Paul Bloom, Oakland, Calif.; Frank Davis, Cincinnati, Ohio; Kenneth Robb, New Harmony, Ind.; George Roekriek, Faribault, Minn.; William Lattin, Jr., Ketchikan, Alaska; E.B. Bonnet, New Orleans, La.; Bob Viets, Harlingen, Texas; Tom Keely, Flushing, Mich.; Turk Harshbarger, Jerome, Idaho; Margaret Weatherly, Anchorage, Alaska; Chuck Middleton, Ketchikan, Alaska; Leonard Vandenberg, Kalamazoo, Mich.; Stacy Dobrzensky, Oakland, Calif.; Col. Robert D. Feer, Galena, Alaska; Adm. James Russell, Tacoma, Wash.; Walter Lord, New York City; Byrnes Ellender, Billings, Mont. (7th Ferrying Group Association); Dean Brandon, Medford, Ore.; Bob Real, Banning, Calif.; Adm. W.M. Leonard, Virginia Beach, Va.; Al Makiel, Calument City, Ill.; R.M. Weikel, Missoula, Mont.; William House, Valley Center, Calif.; Col. Irving Payne, West Long Beach, N.J.; Capt. N.G. Terry, Jr., San Antonio, Texas; and Art Jones, Sequim, WA.

PHOTO SOURCES

AAC—Alaskan Air Command
AMHA—Anchorage Museum of History & Art
AP—Associated Press
ASL—Alaska State Library
GA—Glenbow Archives
JRC—Adm. James Russell Collection
LC—Library of Congress
NA—National Archives
PABC—Public Archives of British Columbia
PAC—Public Archives of Canada
RF—Richard Finnie Collection, Yukon Archives
USA—U.S. Army Archives
USAF—U.S. Air Force Archives
USMC—U.S. Marine Corps Archives
USN—U.S. Navy Archives
YA—Yukon Archives

The Aleutian Campaign Not A Diversion To Draw The American Fleet From Midway

by Walter Lord*

*Author of *Day of Infamy* about the Pearl Harbor attack and *Incredible Victory* about the Battle of Midway.

November 16, 1968

The Aleutian phase of the Japanese Midway operation was more a political sop than anything else. None of the reviewers picked this up, yet I felt that it was one of the most interesting points that I uncovered. Hitherto, all accounts of Midway had always stressed that the Aleutian operation was a "diversion" to draw our fleet away from the real target, Midway. Yet this never made sense to me, because it would have drawn our Hawaii-based ships toward there rather than away from there. Besides, everyone agrees that the basic objective of the Japanese was to trap our fleet into a decisive Naval engagement, and if that were so, why any diversion at all?

Hence I was fascinated and quickly convinced when Commander Tsunoda, the resident expert on Midway at the Japanese War History Office told me what he stressed were the real facts. According to Tsunoda, it all went back to a feud between the planners of the Imperial Combined Fleet and those in the War Plans Section of the Naval General Staff. In American Naval terms this would be comparable to a feud between Nimitz's staff and King's staff in Washington.

Combined Fleet under Admiral Yamamoto was the real sponsor of the Midway operation. The War Plans Section of Naval General Staff opposed the idea. They felt the plan was much too risky, and also the possibility of the inferior U.S. Fleet attacking at that point was much too small. But Admiral Nagano, who was chief of the Naval General Staff, overruled his own War Plans Section and approved Yamamoto's project. This left the members of the War Plans Section disgruntled and embittered.

It happened that at that time the Japanese Naval Command in charge of the North Pacific area was very anxious for the capture of Kiska and Attu as a safety measure against U.S. air attacks from the north. Hence when the War Plans Section supported this project and felt that it should take place at the same time as the Midway operation, Yamamoto quickly agreed more or less as a way of placating this group. Moreover, during the war games held at the time of the Ceylon campaign, U.S. aircraft theoretically based in the Aleutians had made a successful raid against Tokyo, and this helped strengthen the proposal of neutralizing the Aleutians. It was further strengthened by the fact that the Japanese knew about the B-29 and expected it would be in operation before too long. It all added up to Admiral Yamamoto's approving the Aleutian proposal on April 5, 1942.

Later in my research I was in touch with Commander Tsunoda again, stressing to him that all previous accounts had called the Aleutian operation a diversion. He again said that the Japanese fleet was so strong at the time that no diversion was necessary and that the real reasons were those he had outlined.

AUTHOR'S NOTE: The Americans did in fact bomb Tokyo with the Doolittle Tokyo Raid of April 18, 1942. At the time the Japanese didn't know where the bombers came from. The Aleutians was one possibility. In fact, they flew off the deck of the carrier *Hornet*, 600 miles from Tokyo, a highly risky maneuver. This raid had some influence on the upcoming battle off Midway Island and the Aleutian invasion.

Contents

Review at Fort Richardson in 1941 for Lt. Gen. John L. DeWitt, commander of the Western Theater of Operations. AMHA

RMR Brass & Bugle Band (Active Forces) on parade while stationed at Prince Rupert, British Columbia, 1941. PABC

BAND. A.F.
E RUPERT 1941.

CHAPTER ONE
NORTH COUNTRY
AT WAR

HEADQUARTERS ALASKA DEFENSE COMMAND
Fort Richardson, Alaska
October 14, 1941

More than a year has passed since the Alaska Defense Command first came into being. That year has seen our numbers increase from a mere handful of men camped in snow-covered tents to a respectable force determined to meet hostile enterprises and deal with them effectively. It has seen a vast construction program, the building of air bases, the fortification of these bases and the initiation of a training program calculated to weld our units into a fighting machine.

Our year in Alaska has witnessed more than this. It has seen men from Southern States become hardened to a severe climate and enjoying the outdoors on snowshoes, ice skates and skis. It has seen men accustomed to luxurious living and highly developed artificial amusement centers laugh off minor discomforts and inconveniences and display commendable initiative in developing recreational facilities from the resources at hand. It has seen a minimum of whimpering and a maximum of straightforward American manhood among our officers and soldiers. For those who have built up this manly spirit that exists in our command, I have nothing but the highest of praise, and I have every confidence that their fighting qualities can be counted on in an emergency.

With the ever increasing seriousness of our international situation, it has become necessary to reinforce Alaskan garrisons at a rate far beyond the ability of construction forces to provide the comforts and conveniences normally enjoyed by peacetime garrisons. Many of our troops are, and will be for some time to come, living under conditions which while not comparable to actual field service, are nevertheless less comfortable than can be expected under normal conditions. This is taken as a matter of course by every good soldier and in no way dampens the spirit of a man of fortitude and patriotism. At times, perhaps, it may cause a little temporary grumbling on the part of individuals who have been softened by luxury and have not yet come to a full realization of the fact that a nation and institutions built by manhood and fortitude can continue to exist only so long as it is defended by men of like fiber.

Ample evidence exists that the enemies of our country are, at the present moment, conducting an insidious campaign of propaganda calculated to undermine morale by attempting to make our soldiers feel sorry for themselves, become disgruntled and complain of mistreatment. Our papers, our magazines and some of our associates are full of subtle propaganda of this nature. If we are not on guard against it, we are likely to play into the hands of our enemies.

I feel confident that a word of warning will suffice in this matter. We are here on a serious mission but, after all, we can have plenty of fun if we look for it and don't wait for it to look for us. Let your letters home be cheerful, harden yourselves against minor discomforts, and let your enemies learn not only that you can "take it" but that you are prepared to hand out to them a good deal more than they can take.

/s/ S. B. BUCKNER, Jr.
Major General, U.S. Army.,
Commanding

/jws
DISTRIBUTION: "A" and "B"

Pacific Coast Militia Rangers (local militia in Dawson) marching along Front Street in Dawson, Yukon Territory, 1941. YA, HARE COLLECTION

The 924th Quartermaster Company Boat (Aviation)

Due to Alaska's unusual defense requirements and remoteness from the continental U.S., some military units were formed that did not fit the normal mode of operations. The Army Air Corps established the 924th Quartermaster Company Boat (Aviation) as a seaborne rescue operation in Ketchikan in February 1942. About half of the 500 men eventually recruited were Alaskans who had had previous maritime experience. Their duty was to patrol and perform rescue missions for downed pilots along Alaska's long coastal area from Annette Island to the Aleutian Chain.

Maj. Everett Davis, commander of the fledgling Alaska Air Force, came up with the idea for rescue boats soon after he arrived at Elmendorf Air Base in 1940. With weather conditions in Alaska far different than the pilots in his command were accustomed to, Davis checked with the Air Corps Supply Depot in Sacramento to see if there was any type of small vessel that he could obtain to use in rescue operations for downed pilots in Cook Inlet.

He was told that two 22-foot Chris-Craft speedboats were already on their way north to be placed into service. And additional contracts were let for much larger craft.

Several months before the Pearl Harbor attack, Lt. Gordon Donley was placed in charge of the two boats, and he proposed a plan to form a squadron of the boats that were being built. He enlisted as many Alaskans with small boat experience as he could and received help from the U.S. Coast Guard in Ketchikan.

Twenty-nine men were in the initial unit and they were housed at the New England Fish Company cannery in Ketchikan. They were later moved to barracks at Ward Lake, but when native evacuees started coming in from the Aleutians after the Dutch Harbor attack, the men were transferred to Annette Island.

When the unit was formed in 1942, it had two 42-foot boats for training. When larger vessels became available at California shipyards, they were brought north by men of the unit.

In all, the 924th had five small speed boats, one 39-footer, five 42-footers, five 85-footers, 14 104-footers and one 150-foot aircraft retrieving and supply vessel.

For over two years, these boats patrolled the entire Alaska coast, completing over 100 missions and assisting over 200 people—both downed fliers and other troops. They never lost a man or vessel in these operations. This is a real tribute to these men, who were operating in some of the roughest waters and worst weather conditions in any theater of war.

In 1943, the 924th was officially changed to the 10th Army Air Force Emergency Rescue Boat Squadron. The squadron was disbanded in August 1945, and all the boats were sold. One, the P-115 (a 104-footer), was converted to a fishing boat and returned to Alaska.

The first reunion of men who served in this unit was held in Anchorage in October 1986 in conjunction with the 11th Air Force Reunion.

Lumber Operations

Extensive military construction in Alaska demanded the use of vast quantities of lumber. Numerous small logging and sawmill operations were carried on by the Army to meet local needs. However, the total output from such sources was but a fractional part of the demands. Lumber, in the quantities needed, was shipped from mills operating in the Pacific Northwest—particularly Oregon and Washington. In view of the lack of adequate shipping space and the long haul involved, it was necessary to augment even this source.

The combined efforts of southeastern Alaska lumber mills produced an average monthly total of approximately seven million board feet of lumber during the summer months. In order to take advantage of this additional source, it was decided to contract for practically the entire output. This was done, although in several cases only a portion of a mill's entire output was contracted for. The demands of other governmental agencies as well as civilian needs has to be met. These operations required coordination and in March 1943, Mr. James W. Huston, then Resident Engineer at Juneau, was appointed Lumber Coordinator, acting under the Commanding General, Alaska Defense Command.

Lumber requisitions from both the District Engineer and from this Headquarters were passed on to Mr. Huston for fulfillment. He placed the requisitions on order with the mills and then arranged for the shipment of the lumber to the various Alaskan projects when the orders were ready for shipment. Authority was granted to make lumber releases to governmental and civilian agencies; however, civilian releases were not to be in such amounts as to jeopardize cutting schedules. When the orders were complete, the lumber was turned over to the Army Transport Service for shipment.

In addition and to further supplement the supply, Lend-Lease arrangements were made with the Russian Government to furnish approximately 22 million board feet of rough lumber. The first shipment arrived and was discharged at the ports of Seward and Fort Randall in January 1943. Plans were under way, as of November 1943, to obtain an additional 20 million feet under this reverse Lend-Lease arrangement.

Danger Bay Sawmill on Afognak Island, operated by the 799th Engineering Forestry Company, 1942 and 1943. The old sawmill was moved in 1947-48 to Afognak Straits near the Afognak village. It was in operation until 1964 when the Alaskan Tidal Wave destroyed it. COURTESY GEORGE ROCHRICK, FARIBAULT, MINNESOTA

Log pond and chain for pulling logs into the mill.

Mess hall at lumber operation. Constructed in 1943.

A stiff leg or hoist, used to hoist small boats out of the harbor.

A power barge used to ship lumber down the chain.

Rest period for troops somewhere in the Aleutians, 1942. USA SC 140056

The Military's First Radio Station

In the United States, commercial broadcasting supplied the news, sports, and entertainment, only occasionally directing programs toward the soldier audience in those areas where a concentration of military facilities existed. In Panama and the Philippines, soldiers could listen to English language stations which existed to satisfy the needs of United States civilians working in the country for the American government and commercial interests. By the late 1930s, KGEI in San Francisco was beaming shortwave broadcasts to the Philippines with programming oriented to the U.S. military.

After the Japanese attacked the Philippines on December 8, 1941, the American radio stations went off the air, destroyed either in the initial assaults or by the retreating U.S. and Filipino forces. As these troops left for Corregidor, they did carry away some equipment from the stations. From these scattered pieces, the soldiers were to quickly put a station on the air to counteract the propaganda station which the Japanese set up after they captured Manila. *Voice of Freedom* came into being through the efforts of Manual Quezon, President of the Philippines, General Douglas MacArthur, and Carlos Romulo, publisher of the *Philippine Herald*. Once on Corregidor, Quezon saw the need for a station to provide a means of establishing communications with the Philippine people and the American forces on Bataan. Agreeing with the idea, MacArthur directed on January 1, 1942, that the station be put on the air in 48 hours and provided the name, *Voice of Freedom*.

Once in operation, the station broadcast three times a day. The programs included news commentaries, items of local interest and records which the retreating forces had apparently brought with them. Carlos Romulo also broadcast appeals to the Filipino and American people to unite against the Japanese invaders. As one American officer noted, most of the programming was propaganda "so thick that it served no purpose except to disgust us and incite mistrust of all hopes." Part of the reason for the awareness of the deteriorating military situation in the Philippines was the broadcasts from KGEI, which beamed a "Freedom for the Philippines" program each night to which most of the men listened until the capture of Bataan on April 8.

The short-lived *Voice of Freedom* station does not in fact lay claim to the title of the first United States military radio station. By the time it began broadcasting on Corregidor in January 1942, soldiers stationed in Alaska had put two radio stations on the air. Responding to the increasing tensions with Japan, the War Department had begun to send troops to Alaska in early 1941. The units stationed in widely scattered locales found themselves with little to do in their spare time. Alaska had few commercial radio stations, none of which reached the remote military bases. In mid-March 1941, two servicemen at the military installation in Sitka began broadcasting to their fellow soldiers in an attempt to fill a void in news and entertainment. Using make-shift equipment and the call letters KRB, the men played records which they scrounged from soldiers and recruited local talent to play live music and perform short skits. Ultimately, the FCC found out about the unauthorized station and ordered it shut down.

Likewise, at Fort Greely, on Kodiak Island, the soldiers took it upon themselves to start a radio station to fill the men's need for news and entertainment. Capt. William Adams, the base finance officer provided the impetus in October when he put a notice in the post paper of a meeting for all those who might be interested in forming a radio station. About a dozen men turned up and were divided into an engineering committee to work on assembling a small transmitter and a production committee to develop when they "broadcast" a variety show using a crystal mike set up in the lounge of the officers' quarters to carry a live band, singers and a skit by cable to the mess hall.

The ingenuity of the men and their enthusiasm quickly encouraged the expansion of the operation into a full blown radio operation. Civilian workers on military construction projects on Kodiak contributed money raised in three lotteries in November and J.C. Henry, the contractor's general superintendent used it to buy necessary equipment in Seattle. To house the new station in permanent headquarters, the contractor and his men volunteered their time to build a station on an empty piece of land near Lake Louise. By the middle of December, the soldier/broadcasters were able to begin unofficial, test operations a few hours a day with the programs reaching into the town of Kodiak.

KODK, as the staff named the new station, began full-time operations on January 1, 1942, broadcasting from 7 a.m. to 10 p.m. Initially, the schedule consisted primarily of recorded music and newscasts, but soon began to include a variety of live programs ranging from bands and singers to plays, using both military personnel and local talent whom the station gladly used irrespective of their ability. The quality of live performance went up briefly in March when comedian

Joe E. Brown arrived in Kodiak on his one-man, 33-day tour of Alaskan military facilities. KODK was the only radio station in operation he found during his travels and he appeared on the air several times during his stay.

For the most part, the station had to make use of records it could locate among the men on the base. In the first days of operation, it took only four hours to run through the entire record library, but the situation improved as people brought in their own discs. Joe E. Brown also contributed to the programming after he got back to Hollywood by having his friends in the entertainment business begin to send transcriptions of their radio broadcasts to KODK. The station further increased its range in May when it did its first remote, covering the dedication of the new chapel by hooking an amplifier into a telephone line. Subsequently, the station carried the Sunday services to men on duty every week.

Each of the outfits at Fort Greely was assigned certain times in which it could put on its own radio show. As a result, the station was able to carry programs ranging from Mountaineer music to sentimental cowboy songs to band music. The "Kodiak Press Club" put on a series of extravaganzas, running the gamut from murder mysteries to tales of thwarted love in Kodiak fishing villages. In the end, the station was able to survive and prosper through hard work and the type of planning which produced balanced programs providing radio fare for all segments of its audience. In November, KODK moved to temporary quarters in the old post library building while its facilities underwent remodeling to improve broadcast quality. The three studios were better soundproofed and the control room was set on four concrete blocks to assure steadiness of equipment. On December 5, the station returned to its renovated building with the new call letters WCVQ and an official operating license from the FCC.

By then, both independently of any knowledge of KODK's existence and later by example, other stations began to appear on military bases throughout Alaska. At Sitka, in February 1942, soldiers again started a station to provide entertainment and news to the bored soldiers at the remote facility. Pvt. Charles Gilliam, a radio technician in civilian life, had picked up a supply of radio parts in Seattle, while in transit to Fort Ray at Sitka. Once there, assigned to the artillery radio facility, Gilliam and Pvt. Robert Nelson, responding to the lack of leisure time recreation, rigged up a small transmitter and began broadcasting records directly from an old phonograph. They had no micro-

phone hooked into the system to make announcements or identify the source of the music and so the "broadcast" which reached only the nearby barracks had no call letters, no news, and no schedule.

Encouraged by the response from the men, the fledgling broadcasters expanded their operation and put the call letters GAB on the side of the radio shack from which they initiated their programs. Donations began to come in to help improve the facility and on April 6, having acquired a "live" capability, the station became KRAY. As with KODK, early programming was loosely structured and informal. Soldiers assigned to regular military duties worked at the station during their off hours, usually learning their jobs as they went along.

As KRAY grew in size and popularity, the commander of the base, Col. Walter Shoaff approved construction of a permanent facility which contained three studios and four offices with the main studio seating 100 people for live broadcasts. In its new building, the station officially went on the air August 16 with an hour and a half live variety show including several bands, solo performances, and a dramatic skit. As at Kodiak, local citizens contributed to the programming. Broadcasting from 11 a.m. to 10 p.m., the station received a license from the FCC and the official call letters WCVX on November 19, 1942.

Like KODK and the other stations that were springing up, KRAY initially had problems acquiring enough recorded material to sustain its operation. The transcriptions of commercial network shows, often arriving months after their stateside broadcasting, did help fill the stations' schedules, even though they appeared on an irregular basis. A $1,000 donation from local Sitka residents and clubs helped pay for a Long-Worth transcription library for the station which a local citizen described as "one of the greatest things ever to happen to Sitka."

Such means of acquiring recorded material could not, of course, provide sufficient programming to satisfy the voracious needs of even the small Alaskan stations. Their appearance, however, indicated both that the need for regular radio programming to provide news and recreation existed and that despite the obstacles, the ingenuity of the soldiers in the field would find a way to put stations on the air wherever possible. Nevertheless, the haphazard, uncoordinated development of the first Alaskan stations demonstrated the need for an organized broadcast operation to improve morale and satisfy military requirements for reaching troops with command information and education.

November 10, 1942

Subject: Censorship in Alaska.

MEMORANDUM for the Secretary.

Censorship in Alaska has been and is, to my judgment, unduly repressive, wasteful—since many people are employed in carrying out its provisions—and wholly unnecessary. Censorship falls under five heads:

1. Outgoing news and dispatches. This is controlled by the Army and Navy. During the first six or seven months after our entry into the war, the high military command felt it advisable to throw a blanket over Alaska, to obviate all mention of Alaska that even remotely suggested its relation to the war, prevented regular news men from sending out any stories, censored even the official news release of the Alaska War Council, the announcement extending the rubber drive, etc. and kept Alaskans in complete ignorance of events concerning Alaska that were being published elsewhere in the United States. I am happy to say, however, that this situation has now been largely corrected as a result of discussions with General DeWitt. While there is still room for further improvement in the handling of the news, I am convinced that the military authorities have completely altered their attitude and that we are now headed for a desirable news policy. Nothing needs to be done here for the time being.

2. Incoming news dispatches. Some news dispatches disseminated throughout the United States are censored by the Office of Censorship in Seattle. The Army and Navy now take the position that anything that has been published in the United States should be sent to Alaska. Nevertheless, the Office of Censorship has taken upon itself to delete certain matters. The President's speech was held up by the Office of Censorship for several hours, likewise a speech by Congressman Magnuson delivered in Seattle, which was sent out by the Associated Press and United Press but was held up by the Office of Censorship. There would seem to be no excuse or justification for this civilian agency moving in where neither of the military services have any desire to tread.

3. Incoming newspapers and magazines. Newspapers and magazines coming from the United States are clipped by the Office of Censorship in Seattle. There is no justification whatever for this. General DeWitt expressed to me categorically his disapproval of this performance, and his willingness to be quoted—that no justification or military necessity existed for this policy. My copies of the Washington Post, Time and News Week have been cut. This policy should be completely abandoned, and the great army of newspaper and magazine clippers dismissed for more useful work.

4. Mail. All letters to and from Alaska are subject to censorship in Seattle by the Office of Censorship and is, of course, in addition to the military censorship exercised by the Army and Navy solely for mail to and from members of the armed forces. Needless to say, this latter is universal practice for armed forces and does not concern us. The civilian mail censorship, however, is wholly unwarranted. There is no valid reason why Alaska mail should be treated any differently than California, Washington or Oregon mail. I suspect this originated as a general policy for the territories, and whatever may be the justification or lack thereof for other outlying islands, I feel definitely that this policy should not apply to Alaska. General DeWitt is in agreement with this position. I could elaborate instances of the poor execution of this policy—the fact that identical letters, carbon copies, are treated differently in the same office—but I would like to rest my case on the obvious lack of need, in the waste of time in reading all these letters, and in the needless prying and snooping that takes place in consequence. Finally, the mail service, already suffering greatly through inadequate transportation facilities and shortage of Post Office personnel, is further delayed by censorship.

5. Kodachrome photos. Taking colored photographs has become a widespread hobby and thousands of people enjoy taking color pictures in Alaska. All of these pictures have to be sent either to the Eastman Kodak Co. at Rochester, New York, or at Los Angeles, California, to be developed. There is no censorship of these pictures for anyone in the United States, but pictures taken in Alaska are censored and pictures which they conceive to have some military aspects are not returned to the senders. Their judgment in this matter is wholly fantastic. Among the victims of this censorship have been Major General Simon B. Buckner, Jr., head of the Alaska Defense Command, who complained to me bitterly about this censorship. General Buckner told me of one picture of a sled which had been removed from his pictures. Presumably, the idea was that he would send this picture of a sled to an enemy who would then find out that sleds were being used in Alaska. In my own case, pictures that had no possible relation to the war were removed. The complaint is widespread in Alaska. I know the case of one man who sent four rolls, a total of 80 pictures, and got back 7. He wrote a violent letter to the Office of Censorship and got them all back which would, at least, indicate that the Office of Censorship did not have a clear understanding of its task.

It seems clear that if an enemy agent were trying to photograph strategic objectives in Alaska, the one medium he would not use would be Kodachrome which he cannot develop himself but which must be sent to

Eastman to be developed and where any unusual or suspicious photographs would be detected, but that he would use ordinary black and white and develop the films himself. Both General DeWitt and General Buckner stated to me that they considered this censorship wholly unnecessary.

We have, therefore, in Alaska four forms of censorship imposed by a civilian agency which the military does not desire or require. These forms of censorship are distinctly detrimental to the morale of the people of Alaska. They greatly add, and unnecessarily, to the burden of life there. In addition to that, they must employ much personnel wholly uselessly. They are among the many irritations which would be cheerfully borne if their existence were justified, but which being rightly considered needless by their victims, serve to lessen the faith in and loyalty to our government which should instead have the fervent and enthusiastic support of the entire people.

I therefore desire, Mr. Secretary to have the full backing of the Department in trying to eliminate these unnecessary forms of censorship. I would like first to discuss the matter with Mr. Byron Price and his staff. If relief cannot be secured there—which seems probable since the agency that voluntarily cuts down its activity and diminishes its jurisdiction is rare—it may be necessary to seek appropriate action higher up.

Ernest Gruening,
Governor.

Approved: NOV 18 1942

Secretary of the Interior

Col. Benjamin B. Talley, engineering officer who planned and supervised the construction of Army installations in Alaska, received the Distinguished Service Medal from Maj. Gen. Simon B. Buckner, Jr., commanding general of the Alaska Defense Command at his headquarters in 1943. LC

Brig. Gen. B.B. Talley today.
COURTESY LYMAN WOODMAN

Col. J. Weed, Transportation Corps in Seattle and Col. Talley, Corps of Engineers, on the old Army dock in Anchorage after checking a cargo vessel heading for Adak in 1942.
COURTESY LYMAN WOODMAN

In June 1942 the nearly 500 Aleut inhabitants of the Pribilof Islands (St. Paul and St. George) were evacuated to southeastern Alaska because of the Japanese threat in the area. The Aleuts living on Atka were also evacuated. The natives of Attu were captured by the Japanese invaders and interned in Japan. NA 80-G-12163, 80-G-206196, 80-G-206197

Headquarters Alaskan Department
PUBLIC RELATIONS OFFICE
APO 942, c/o PM, Seattle, Wash.

FOR IMMEDIATE RELEASE

HEADQUARTERS, ALASKAN DEPARTMENT—American's only War refugees, the Aleuts, have recently been returned to their homes by the Army. Under the direction of Don C. Foster, Superintendent of the Alaska Indian Service, four hundred Aleuts boarded an Army Transport ship at Juneau and headed West, to the Aleutians. Never in its service in North Pacific waters, had the D.W. Branch carried such a happy human cargo. The soldiers and sailors couldn't understand why these people should ever want to return to the wind-whipped rocks, but the Aleuts smiled—They were happy—They were going home.

It had been almost three years since the Jap occupation of Attu and Kiska caused the Army to evacuate these people to the mainland. The scorched earth policy was applied to their homes to leave nothing for the Nips, and that fact alone brought the only touch of sadness to these people who were now returning to blackened ashes and a long term of rebuilding.

The Army is doing much to return to these people, all that they possessed before the evacuation in June, 1942. They are supplying the lumber and tools necessary to rebuild the villages, and have arranged to pay the men $50.00 per month until the reconstruction is completed. In the meantime, each family has been given a Quonset hut for their temporary home and Army rations will keep them as well fed as they have ever been. Bedding and other necessities are being supplied, and the Army and Navy intend to replace lost items, even to guns and dories, so essential to these people whose livelihood depends mainly on hunting, fishing and basket-weaving.

Although a few of the young women married and remained on the mainland, the three years which the Aleuts spent in Alaska only increased their dislike for it. They still retain a dislike for trees, large towns and most of the things that civilization offers. They want no more than to fish, hunt, farm and live happily in their own little villages, each complete, even to a Russian Orthodox church.

In early March of 1945 I was told to pack my gear as I was being transferred from Dutch Harbor. I did so and was told to report to the Naval Air Station. At that point I found out my destination was Hula Two. I boarded the plane, and was flown to the Army airfield at Cold Bay, Alaska.

I was one of a few that were picked at random from Dutch Harbor. Others came from outposts along the Aleutians, Alaska, stateside and other various points. We were there to clean up and put back into operation an abandoned portion of the Army post. We cleaned quonset huts, mess halls, bakeries and all other buildings in the vicinity. If I have my directions correct, this would be west of the Army airfield at Cold Bay. We had no idea of what we were preparing for as the base was classified Top Secret and orders came direct from Washington and Moscow.

After about two weeks, a freighter flying the Russian flag came into harbor and unloaded around 2,000 Russian Navy personnel, officers and enlisted men. Our job just turned out to be to train the Russian personnel to operate all types of landing craft, LSTs, mine sweepers and everything needed to launch an invasion. When the crews were familiar with their work, they would man the craft, head for Russia and more craft and personnel came in and the process was repeated. Russia at this time was still at peace with Japan as this was still about five months before the end of the war. Russia was to invade the Japanese mainland from the north. This was the reason for the Top Secret classification.

In early August the Bomb was dropped, the war ended and it was all unnecessary.

Kenneth Robb

Yeoman 2/C, Supply Department—
Hula Two Project.

Now resides in New Harmony, Indiana

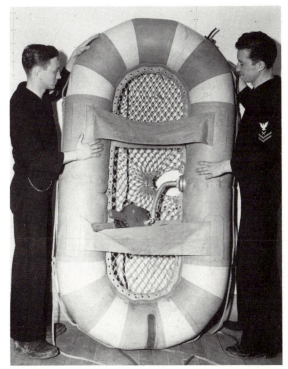

Japanese life raft picked up by an American submarine in the North Pacific, June 1942.
NA 80-G-206155

An Army chaplain reads the service at the burial of a Japanese flier shot down in the Aleutians. LC

The Whitehorse refinery under construction in October 1943. The caustic treating building with the alkylation unit is being built, along with the piping trench in the foreground. RF

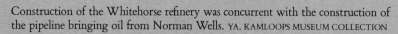

Construction of the Whitehorse refinery was concurrent with the construction of the pipeline bringing oil from Norman Wells. YA, KAMLOOPS MUSEUM COLLECTION

The Canol oil refinery tank farm. USA SC 231562

The Standard Oil Co. refinery at Norman Wells, Northwest
Territories, was built years before the advent of World War
II. YA, KAMLOOPS MUSEUM COLLECTION

CHAPTER TWO
CANOL PROJECT

Oil To Alaska*

This story of the Canol Pipeline Project is excerpted from a pamphlet published in 1943 and written by C.V. Myers. There has been some mild editing to clarify facts and some superfluous information has been deleted.

The entire Canol project was under the supervision of Brig. General L.D. Worsham, Division Engineer in charge of all engineering projects in Northwestern Canada and Alaska.

General Worsham and his corps of engineer officers supervised the work of the civilian contractors and directed their efforts throughout the entire course of operations.

The Edmonton District was supervised first by Lt. Col. P.Z. Michener, and later by Lt. Col. Robert W. Lockridge.

Working under the Edmonton District were the area engineers at the various points—Captain Alfred S. Holmberg at Waterways, Captain Edgar J. Murphy at Peace River, Captain W.T. Warren at Fort Simpson, Captain R.E. Westling at Norman Wells, Lt. Col. Benjamin Rogers, and later Major John K. Borrowman, at Camp Canol.

The Whitehorse District was under the supervision of Col. James V. Johnston and his assistants.

Besides Bechtel-Price-Callahan, other civilian contractors on the job were, J. Gordon Turnbull and Sverdrup & Parcell, The Imperial Oil Company of Canada, Marine Operators and Noble Drilling.

Altogether they comprised a team which in twenty months was able to conquer an undeveloped area half the size of the United States, pioneer approximately 2,000 miles of road, and lay 1,800 miles of pipe over barren territory.

This is the story of how it was done.

"What is it all about anyway—this CANOL?"

It was the summer of 1942 in Edmonton. The man on the street corner spoke to the stranger beside him, and pointed to the big truck rumbling by. It had the word CANOL painted on its side in large gold letters.

"Bless me, if I know," said the man. "I work there, but I still don't know. Building a pipeline or something like that."

"But where are they building it to?"

"I hear it's right across the North-West Territories."

"Just swamps, and muskegs, and mountains up there. No towns, no roads or railroads. I don't believe they can build a pipeline there."

"Maybe they can't. I dunno."

"Maybe it's something else altogether. But what do they mean—CANOL?"

The Canol Project began in June, 1942, but strict Army censorship kept CANOL a mystery name until well on into 1943. People knew about the Alaska Highway. They did not know that the project which would be a large factor in determining the value of that highway, which would cost

several times as much money, the like of which had never been attempted before—they did not know that this job was already under way. No fanfare heralded the beginning of the Canol Project.

Even the men who endured the extreme temperatures, the swamps, the flies, had no clear conception of what it was all about. Employees who worked at Whitehorse, or Prince Rupert, Fairbanks, Skagway, Waterways, Peace River, Canol, or Edmonton, could have no idea of how they fitted into the master plan which embraced one of the most tremendous undertakings ever attempted by man.

"He who holds Alaska holds the world."

Colonel Mitchell said it. No one paid much attention. Apparently the Japanese believed Mitchell, for in 1942 they were based in the Aleutian Islands pointed at Alaska.

With both Germany and Japan now being crowded back into their corners, it is hard to remember the panic that grew to high pitch after Pearl Harbor, the blackouts along the coast, the threat of bombing. It was not hard to envision a Japanese attack then, and the American fleet lay crippled. Alaska was in peril. Could the crippled fleet keep the coast route open? How could men and materials be moved to Alaska if the fleet could not keep it open?

The Alaska Highway seemed to be the answer. But war requires hundreds of thousands of barrels of oil, and if the sea traffic were cut how would this oil be supplied? Thousands of miles over a highway already strained to capacity?

There was one partially explored oil-field—at Norman Wells on the Mackenzie River. If the oil could be brought to Whitehorse, distribution from there on would be a relatively simple matter. Especially with the aid of the Alaska Highway to take the oil north or south. And the Alaska Highway was already building.

If there was any answer to the problem poised by the Japanese threat, Norman seemed to be the answer.

In the spring of 1942 the Army picked its contractors for the job. The W.A. Bechtel Company and the W.E. Callahan Company were old-time constructors with well established reputations. The H.C. Price Company was an outstanding welding organization backed by years of experience. These three combined into Bechtel-Price-Callahan, the sole purpose of whose existence was to build the pipeline, and bring the oil from Norman Wells across the mountains to Whitehorse. The Imperial Oil Company, under the direction of U.S. Engineers, undertook to develop the field to its capacity.

The project was named CANOL, after Canadian Oil. Camp Canol would be established across the river from Norman Wells.

With very little to go on because of the rugged and unexplored nature of the country, but with the urgent pressure of necessity, the CANOL vision was undertaken.

Oil rig on Goose Island in the Mackenzie River between Norman Wells and Canol Camp, February 1944. RF

The constructors moved in in June. They knew generally what the conditions would be, but little more. They did not know because no one in the world knew. They knew only that the job had to be completed by Christmas.

They knew they would have to rush it from both ends. They would have to start in at Canol and at Whitehorse. In order to maintain Whitehorse, they would have to establish a base at Prince Rupert.

Freight and supplies for Whitehorse would come to Edmonton by rail. Continuing on to Prince Rupert they would be reloaded there into barges and shipped by sea along the coast to Skagway. Then by rail again to their destination at Whitehorse.

As long as the west coast route remained safe, other supplies could be loaded at Seattle and Vancouver, shipped directly to Skagway, then up the White Pass & Yukon Railway to Whitehorse. Lines of communication with Whitehorse were therefore well established routes, and as it proved later, secure.

The constructors knew the water communication system with Canol.

With Edmonton as the mother base, a giant pincers could be applied on the unknown intervening area between Canol and Whitehorse.

But the intervening area was to prove itself a hard nut to crack. A nut so hard that it would take the efforts of 10,000 men to smash it, and 20 months instead of six.

Canol was the weak end of the pincers. Fifteen hundred miles north of Edmonton by the ordinary water route. No railroad, road or trail of any kind. The end of steel was at Waterways, Hudson's Bay Post, 300 miles north of Edmonton. A thousand miles of inter-connected rivers and lakes led then to Norman Wells.

Water transportation opens about the first of July. By October 1st it is all over. Three months to ship the necessary supplies. Three months more to push the pipeline through.

Between Whitehorse and Canol lay the Mackenzie mountains which form a watershed between the Mackenzie and Yukon rivers. Starting out at nearly sea level at Canol you go over the mountains, which rise to almost 9,000 feet, and then back again to low altitude at Whitehorse.

Reconnaissance began immediately. First by airplane, then by dog team and on foot. Northern fliers were consulted, every pioneer who might know something about the conditions that would have to be met.

Within two weeks the Mackenzie Mountain Range and surrounding territory had delivered the Canol Project one of the greatest shocks it was ever to receive. Completion by Christmas of 1942 would be utterly impossible. The country was rugged beyond all stretches of the imagination. Conditions generally were even worse than anticipated.

So the plans were revamped. Schedules changed. The urgency of the work had not diminished. It would have to go ahead.

In the meantime the base at Waterways had been established. The fight against time to get all the freight to Canol before the three months' season closed was already in progress.

A man is trying to push a bookcase. He is standing out from it at arm's length and pressing on the bookcase with his fingers. He cannot exert any of his strength. He cannot move the bookcase.

Before he can move it he will have to get up to it. If he can get behind it with his shoulder he will have no trouble. If the bookcase is surrounded by furniture, he will first have to move the furniture. But he has to get there.

The main office of Bechtel-Price-Callahan, the main Canol contractor, on Jasper Street and 109th Street in Edmonton, November 1942. RF

Punahau Base (formerly a Jesuit College), the Edmonton headquarters of the Northwest Service Command, 1942. This is now the Charles Camsell Hospital. RF

Prince Rupert, British Columbia, became an important trans-shipping point for Canol project equipment because of its rail link with interior British Columbia and Alberta. RF

BPC carpentry shop in Edmonton at 105th Street and 81st Avenue, November 1942. Line camp cabooses are shown being constructed. RF

Milepost at Carcajon River, January 1944. RF

Pushing a pipeline through from Canol was like trying to push a bookcase at arm's length. First you had to get there. That was the purpose of Waterways—to get there.

The camp at Waterways opened about the middle of June 1942. By July 7th, 285 men were on the job, building the camp to house the men, and the office to supervise and pay the men, who would build the camp for the men, who would unload the freight from trains and load it again onto barges.

The camp was erected on the river flat about a mile down from the town of Waterways with its 400 people. Because of the level prairie-like nature of the ground it was called Camp Prairie. Behind to the west lay the mountains and the uninhabited hinterland. To the north the town of McMurray with 250 inhabitants. Along the front ran the river.

The only automobile road in the whole country was for a distance of five miles between the towns of McMurray and Waterways. About once a month the Hudson's Bay boat made the trip north with freight and mail for Norman Wells and Aklavik. The only communication in from the south was the single track railroad of the N.A.R. (Northern Alberta Railroad).

The Athabasca River flows into Lake Athabasca. The Slave River drains Lake Athabasca into Great Slave Lake. Out of the western end of Great Slave Lake the Mackenzie River runs for a thousand miles down to the ocean. A hundred miles south of the Arctic Circle the mighty river passes Camp Canol in a stream bed four miles wide and at an elevation of about 325 feet above sea level. It lumbers by at the rate of five miles per hour, down to its Arctic destiny, discharging itself into the sea.

Getting to the Mackenzie is not as simple as a glance at a map would indicate. At Fort Smith, just north of the Alberta boundary, transportation is confronted with a stone wall. Literally a stone wall, for here a very hard limestone ridge cuts across the country. This ridge refuses to be worn down, and slows up the river behind it, and precipitates the river beyond it, in a series of rapids, which drop 125 feet.

These are the rapids of the drowned, the dead horse rapids, and many others. No boat can pass over them. Every barge has to be unloaded. The freight has to be transported by truck or wagon across the portage of 16 miles, and loaded onto other boats waiting to receive it.

Until July 1942, all northbound freight had been handled in this way. But in the wild race to move 30,000 tons in the brief three-month period, the constructors for the CANOL project saw defeat staring at them from the rapids.

But how was the delay to be overcome? There was no time to blast, to dredge, to dam. And yet the boats must pass. Of course, there was only one other alternative—the land. Huge trailers were built, trailers big enough to accommodate barges weighing up to 300 tons. These massive rubber-tired platforms were then pulled down to the ways at the water's edge to accept their bulky cargo.

The barges arriving at Fort Smith from Waterways were unloaded at the portage. Loaded trucks drove down onto dry ground. Caterpillars rumbled off the deck. Bulky freight was hastily transferred to waiting vehicles. The caterpillars pulled the barges bodily out of the water onto the big trailers. Then the caterpillars would hook onto the trailer and tow it across the 16 mile stretch.

Down it would go into the water again. The caterpillars would drive back onto the deck, followed by the trucks laden with freight and fuel. Within ten hours from the time of arrival at Fort Smith the same barge would again be on its way up the Slave River, Canol bound.

At Resolution Delta a second change-over had to be made. Here the Slave River enters the lake in a wide delta, and river conditions change suddenly to conditions approaching those met out on the open ocean.

Great Slave Lake is the fifth largest fresh water body in the world. The wind whips across its 12,000 square miles, lashing it to a fury, and the waves rise 20 feet in the air, and beat with impact against the shore.

On the river, barges were pushed by the tug-boats. They were lashed securely out in front and at the sides, perhaps as many as five or six to a tug. But on Great Slave Lake it is a different story. Such a combination would be smashed to pieces by the raging choppy swell.

At Resolution Delta all the barges were unlashed. Strung out at the end of 300 foot cables, one after the other, three to a tug-boat, the tiny convoy moved out for its 150 mile trip across the lake.

At Wrigley harbor, on the opposite side, a change-over again was necessary. The barges were unhooked, lashed once more securely to the tug, then into the placid water of the eight-mile wide Mackenzie, and off on the 500 mile trip down the river as a single unit to bring supplies to the infant camp at Canol.

But all this took time. It all took organization. It was all a part of the "getting there." The real job had not yet commenced.

There was something more to the "getting there." When it was found that the prospects of completing the job before Christmas were absolutely hopeless other provisions had to be made. If a camp was to be sustained all winter at Canol, some means of communication would be absolutely necessary. The only communication possible would be by air. But planes require landing fields. Over a distance of 1,500 miles, emergency landing fields at least.

And so a system of airports had to be established. Construction started early in the fall at all points. Eight airports up the line, Embarras, McMurray, Fort Smith, Resolution, Hay River, Providence, Simpson and Wrigley. It was all a part of "getting there."

And all these camps had to be transported bodily, and the

Canol Camp Album

Canol Camp on the south bank of the MacKenzie River was, by 1943, a small town of over 2,000 people, with many buildings with central heating and electric power. The camp-site was moved from the river's edge to a level location farther up on the 30-mile flat that sloped toward the mountains.

ALL PHOTOS COURTESY MRS. INGRID CURTIN

Administration Bldg.

Dinner time at Cano...

Igloos

Mess Hall

Barracks at Canol

Pay Day

equipment to clear the trees, to make muskegs into landing strips, and the men to do the job, and the food and housing the men would require. And warehouses at these points, and shops, and a winter's supply.

All this freight was in addition to what was required by Camp Canol. There was three months to do it in.

Waterways was only incidental to Canol. Yet Canol was dependent upon it. An unexpected set-back to Waterways was a set-back to Canol. And an unexpected set-back, almost at the very beginning.

The constructors had believed, and the U.S. Engineers had believed, that the river transportation equipment already in existence would be ample to meet their requirements. They found themselves to be misinformed. The barges simply were not there. Not half the number required to move the vital freight to Canol.

And anything that stopped the movement of freight was nothing short of disaster.

The two last barges in tow on Great Slave Lake reared and plunged at the end of their cables. These barges carried vital supplies. They carried tractors for the men who would be isolated at Camp Canol during the winter months. They carried parts, food, clothing and tools. And nature, as if aware of the precious contents, churned the lake in her fury. The barges rose on the crests of colossal waves, then plunged unmercifully out of sight in their troughs. The men in the tug-boat ahead saw that their cargo was doomed, and cut loose the cable.

The barges capsized, spilling forth their contents into the hungry waters. Now the vital supplies could never be shipped in time!

And 10,000 tons of freight had missed the boat. Yet the supplies had to be moved. The camp at Canol was already established. It was like an infant isolated from the world. It could not be deserted. Some way, somehow, supplies must still go north.

Female office workers at Canol Camp, February 1944. No women were employed at the outlying camps. RF

BPC mess hall at Canol Camp, 1944. RF

Something had to be done, and done at once.

A barge building program was immediately undertaken. The camp at Waterways swelled to over 500 men, with more coming in. Great floodlights illuminated the yards at night, and the pitch of daylight activity never slackened. Soon the barges were sliding into the water. Ten additional tug-boats were brought in by rail. The freight moved on.

And so during the summer and throughout the fall Waterways became a hive of industry. Day and night it hummed with the steady pounding of hammers, the putting of tug-boats on the river, groaning monsters of caterpillars, the constant whine of sawmills.

Suddenly all activity ceased.

Night had dropped down like a curtain over the north. The rivers slackened and stopped. Freeze-up had arrived!

Thirty thousand tons of supplies were to have gone up the Athabasca. Despite the barge building program, less than 20,000 had passed across the docks at Waterways.

Men Against Mountains

Fifty thousand years ago a sheet of ice nearly a mile thick passed over the Mackenzie Basin and came down almost to the border of the United States.

Fifty thousand years ago Nature was dreaming up trouble for the modern pipeline layers. With a head start like that small wonder Nature won the first few rounds thumbs down.

No one knew exactly what Nature had been up to until the first reconnaissance was undertaken. Then they found her out.

Imagine a sheet of ice to a height of 4,000 or 5,000 feet, and many miles across. Not so long ago fighter airplanes were flying at 5,000 feet. Imagine such a thickness of ice, and imagine what it would do to the ground underneath as it advanced. Every bit of soil was scraped from the surface of the

A trailer train convoy along the Canol road in the Yukon. This turned out to be the most practical way of transporting housing and construction units along the pipeline route. RF

Canol Camp, 1942. RF

land, leaving only the bare live rock behind. Mountainous boulders, frozen into the bottom of the glacier, gouged great holes in the face of the earth.

Then in 30,000 years or so the glacier receded, and disappeared. It receded by melting, of course, at its south end first.

But the glacier had stripped the earth. The northern soil lay now in the south, and in the north lay a surface of bare, gouged-out rock.

The hollows in the rock became gradually filled with water. And so in the north thousands of shallow lakes abound. Seen from an airplane in the winter time it is like a mottled mass of light and dark.

The glacier destroyed any orderly drainage system that might have existed before. And no decent drainage system has as yet developed. Consequently muskegs, swamps and bogs, prevail in great number. And in the swamps and bogs the mosquitoes breed and flourish.

But that is not all. Not only did Nature create such almost impossible conditions, she also cunningly contrived to conceal what she had done.

For over all the surface there grows a carpet of moss. In 20,000 years since the glacier disappeared, the rock has been pulverized enough by erosion to form a fine dust or silt. For many hundreds of years the moss has been growing on the silt until now it has attained a depth of ten to 18 inches.

This moss acts as an insulator. The frozen silt and ice beneath it never thaws; the boggy underlying holes refuse to freeze. A man walking over the ground finds the surface over the boggy holes identical with the surface over the solidly frozen foundation of permafrost. The bogs await the unsuspecting caterpillar following the man. The 20 ton monster lumbers on. Suddenly it drops, sinks into the muskeg, and may disappear completely from sight.

This mossy condition prevails throughout the region, in the mountains, the valleys and on the plateaus. It is an ever

constant hazard to heavy equipment. Dozens of pieces were rescued when they had all but disappeared.

The only advantage gained from the moss and silt is that it forms the base on which the scanty timber grows. Moss and timber both are scooped into piles to make the road-bed through the mountains.

These conditions were discovered early in the fall of 1942. They took little reconnaissance. They were no encouragement to the constructors and the men who had still to find out about the conditions in the unknown Mackenzie Range.

Before the pipeline could go through a road must go through. Before a road could go through a survey must be made. Before a survey could be made a route must be chosen. Before a route could be chosen the mountains must be explored.

The first man over the mountains from the east side was Guy Blanchet, employed first by Bechtel-Price-Callahan, and later by the Architect Engineers, J. Gordon Turnbull and Sverdrup & Parcel.

On October 25, 1942 Blanchet set out with three Indian guides and dog teams to make the 250-mile journey and find a way through.

Blanchet had explored the first trail from the east side. Three days before Christmas, in a temperature of 60 degrees below zero, the first road construction crew set out from Canol.

They numbered 23 men under the direct supervision of J.B. Porter, General Superintendent for the Constructor. It was a train of nine cabooses and sheds drawn by caterpillar tractors. They had an office and radio cabin, repair shop, grease shop, two messhalls, bunkhouses, kitchen and kitchen store room. The sleigh-mounted cabins were ten by 20 equipped with stores and emergency repairs and supplies.

Diesel fuel froze to the consistency of vaseline, and would not pour. Light motor oil became as hard as cup grease. The

Telephone Line Construction

Camp of Miller Construction Company, a subcontractor of the Canol and Alaska Highway projects, building the telephone lines. This is at Johnsons Crossing, Yukon, the starting point for the Canol road north.
AUTHOR'S COLLECTION

Telephone linemen at work along the Alaska Highway between Tanacross and Cathedral Rapids, Alaska, October 1943. The four-inch fuel pipeline is shown. This pipe, which was never buried except at road crossings, extended from Whitehorse north to Fairbanks and south to Watson Lake, Yukon, along the highway. An additional fuel line extended north from Skagway to Whitehorse to supply the east-west line. RF

This view shows the Alaska Highway, telephone line, gas pipeline and oil pipeline just south of Whitehorse.
AUTHOR'S COLLECTION

Construction crews employed by the Miller Construction Company along the Canol road and the Alaska Highway built the longest continuous telephone line in the world.
COURTESY RUSSELL GETTLEMAN, GREEN BAY, WISCONSIN

best grade of anti-freeze froze solid in the tins.

The walls of the some-day-to-be famous Dodo Canyon rose vertically 400 feet above them. As they progressed the height of the walls increased to 700 feet. The bottom was rocky with coarse gravel. Sleigh runners scraped on the jagged surface and wore out in no time.

Sometimes tractors stopped as often as every 15 minutes. Intense cold caused condensation. Condensation caused ice. The ice lodged in the fuel system and cut off the fuel supply. In 70 below zero temperatures mechanics had to get out and clear the lines.

The cold rendered the sleigh runners as brittle as cast. Time after time they broke. Welders and mechanics repaired them, and again the snail pace continued.

Motors had to be kept running 24 hours a day. To stop a motor once and let it get cold meant stopping it for good.

In Dodo Canyon underground hot springs kept the ice thin and treacherous. Twenty ton caterpillar monsters would drop through the ice and have to be hauled out by other caterpillars. Fuel sleighs overturned on steep grades.

Three days after New Year's, an hour before dinner the temperature stood at 35 below zero. Five minutes later it was 15 above zero. The thermometer had risen ten degrees a minute. By noon it was 35 above. Four days later it had climbed to 39 above, and the snow in the canyon actually began to melt.

Then it dropped to 15 below suddenly, and culminated in such a terrific blizzard that for two days the train dared not move an inch from where it stood.

Bulldozers attempting to clear the road ahead struck large rocks frozen solidly. Steel snapped. The rocks could not be moved. It was necessary constantly to snake around obstructions of every kind.

In 47 days Porter broke trail 106 miles into the Mackenzie Mountains, and had climbed from almost sea level to an altitude of over 5,000 feet. On February 6 he found himself out of radio communication with Cañol and almost without fuel. As caterpillars bringing it up to him would use up tremendous quantities en route, he had little prospect of securing more. He decided to use his dwindling supply for the return trip. The next day he turned back taking whatever equipment he could and leaving the remainder to be picked up in the spring.

In the meantime another gang of men had crossed the Mackenzie on the ice to Norman Wells and were forging south in an attempt to make junction with the other company forces who were struggling to bring forward the 10,000 tons of freight that had failed to pass the docks at Waterways before the freeze-up arrived.

With the failure of 10,000 tons of vital freight to leave Waterways a crisis had developed. It could not be shipped by river, it could not be shipped by rail, road or air. Yet it had to be shipped.

There was only one way out. A road would have to be built. An overland route. A trail would have to be blazed through a thousand miles of bush, frozen muskeg, still silent rivers and lakes, over ridges and rocks.

In one respect the Constructors were fortunate. The freight had not arrived at Waterways. It was either in Edmonton or on its way up from the States. Within limit the location of the winter road was a matter of free choice.

The route from Waterways north would be impossible. But there was a rail line as far north as Grimshaw, a little town a few miles beyond Peace River. A passable road led north for about 80 miles. Beyond, a sort of tractor trail had already been blazed a distance of almost 500 miles as far as Hay River Post.

On October 3, 1942 Edward V. Lane, Chief Engineer for Bechtel-Prince-Callahan, directed Project Manager, J.P. Shirley, Jr., to build the winter road. The order read in part:

"This covers the construction and operation of a winter road from Grimshaw, Alberta, to Hay River, North-West Territories, Providence, Fort Norman and Norman Wells, with the view of hauling 9,000 tons of freight during the winter season over this road."

The work-order read further: "This work should be handled concurrently with other work on the east end of the project, and since it can be begun at a rail head, it will presumably interfere with none of the existing work."

All materials for the job were immediately requisitioned, 130 more caterpillar tractors, 600 pairs of freight sleds, 23,000 drums of diesel fuel and much more.

A representative was dispatched to Washington to clear all priority materials. A second representative went to the manufacturing plants in the States to expedite the construction and delivery of the sleds.

By October 15 the Peace River base was rolling. Men were hastily transferred from Waterways and met by the outgoing Peace River train ten miles out of Edmonton. This move was to insure against any delay which might result from vacation-minded employees.

But the Peace River project had hardly been undertaken before the immensity of the undertaking became clear. Besides the base at Peace River it would be necessary to have many camps and supply bases to service the forthcoming tractor trains, to serve as centers of refuge in cases of emergency, and as a protection against the severe and unpredictable adversities of the North.

The material for these secondary camps would have to emanate from Peace River, which was itself as yet hardly begun. Electric power would have to be provided at each camp; emergency repair equipment, hospital facilities, fuel to replenish empty tanks, supplies of all kinds, warehouses to hold the supplies, lumber and prefabricated housing material to build the camps. These camps would literally have to be loaded and hauled bodily to their locations.

And all this freight would be in addition to the 9,000 tons.

Carpenter shops in Edmonton swung into double shift. A mass production factory was set up inside a large circus tent, with two assembly lines of parallel sets of planks. Materials were piled all along the way, skids, lumber for the sides, the roof and the right type of nails at the right spots. Carpenters worked on both sides and on top.

At the end of the line the cabooses were hauled out and fitted with bunks, cupboards and stoves. Carpenters applied last minute finishing touches as the cabooses were being towed to the rail loading docks.

The following night these same cabooses would be in Peace River housing other carpenters from the cold. Within a few weeks their destiny would lead them for 1,000 miles over a lonely uninhabited wilderness, across rivers, over lakes and frozen swamps and finally into the valley and across the Mackenzie to Camp Canol.

The camp was one problem, building the road was another. To complete it in time to move the freight before the spring thaw would require progress at the rate of ten miles per day. Road crew No. 1 was finding it impossible to meet more than half of this objective. Crew after crew was dispatched to overtake its predecessor, to assist, and to carry on. On December 18 the thermometer sank to 65 below. On that record day of cold Road Crew No. 5 ventured forth beneath a cloud of steam and smoke. Not one tractor train had yet left Peace River.

The dozers pushed relentlessly forward. The crews progressed ever further afield. Winter grew bitterly cold. Supplies began to run low.

Lack of communication was an ever-present handicap. Messages serviced by the short-wave radio telegraph of the U.S. Army depended upon weather conditions, and were sometimes delayed as much as three or four days.

And food could no longer be supplied by truck. Eggs, milk, vegetables, liquids, or fruit of any kind, froze almost instantly. A new method had to be devised, to supply the men who were making the road, over which would move the freight, to supply the men at Canol.

But the problem of supply and the problem of building the road, were both only incidental to the problem of moving 9,000 tons of freight.

Nature was blocking the attacks upon her stronghold with every method at her disposal. She had not only come down with the severest winter ever known to the pioneers of the North, but she had denied the only asset she had to offer—snow! Huge caterpillars strained over the bare earth in places, almost pulling the runners from beneath the sleds.

The freight simply could not move.

On December 23 when the first freight tractor train left Peace River, it had become apparent that tractor trains could never do the job. Snow had already delayed too long. It

CANOL OIL PIPELINE

#1 Canol Camp to Whitehorse—4-inch, 500 miles.
#2 Skagway to Whitehorse—4-inch, 110 miles.
#3 Carcross to Watson Lake—2-inch, 297 miles.
#4 Whitehorse to Fairbanks—3-inch, 600 miles.

THIS IS THE CANOL PROJECT

It covered an undeveloped area one half the size of the
2,000 miles of road were pioneered Los Angeles to De
1,800 miles of pipeline were laid Denver to New York
An Unknown mountain range was conquered.
Over 25,000 men worked on it.
It took 20 months.

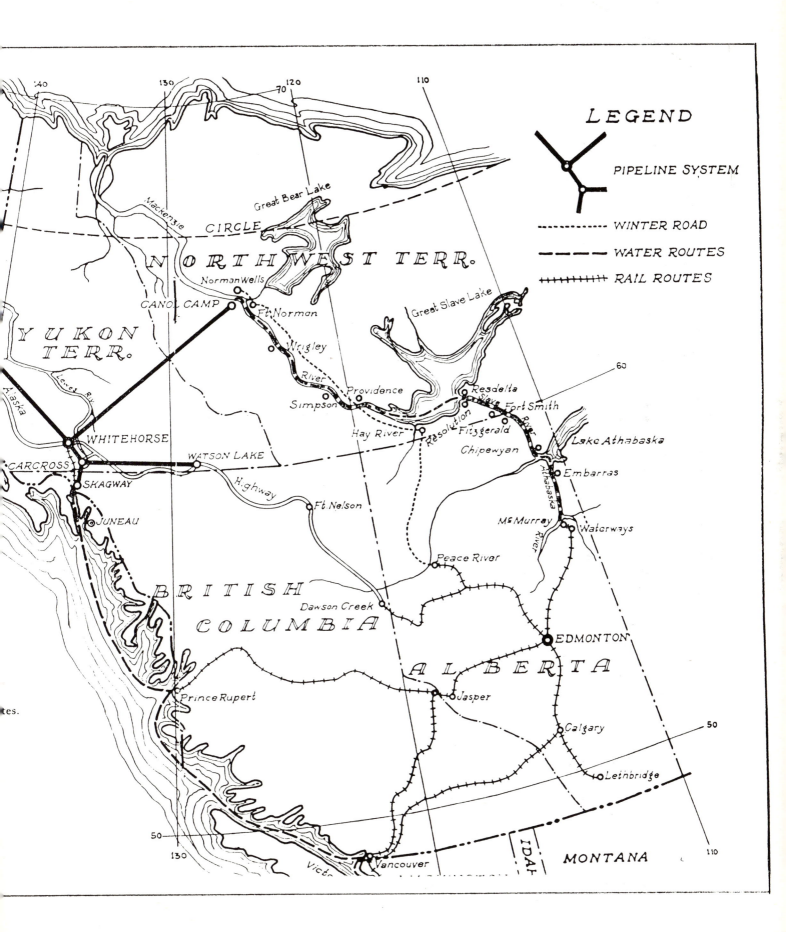

LEGEND

PIPELINE SYSTEM

- - - - - WINTER ROAD
— — — WATER ROUTES
+++++++ RAIL ROUTES

CIRCLE

NORTHWEST TERR.

Great Bear Lake

Mackenzie

NormanWells

CANOL CAMP

Ft. Norman

Wrigley

YUKON
TERR.

River

Providence

Simpson

Great Slave Lake

Resdelta

Slave   Fort Smith

Resolution

Fitzgerald

Chipewyan

Lake Athabaska

Hay River

Embarras

Lewes Riv.

Alaska

WHITEHORSE

WATSON LAKE

CARCROSS

SKAGWAY

Highway

Ft. Nelson

JUNEAU

McMurray

Waterways

Athabaska River

BRITISH

COLUMBIA

Peace River

Dawson Creek

EDMONTON

ALBERTA

Prince Rupert

Jasper

Calgary

Lethbridge

IDAHO

MONTANA

Victo

Vancouver

might delay longer.

The prospect was disturbing, frightening. Was the whole Peace River venture to develop into one colossal blunder? The realization that it was tottering on the brink of failure brought a sinking feeling, a touch of desperation.

There was only one possible way out—trucks. But the road as constructed had been built with the thought of tractors only. Could trucks carrying anywhere from two to ten tons take the beating such a trail would inflict?

Road crews went to work with redoubled effort to improve the road. Every available truck was secured. Private carriers volunteered.

Convoys began moving out of Peace River, and slowly the tide of battle turned. The trucks were getting through. In the severest winter on record, in temperatures of 50 and 60 below zero the convoys crawled along the earth like ancient caravans;—unloaded, and returned for more. Huge stacks of freight piled in the yards at Peace River began gradually to dwindle and disappear.

The trucks moved only as far as Mills Lake. But that was half the distance. Part of the freight could be taken the rest of the way by tractor train, and the remainder could be moved down the Mackenzie fully six weeks before the ice would honeycomb and rot on the surface of Great Slave.

In the meantime the tractor trains trudged on, some of them 24 hours a day. Cooks prepared meals inside the moving cabooses.

And then there were the long bare stretches of mud when the Chinooks plagued the tractor trains.

In spite of the difficulties operations were pushed through. The leading road crew from Peace River made junction with the men working down from Canol, near Blackwater Lake.

Now the road was open, and now the trains moved through.

A great exodus of men from Peace River poured into Canol, as winter rapidly gave way to spring.

The last freight left the great winter base on April 4. Ten million ton-miles had been accomplished! The operation had cost in trucks and tractors and equipment. But the operation had been a success. The critical situation caused by the failure of freight to leave Waterways had been overcome.

Eight thousand tons of pipe lay piled at Resolution Delta on Great Slave Lake.

It had been brought up the Slave River on ponton rafts. Pontons are like pontoons used on airplanes, except the ponton is open at the top. The army had a large number of these rafts which could not be used to transport ordinary freight, so it was decided to utilize them in transporting as much of the pipe down river as possible. The pipe was piled at Resdelta to await shipment when all urgently needed materials had been brought forward.

The Mackenzie River breaks up in May, but on Great Slave Lake the ice lingers and rots. So lake navigation does not open until July.

If the pipe could be brought across the lake while the ice was still solid, it could then be taken up the Mackenzie in May, and six weeks' time would be saved.

But the constructors were more than fully occupied with the many other points on the project, and the vitally important job of moving the freight from Peace River north. At the same time the bases at Prince Rupert, Skagway and Whitehorse were in full swing, involving tremendous construction and strain on resources and equipment available.

An arrangement was made with an Edmonton sub-contractor, Ingraham Bros. They were to undertake to move the 8,000 tons of pipe, but Bechtel-Price-Callahan would assist in every way possible, supplying fuel at cost, parts and considerable equipment.

A huge lake like Great Slave Lake does not present a smooth surface of ice like a skating rink. If you set a glass of water outside in sub-zero weather the water will expand and break the glass. But a lake is contained within its shores, it cannot burst its container. Nevertheless, the water must expand, and there is only one possible direction—upwards.

A train might travel 150 miles across the lake over smooth ice, in record time, only to find itself blocked on its return, by innumerable ridges and impassable drifts.

At first much time was lost by the constant meandering of the trains being forced each trip to take a different route across the ice. Trains of loaded sleighs were forced to travel as far as 50 miles out onto the lake, snaking back and forth in an effort to find a way through.

With the aid of a snow plow at the head of every train or group of trains, and with the maintenance of one definite road, freighting progressed rapidly through March and April.

Then came an unprecedented thaw. On April 20 loads were travelling in nearly two feet of water on the surface of the ice, which, although it was still thick well out on the lake, was getting extremely dangerous near the shore.

During the last days there was some anxiety in getting both men and equipment safely ashore, but convenient land points were found, and all pipe and equipment safely stored until it could be moved by water later on.

Over 5,000 tons of pipe had been freighted across the ice towards Mills Lake, where in mid-May it could be loaded onto barges and taken up the Mackenzie.

Thus the danger of an early summer shortage was averted.

With the influx of hundreds of men and machines from Peace River, in addition to hundreds of men flown in by air, Canol in the spring and summer of 1943 became a huge thriving center. Then in May river traffic opened up, and the base began to mushroom as amazingly as Peace River.

The campsite was moved from the river's edge to a level

location further up on the 30-mile flat that sloped toward the mountains.

A large office building to take care of payrolls and the administration of a 2,000 man camp was put up, an 800 man messhall capable of two or more sittings at each meal, warehouses for supplies of food, cigarettes, clothing and all the requirements of a civilization of 2,000 people. Besides this, all the repair services, stock rooms and material necessary for the tremendous amount of equipment used in pushing a road and pipeline through a piece of the most rugged territory found anywhere on earth.

Under the direction of Everett Seabury, Project Manager for the Contractor, the road and pipeline pushed forward during the spring and fall, in spite of swamps, muskegs, mosquitoes and flies.

The method of making the road was to use giant bulldozers to scrape off the surface of 18 inches of moss and scrubby timber growing upon it, and push it all together into a pile to form a roadbed roughly 22 feet wide. The insulating moss prevented the bottom from thawing, and so guaranteed a permanently frozen solid foundation.

After this primary grade was built, loads of sand and gravel were packed upon it to make a firm all-weather road. Sometimes when making a side-hill cut, the whole side-hill of moss and trees would slide upon the slippery ice-like base on which it lay, and come hurtling down upon the newly built grade.

Behind the clearing crews moved the trucks with gravel. Behind the finishing crews came the trucks with pipe, laying it along the road. Behind them the welding crews. Behind the welding crews came the telephone crews, digging holes, sometimes in rock, sometimes in swamp where special supports were necessary, and sometimes in frozen ground. Behind the pole crews came the wire stringers, and all groups forged forward to make the anticipated junction with the men working towards them out of Whitehorse from the west.

At Canol the Mackensive is four miles wide and from 50 to 70 feet deep, depending on the season. Norman Wells is on the east side of the river. There the pipeline begins. The Mackenzie is the first formidable barrier to be overcome.

The problem was to lay a length of 20,000 feet of pipe on the river bed below.

Pipe was welded together in single lengths of about a fifth of a mile. Out in the river between Camp Canol and Norman Wells lie two small islands, Bear and Goose Islands. A cable was hooked to the first length of pipe, and the other end to a tractor on Goose Island. The tractor then backed up on the island, hauling the pipe down into the river until its far end rested on the shore. Here the next end was welded to the first. Again the tractor moved west. By taking new holds, length after length was welded on until the entire four miles of pipe lay on the bed of the river, its ends extending up

on either shore. On both shores deep trenches were dug in the banks of the river, and the pipe was let down into the trenches and covered.

The Canol Project has laid the Yukon low. The Canol Project and the Alaska Highway have tied the Yukon down with a net of pipelines and a road. At last it has been tamed, made docile, and now it bows to the will of man.

The Alaska Highway really broke the Yukon first.

To begin with, there was a road from Edmonton to Dawson Creek. The U.S. Army moved in, put its shoulder forward, and in a few months pushed the road through for 1,600 miles to Fairbanks. In this respect the Highway differed from the Canol Project, but it was of immeasurable assistance.

It connected Edmonton with Whitehorse. After it had been completed, Canol freight could move north without obstruction the year round.

But until it was completed as far north as Whitehorse, supplies and freight went by rail to Prince Rupert, then to Skagway by boat, then by rail to Whitehorse. So Prince Rupert became an important base early in the project, and Skagway, and considerable construction was necessary in the establishment of each, a construction comparable to the establishment of Waterways.

With the completion of the Highway, Dawson Creek became the most important intermediate base for Whitehorse. Prince Rupert and Skagway gradually dwindled. Their facilities as trans-shipment points had already been constructed. One or two hundred men could handle all the freight that came by rail, and by boat up the B.C. coast.

At first Whitehorse's only purpose was to work east to meet Canol.

Then came the contract extensions. The constructors were ordered to put the pipeline through to Fairbanks, to Skagway, to Watson Lake, several hundred miles of pipeline, more than double the mileage on the No. 1 Job between Canol and Whitehorse.

But the great difference lay in the fact that the Alaska Highway had already been built. To lay the pipe along an established road or through well-developed country is no job at all. The extensions to the original project were pushed through in a few weeks, long before the main line between Canol and Whitehorse could hope to join.

In 1942 when the sudden desperate call for Northwestern oil arose, the Norman field was the only field whose possibilities had been even partially investigated. Even so, only four wells were in operation. Five had been drilled. One turned out to be a dry hole and had been abandoned.

No one could say just how good the field would reveal itself to be, but indications were favorable, and geologists were hopeful that the required quota of 3,000 barrels per day could be met.

The oil at Norman Wells is of remarkably good quality.

Canol Camp was a U.S. Army camp on Canadian Territory. Constable Francis and Sid were probably in camp on a good-will visit.

Tank farm at Norman Wells, 1943.

Airplanes were essential in this remote part of the world. They brought in people and supplies and news from the outside. The army contracted with bush pilots familiar with the area for this service.

Barges were used to transport machinery and supplies down the MacKenzie River.

One of the drilling rigs at Norman Wells.

A homemade snowmobile, perhaps one of the earliest built. It was powered by a motor and propeller at its rear.

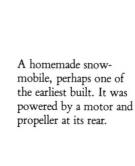

This is all that's left of the Canol Project in the Yukon. Trucks and other equipment were gathered up years ago all along the old Canol Road and brought to this dump near Johnsons Crossing, Yukon on the Alaska Highway.

Army Oil Project in Canada Called Mistake

WASHINGTON — (AP) — The Truman committee bluntly charged Saturday night that the War department's $134,000,000 oil project in Canada was a mistake from the beginning and that its continuance is unpardonable.

Lt. Gen. Brehon Somervell, commanding general of the Army's service forces who upheld the project as a military need, bore the brunt of some of the sharpest criticism yet voiced by the Senate's war investigating group when it declared in a formal report:

"There may be some slight excuse for Gen. Somervell's original hasty decision in view of the tremendous pressure on him at the time, but his continued insistence on the project in the face of these repeated warnings is inexcusable."

To which Senator Ferguson (R., Mich.) added that the attempt to justify the project "by specious arguments impairs confidence", while Senator Kilgore (D., W. Va.) deplored that "thousands of men have toiled through Arctic temperature as low as 70 degrees below zero on a project that never should have been started".

In reply Somervell, quoted from the Bible to illustrate his position:

"And five of them were wise and five were foolish. They that were foolish took their lamps, and took no oil with them: but the wise took oil in their vessels with their lamps."

Somervell also called in his staff Saturday and read to them an excerpt from his annual statement made last March. In it, he said:

"We must get results. We may become impatient with de-

(Please Turn to Page 12, Col. 2)

Canadian Oil for Next War ---Somervell

WASHINGTON, Dec. 20.— (INS)—Lieut. Gen. Brehon Somervill, army supply chief, told Congress today that when the army launched its 100 million dollar Canol oil project in Canada, it created a petroleum reserve for a third world war.

Somervell made this assertion while testifying before the Senate Truman committee, which is investigating charges that the Canol project was a huge waste of public money.

SITUATION DESPERATE.

As chief of supply, Somervell was responsible for the project, and was called before the committee today to explain his stand. He said:

"When we decided to undertake the work, we not only were justified by the desperate war situation confronting the country, but hindsight justifies it even now.

"Instead of finding only two to three million barrels of oil at Norman wells, we have found about 58 million barrels. There are prospects that we will find one hundred million.

"We need all the oil we can get for this war. It also will prove a reserve against the future."

FLEET DISABLED.

The general pointed out that as a result of the Jap raid on Pearl Harbor the American fleet was completely disabled, and added:

"We had lost our fleet as an offensive weapon for months to come. We had lost Guam and Wake. Japanese submarines were shelling our west coast.

"I call the committee's attention to what might have been our plight had the enemy staged a Ploesti raid on the refineries and petroleum stores around Los Angeles."

Canol Oil Project Called Mistake

Continued from Page 1

lays that cooperation with other agencies inevitably entails. Let's not under any circumstances be irked by these contacts—let us not become intolerant of their views and problems and let us not under any provocation, no matter how great, be drawn into useless bickering."

Two members of the committee, Senators Connally (D., Texas) and Hatch (D., N. M.), said in a joint statement they did not agree with the Truman report "in all respects, especially its severe criticism of the War department in undertaking this project at the time and under the circumstances surrounding the case."

The War department issued a statement by Under-Secretary Robert P. Patterson, saying:

"Let us remember first, that we are at war, and the Canol project was a military project, not a matter of peace-time economy. The supply of our far-flung armies and to a great measure that of our Allies has been under the direction of this extremely able officer (Gen. Somervell). Under his direction the original situation of too little and too late has been changed into an extraordinarily efficient flow of munitions, food and medicines.

"The War department has complete confidence in the ability, judgment and performance fo Gen. Somervell."

The Truman Committee, taking cognizance of recommendations from Secretary of the Navy Knox, Interior Secretary Ickes as petroleum administrator and Donald M. Nelson, chairman of the War Production Board, that the United States should abandon the project immediately, salvage what materials it can and take its loss, declared:

"The question as to whether the project is worth completing at the present time must be determined upon the present situation and the estimated future cost of operation, replacements and maintenance.

"What has been done has been done. It is too late now to go back and rectify past mistakes."

It recommended:

1. That no portion of a seven million dollar allocation for further drilling in the Norman Wells vicinity be spent until the War department negotiates new contracts with Imperial Oil Co., Ltd., Canadian subsidiary of Standard Oil of New Jersey and "unless there is clear expectancy that some benefit can be obtained therefrom during the war equal to the cost in materials and manpower involved."

2. That completion of the four-inch pipeline from Norman Wells to Whitehorse and of the aviation refinery at that point be determined by the War department only after it makes "equitable arrangements" with the Canadian government and Imperial Oil for "suitable rights" and can state flatly that "the project in its present state is worth the materials and manpower necessary to complete it".

3. That authority over the entire program for obtaining petroleum—abroad as well as in the United States—be concentrated in Petroleum Administrator Ickes who should have been consulted "before the Canol project was undertaken."

The lengthy report reviewed developments leading up to a directive by Somervell June 30, 1942, based on a recommendation from James H. Graham, $1-a-year engineering assistant and dean of engineering at the University of Kentucky, calling for the project's completion in October of that year.

While it was designed to provide a near source of aviation gasoline and oil for the defense of Alaska at a time when the submarine menace was at its height and the enemy was on the advance everywhere, the committee declared that it will not operate until May, 1944, and that Somervell never thought it would be ready before the Summer of 1943.

Asserting that Imperial Oil advised the War department that there was "no conclusive evidence" the Norman Wells fields would produce even the 3,000 barrels of oil a day then contemplated, the project was undertaken and continued, the committee said

Gen. T. M. Robins of the Army engineers that "ten times the volume of delivery contemplated could be made by barges already available from inland U. S. rivers at one-tenth the cost and effort".

2. A warning from the Standard Oil Co. of California, hired by the War department as a consultant, that the project couldn't be completed by October, 1942, in which it proposed an alternative method of transporting oil products from the United States and storing them in the area with the advantage, it said, that supplies could be brought to the area months before the canal project could be completed.

3. Repeated protests from Ickes against completing the project after he first heard of it "through outside gossip".

Paraffin base oil, it will not freeze down to 80 degrees below zero, and such a temperature has never been recorded even at Canol.

At Whitehorse the crude can be received the year round and refined into first class aviation gasoline. It is available in quantity. It leaves little to be desired.*

---

*As it turned out, by the time the pipeline and refinery were completed in 1944, the war had passed far from Alaska's shores and very little Mackenzie oil was refined before hostilities ended.

As can be seen by these newspaper articles, the Canol project was the most controversial construction project undertaken in the Alaska/Canada theater of war. Certainly by the time of its completion in 1944, the threat of Japanese intervention into the area had long passed and sufficient oil and gas was being shipped north to take care of the decreased military needs. But it is hard to criticize any action in those dark days of late 1941 and early 1942, when the threat of Japanese aggression was great and military commanders had to make some hard, fast decisions.

Dedication of the refinery at Whitehorse, April 30, 1944.
COURTESY LYMAN WOODMAN

The Whitehorse Refinery

In order to save time and materials it was decided to purchase an existing plant. The Bareco Refinery in Corpus Christi, Texas was purchased in September 1942, dismantled, and over 4,000 tons of equipment was shipped north in April 1943. A steam boiler was purchased in Hamilton, Ontario and generators in Pinedale, California. On April 30, 1944 the refinery was dedicated, the same month that crude started flowing through the pipeline from Norman Wells. The crude was of such high grade that it could be used as diesel fuel without refining with a few adjustments. The Standard Oil Company (Alaska) was responsible for the refinery and produced 100 octane aviation gasoline, automotive gasoline, fuel oil and diesel fuel.

In its 11 month operation (April 1944 — March 1945) the Canol pipeline pumped over one million barrels to the Whitehorse refinery.

The Canadian Government had the option to purchase the refinery after the war but didn't exercise it. In 1947 the refinery was sold to Imperial Oil Company, dismantled and shipped to Edmonton for reassembly.

Looking west from atop a hangar showing a large number of lend-lease aircraft, Ladd Field. COURTESY 7TH FERRYING GROUP ASSOCIATION

CHAPTER THREE
RUSSIAN LEND-LEASE

ALSIB: The Ferrying of Lend-Lease Aircraft from Great Falls, Montana, to the War Fronts of the Soviet Union, September 1942-September 1945

Excerpted from a report written by Deane R. Brandon, Gold Hill, Oregon.

On September 3, 1942, two flights of A-20 light bombers led by Lt. Edmund J. Averman and Lt. Albert D. Wickett touched down at Ladd Field, Fairbanks, Alaska. Thus began what was known as the ALSIB operation, in which almost 8,000 lend-lease aircraft were delivered to the Soviet Union over the Alaskan-Siberian route, from which the contraction AL-SIB originated. (In World War II documents, only the first letter in ALSIB was capitalized; for the purposes of this text, the contraction will be capitalized.)

The German armed forces had launched their tremendous attack against the Soviet Union on June 22, 1941. On July 27 of that year, Brig. Gen. Joseph P. McNarney, on duty in England, was dispatched to Moscow with instructions to discuss aircraft deliveries under a proposed American lend-lease program.

Meetings with Soviet Gen. Yakovlev proved unproductive, and Gen. McNarney terminated his visit on August 1.

In September 1941, American Ambassador Harriman suggested to Stalin that American lend-lease aircraft be delivered to the Soviet Union via Alaska using American crews. Stalin replied that the proposed route would be too dangerous. As a result, the Americans believed that all aircraft sent to the Russians would have to be flown over the very long South American-African-Middle Eastern route via Iran. Most of this route would carry the planes through desert sand, a well-known destroyer of aircraft engines. The only other alternative was shipping the aircraft in crates via ship. With the war situation what it was at the time, no method looked very promising.

On November 1, 1941, a member of the American Special Observer Group in England held a conference with Soviet Gen. Poughachev, vice chief (air) of the Soviet Military Mission in London. The Alaskan-Siberian route was again mentioned, but the proposal was received without enthusiasm. The Russians still believed that the shipping route to Murmansk and Archangel on the Arctic Ocean would be better, as would the Middle East route to Iran. In spite of this, America's Col. Griffis was sent to Moscow on November 4, 1941, with instructions to find acceptable aircraft delivery routes to the Soviet Union. His best efforts were of no avail in selling the proposed Alaskan route.

In the meantime, thousands of miles away in Seattle, Washington, a new U.S. Army Air Corps unit was being activated. This unit was known as a "control point" for the ferrying of aircraft from the factories to bases throughout the country. The missions assigned consisted mostly of delivering B-17s from the Boeing factory to various domestic destinations. The control officer was Capt. Lloyd W. Earle, and his unit, based first at Boeing Field and later at 208 James Street, Seattle, consisted of 18 officers and 16 enlisted men.

According to the history of the 7th Ferrying Group, The Northwest Sector of the Domestic Division, Ferrying Command, was activated in January 1942 at the downtown Seattle location. One of the many new military units being organized at the time, it later became the 7th Ferrying Group.

The Ferrying Command of the Army Air Forces had been activated in June 1941 for the purpose of "moving aircraft from factories to such terminals as might be designated by the Chief of the Army Air Corps." Later, the Ferrying Command was redesignated the Air Transport Command (ATC), with a Ferrying Division to deliver aircraft.

At control points selected by the commander of the Ferrying Command were stationed control officers, who were responsible for the assignment of pilots and crews in accordance with existing instructions, including proper clearance and routing over prescribed routes. All flights were made in daylight and only contact (now called VFR) flying was allowed.

After Pearl Harbor, it became imperative to rush men and war material to Alaska. In January 1942, plans were made for utilization of the route through Canada to Alaska. Canadian permission was obtained, and a contract was signed with Northwest Airlines on February 26, 1942, which called for that organization to support the ferrying mission and to haul high priority cargo over the route. Northwest Airlines sent its own personnel north to Edmonton, Fort St. John, Fort Nelson, Watson Lake and Whitehorse, where they performed station maintenance functions using the Canadian facilities. Later, they would set up a communications and meteorological service and a flight control system for their own aircraft.

Maj. Leroy Ponton de Arce was transferred from Long Beach, California, to temporary duty with the Northwest Sector on February 1, 1942. Capt. Earle then became executive officer, with Capt. Homer E. Fackler as operations officer.

A survey flight in March 1942 was the first Air Transport Command activity over the northwest route, although other Air Force commands had been moving aircraft over the route, using the string of primitive airstrips that the Canadian Department of Transport had been developing and those in Alaska that were being developed by the Army and the Civil Aeronautics Authority.

USAAF Air Transport Command Ferrying Division insignia.

How unprepared we were for operations in the far north can be seen from the following report, sent by an AAF officer in early 1942: "Early in January, twenty-five P-40s of the 11th Pursuit Squadron set out for Elmendorf Field (Anchorage, Alaska). On January 12, twenty-two were still en route, three having crashed before reaching the Canadian border. Ten planes had left the United States and were somewhere between the Canadian border and Ladd Field (Fairbanks, Alaska). Nine were at Spokane and three were at Portland. Of the five transports that were to accompany the pursuit planes, three were still at Spokane and two were somewhere in Canada. Thirteen B-26s of the 77th Bombardment Squadron also set out for Alaska at the same time as the pursuit planes. On January 12, nine of them were somewhere between Spokane and Ladd Field and four were still at Spokane. Almost a month later, only thirteen of the P-40Es had arrived Elmendorf Field. Seven had cracked up en route and only four of these were salvageable. Five were still on the way. The B-26s met with even greater difficulties. Out of the thirteen that started for Alaska, five crashed. Four of the crackups took place in what is now known as 'Million Dollar Valley' between Edmonton and Fairbanks. Of the eight that finally arrived, four were grounded at Fairbanks and four at Elmendorf with faulty fuel installations."

The Air Transport Command's northwest route, as finally laid out, consisted of bases of varying sizes, from small detachments to major bases. They were located in a line which began in Great Falls, Montana, continued to Lethbridge, Calgary, Edmonton and Grande Prairie, Alberta; Fort St. John and Fort Nelson, British Columbia; Watson Lake and Whitehorse, Yukon Territory; Northway, Tanacrass, Big Delta, Mile 26 (now Eielson Air Force Base), Ladd Field at Fairbanks, Galena and Nome, all in Alaska. This covered a distance of well over 2,000 miles; it was an additional 500 miles or so from Fairbanks to Nome.

Although the route over Alberta was in prairie country, where there were many farms and small towns as well as the cities of Edmonton and Calgary, the main part of the route was over a vast wilderness of muskeg, swamp and mountains mostly covered with the stunted scrub timber of the far north — spruce, tamarack and birch with willows along the rivers and lakes. For a pilot who was lost or had a failing engine or low fuel, it presented a real problem. There were few places to put down a plane, which meant bailing out via parachute in a real emergency.

In the early part of the operation, there were few radio navigational aids and the normal type of navigation was to follow the recently constructed Alcan Highway.

By the end of April 1942, Northwest Airlines was making regular flights from Minneapolis to Edmonton and on to Fairbanks. Western Airlines began flying the route from Great Falls on the 1st of May, and in about two weeks began regular schedules. United Airlines also began operating on the interior route.

Also in April, Lt. Col. George Brewer, who had surveyed the Alaskan and Canadian portions of the route, recommended that Fairbanks be selected as the "turn over" point instead of Nome. Nome was over 500 miles closer to Soviet territory but was considered very vulnerable to Japanese attack from Aleutian bases. Fairbanks also had better facilities and had an advantage over Nome in the matter of weather.

At this stage, proposal followed proposal in regards to the route. By mid-May, Soviet officials reported that they were willing to accept aircraft delivered to them in Alaska. Plans for the ferrying operations then moved forward in Washington and at Air Transport Command headquarters.

In May 1942, Col. William H. Turner requested that a survey be made of Spokane, Washington, and Great Falls, Montana, with a view to moving the Northwest Sector headquarters out of Seattle. On June 2, Lt. Col. de Arce, Maj. Cleveland and Capt. Alma G. Winn flew to Spokane and then on to Great Falls to make the survey. Great Falls was tentatively selected, and Lt. Cockrell was detailed to make a complete survey of the situation at Great Falls. His report strengthened the decision of the staff to locate there. The three factors in favor of Great Falls were its record of over 300 good flying days per year, its position away from the dangerous coastal defense area and its convenient location to the series of airfields destined to become links in the northwest route.

The designation, 7th Ferrying Group, was first used on June 4, 1942, when the Northwest Sector was redesignated by that name. In the same general orders, Lt. Col. de Arce assumed command of the group. Maj. Lloyd W. Earle was

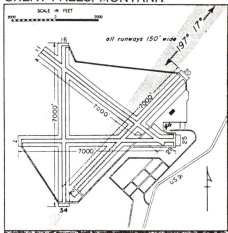

SCALE IN FEET

all runways 150' wide

DESCRIPTION

DIMENSIONS - Four runways: N./S. (16-34) 7,000'
  x 150'; NE./SW. (2-20) 7,000' x 150'; E./W.
  (7-25) 7,000' x 150'; NW./SE. (11-29) 7,000'
  x 150'.
SURFACE - Runways asphalt.
MARKINGS - "GREAT FALLS" on hangar. Wind cone.
LIGHTING - Revolving and stationary beacons.
  Boundary, range lights. Obstruction lights
  on all buildings and towers. 8 flood and 2
  spot lights on parking area.
OBSTRUCTIONS - N. - 90' poles. SW. - 135'
  tower 2½ miles. NW. - 150' towers, 3/4 mile.
  NE. - 510' smokestacks 5½ miles, 60' poles.
  E. - Hangar and Adm. building, steep hill.
  Equipment on field.

FACILITIES

HANGARS - One concrete and steel, 240' x 170' x
  50'; one small wooden, 100' x 80' x 39'; two
  frame hangars.
REPAIR FACILITIES - 2nd echelon minor repairs.
FUEL AND OIL - Gas in quantity, oil. Tank
  trucks.
COMMUNICATIONS - Telephone, telegraph in town.
  Teletype, radio, radio range, control tower.
WEATHER REPORTS - 24-hour service.
TRANSPORTATION - Army car or taxi. Northwest
  Airlines (DC-3), Western Airlines (DC-3 and
  Waco) use this field. Railroads.
ACCOMMODATIONS - Hotels in city. Barracks and
  quarters. Population of Great Falls - 65,000.

NAME AND LOCATION

GORE FIELD, formerly GREAT FALLS MUNICIPAL AIR-
  PORT, 3 miles SW. of town on plateau.
POSITION - Lat. 47° 29' N., Long. 111° 21' W.
MAGNETIC VARIATION - 20° 15' E.
ALTITUDE - 3,645 feet.
LANDMARKS - City of Great Falls, Missouri River
  to E.; copper smelter with 510' smokestack 5
  miles to NE.

WEATHER

PREVAILING WINDS - SW. W. in May, June, July.
  Maximum 66 m.p.h.
PRECIPITATION - 14.85" annually.
TEMPERATURE - 99° F. to -15° F.
VISIBILITY - Fog 30 days annually.

CHARTS - Butte Sectional.
         Big Horn Regional.

GENERAL INFORMATION

OPERATED BY - AAF A.T.C.
REMARKS -

Airmen were housed temporarily at the
Civic Center in Great Falls.
COURTESY 7th FERRYING GROUP ASSOCIATION

the first member of the new group to make a survey flight over the route.

A memorandum from headquarters to the commanding officer of the 7th Ferrying Group directed that, "You will take necessary action to organize and operate a ferry route between Great Falls, and Fairbanks, Alaska."

In the meantime, as a result of the Japanese attack on Dutch Harbor that started June 3 and the invasion of Kiska and Attu which followed, 10 domestic airlines were on emergency runs to Alaska by the end of June. The pilots and crews of the 7th Ferrying Group and the crews of the tactical units flew aircraft north at an ever increasing rate, most going to support the developing Aleutian campaign.

On June 16, 1942, the commanding general of the AAF directed that a ferrying route to Alaska be developed. General order number 11, dated June 22, 1942, transferred the 7th Ferrying Group from Seattle to Great Falls. The Seattle per-

sonnel moved to Great Falls and shortly, officers and enlisted men began pouring in from various bases, including large numbers of enlisted men from the AAF Basic Training Center at Jefferson Barracks, Missouri. The first arrivals, under the direction of Maj. Frank C. Svoboda and Lt. Arthur Rush, had their first three meals at the Park Hotel.

There was no base or barracks to house the troops, so arrangements were made with the city to house the troops at the Ice Arena in the Great Falls Civic Center. Tents also were erected at the Fair Grounds. Newly arrived officers made their own housing arrangements. While plans went ahead for the construction of an air base on the Great Falls Municipal Airport, known as Gore Field, others were working on plans for another base just east of the city, which became known as East Base and today is known as Malmstrom Air Force Base.

On July 11, 1942, the 385th Air Base Squadron was acti-

25th Squadron formation at Gore Field, 1943. Maj. Breckenridge is pinning Air Crewman's wings on M/Sgt. Byrnes Ellender. COURTESY 7th FERRYING GROUP ASSOCIATION

Original dance band at Gore Field, 1942. COURTESY 7th FERRYING GROUP ASSOCIATION

Dayroom of the 7th Ferrying Squadron at Gore Field, January 1943. COURTESY 7th FERRYING GROUP ASSOCIATION

vated under Capt. W. Luker. This unit was responsible for the operation of the base. Other units were activated as needed.

On July 20, 1942, the 7th Ferrying Group began sending detachments north to airports at Lethbridge, Edmonton, Fort St. John, Watson Lake and Whitehorse. These detachments were from the 383rd Air Base Squadron, which had been activated for northern assignment. Headquarters of the 383rd was at Edmonton. During the three-year life of the ALSIB operation, there were many changes in unit designations with some units only lasting a short time before being inactivated.

Col. Alva L. Harvey and a 13-member group departed Washington, D.C., on July 31, 1942, in a B-24. With special Russian permission, they flew the entire proposed ALSIB route with a stop at Billings, Montana, and then on to Moscow via Edmonton, Fairbanks, Nome, Volkal, Seim-chan, Oimekon, Yakutsk, Kirensk, Krasnoyarsk, Novosi-birsk, Omsk, Sverdlovsk and Kazan. They were met by a Russian escort at Fairbanks on August 14, but the Russians decided that it was not practical to fly the B-24 into the Soviet Union, so the mission was reduced to seven members and proceeded on to Moscow in two Soviet aircraft.

The Harvey mission was able to obtain considerable information about Soviet airfields, including the fact that all the fields from the Bering Sea coast to Kirensk were new, with the exception of Yakutsk. From Krasnoyarsk to Moscow, all the fields were modern and well equipped by the standards of the time. However, information obtained indicated that the supply situation was much in doubt, even down to the drinking water at the bases.

Finally, the Soviet government agreed to the establishment of the Alaskan-Siberian route. It was agreed that within three weeks, the AAF would deliver 50 A-20s, 12 B-25s, 43 P-40s and 50 P-39s aircraft to the Russians at Ladd Field. However, this proposal was soon revised downward when Maj. Gen. Alexander I. Belyaev, chairman of the Soviet Purchasing Commission, indicated that the Siberian bases were as yet unable to handle so many aircraft.

PRESCRIBED NORTHWEST ROUTE ORGANIZATION,
AUGUST 14, 1942
ARMY AIR FORCES
AIR TRANSPORT COMMAND
FERRYING DIVISION
7th FERRYING GROUP

383rd AIR BASE SQUADRON	384th AIR BASE SQUADRON	385th AIR BASE SQUADRON
Edmonton, Alberta	Fairbanks, Alaska	Great Falls, Montana
DETACHMENTS	DETACHMENTS	DETACHMENTS
Fort St. John	Northway	Lethbridge
Fort Nelson	Tanacross	Kamloops
Grand Prairie	Big Delta	Prince George
Watson Lake	McGrath	Calgary
Whitehorse	Galena	
	Nome	
	Anchorage	

Gore Field was not immune to aircraft accidents. Here a P-38 has crashed on the runway in 1943.
COURTESY TURK HARSHBARGER, JEROME, IDAHO

An A-20 crashes at Gore Field. It has the Russian star already painted on it. COURTESY TURK HARSHBARGER, JEROME, IDAHO

A lend-lease C-47, foreground and a B-25, background, await departure at Gore Field for Alaska. These also have their Russian markings painted on the fuselage. AAC

An AT-6 trainer with ski-wheels mounted for snow landings at Gore Field, 1943.
COURTESY TURK HARSHBARGER, JEROME, IDAHO

This photo taken at the U.S. Air Base at Great Falls, Montana, during the war years, shows George "Racey" Jordan, then an Air Force major (right, rear) at a review honoring Eddie Rickenbacker (left, front row), Jordan's World War I comrade. Left to right front row are: Rickenbacker; Lt. Col. Harry Johansen, commanding officer of the 7th Ferrying Group; Col. R.L. Meredith, commanding officer of the base and Col. N. Kotikov, U.S.S.R. Air Force Mission Head. Maj. George O'Neill, control officer of the base is next to Jordan (left, rear). On a Fulton Lewis, Jr. nationwide broadcast, Jordan stated that he saw Russian officers board planes at the base carrying detailed atom-bomb secrets and quantities of uranium. Two congressional committees ordered investigations of the charges and Jordan eventually wrote a book about his charges.
COURTESY BETTMANN NEWSPHOTOS

In mid-August, action was taken to create a command to be known as "The Northwest Ferrying Route," with Col. de Arce, C.O. of the 7th, as "route commander." The 384th Air Base Squadron was activated at Fairbanks, and soon the route was covered, with the 383rd having detachments at Fort St. John, Fort Nelson, Grande Prairie, Watson Lake and Whitehorse, while the 384th had its detachments at Northway, Tanacross, Big Delta, McGrath, Galena, Nome and Anchorage. Maj. Raymond F. Kitchingman, as C.O. of the 384th at Ladd Field, had the responsibility of turning over the delivered aircraft to the Russians. Because of his strategic position, he was required to report fully and often to Gen. Tunner at Ferrying Division headquarters in Cincinnati, Ohio.

The first Russian arrivals at Ladd Field were Col. Piskounov and Mr. Alexis A. Anisimov, members of the Soviet Purchasing Commission, who arrived on August 26, 1942. Two Russian aircraft arrived on September 4, bringing more mission members.

The Russian ferry pilots, the first of many to come to Ladd Field over the next three years, arrived on September 24. As far as can be ascertained, the Red Air Force did not assign pilots to extended duty ferrying ALSIB aircraft. The pilots were ordinary combat pilots who were given the ferry trips as a "rest from combat" or reward. The majority of these pilots and crews were older, tougher and more serious than their American counterparts.

After five days of intensive transition training, Lt. Col. Paul V. Nedosekin took off westward, leading the first flight of 12 A-20s on October 9.

Transition training of the Russian pilots was to be conducted by American personnel at Ladd Field and at Big Delta. At these two stations, the pilots would be checked out in the particular type of airplane that they were to fly home to the Soviet Union.

The Soviet Mission were very anxious to obtain the aircraft and advised that they would waive winterization requirements on all aircraft delivered before October 1.

Maj. Kitchingman received a bombshell on September 27, in the form of a telegram from Col. de Arce that read: "Return all transition pilots to their home stations immediately upon completion of transition duties with Russians." Other personnel, including civilian technical representatives, received similar orders.

Word was then received that the northwest route would not be used after all. Gen. Tunner gave Maj. Kitchingman permission to turn over to the Russians the 14 A-20s and the 30 P-40s then at Ladd Field, but was told to hold the six C-47s pending further orders.

As of October 12, deliveries of lend-lease aircraft over the route were again authorized. The anticipated number of deliveries during October was 15 B-25s, 50 A-20Es, 60 P-39s and 20 P-40s. On October 17, the Air Transport Command activated a new unit designated the Alaskan Wing. Alaskan Wing ATC assumed full control of the route and ferrying operations north of Great Falls on November 1, 1942. The proposed "Northwest Route" command was abandoned, and the responsibilities of the 7th Ferrying Group for facilities north of Great Falls ceased.

The Alaskan Wing established its new headquarters in Edmonton, Alberta. First commander of the wing was Col. Thomas L. Mosley. Executive officer was Col. George E. Gardner, former vice president of Northwest Airlines.

Meanwhile, the 384th Air Base Squadron, with headquarters at Fairbanks, had placed detachments at Big Delta, Tanacross, Northway, Galena and Nome.

In February 1943, the commanding officer of the Alaskan Wing had the 16th Army Airways Communication Squadron take over all aeronautical radio installations. Northwest Airlines tried, in vain, to retain control. Records show that by March 1943, over 400 lend-lease aircraft had reached Fairbanks; 369 passed the checks of the Soviet Mission there, and had been accepted and flown away by Russian pilots. The accepted planes included 106 A-20s, 34 B-25s, 151 P-39s, 48 P-40s and 30 C-47s.

The winter of 1942-43 saw the Alaskan Wing increase its strength more than two-fold. By the end of March 1943, the wing had 240 officers and 1,497 enlisted men on its rolls.

On April 13, 1943, Col. Mosely was transferred to command of the North African Wing ATC, and Col. Dale V. Gaffney, C.O. of the Cold Weather Testing Detachment at Ladd Field, was offered command of the Alaskan Wing. He took over command of the wing at its headquarters in Edmonton, and four months later was promoted to brigadier general.

Two new ferrying squadrons were activated in the 7th Ferrying Group on April 15, 1943. They were the 90th, under Capt. Joseph L. Sullivan, and the 307th, under Maj. Reesor M. Lawrence.

During the course of 1943, much time and energy was spent in trying to expand operations and facilities of the Air Transport Command in Alaska and Canada. There was not only conflict between the Alaskan Wing and the 7th Ferrying Group, but also friction between the Wing and the Alaska Defense Command, Canadian Department of Transport, Canadian Joint Board of Defense, the Army Engineers and the U.S. Civil Aeronautics Authority.

Gaffney, now a brigadier general, soon became known as "The Screaming Eagle of the Yukon," but the ATC finally got the warehouses, repair shops, laundries, bakeries, mess halls, barracks and the latrines that it needed.

By the summer of 1943, there were many Russians stationed at Fairbanks, Nome, Galena, Edmonton and Great Falls. For the most part, the Russians and Americans got along well, although it was obvious that Soviet personnel had been warned against fraternization with American personnel. In turn, many American officers and men were highly prejudiced against the Russians due to years of warnings against the "Red Menace."

As could be expected there were aircraft losses, not only on the trip north but from the factories to Great Falls. Strangely, the Search and Rescue organization was slow to develop. Air crews were taught survival techniques and equipped with what was then the best flying and emergency gear available.

On July 20, 1943, women entered the ALSIB picture when the 880th WAAC Company was activated at Great Falls. As time went on, they worked at jobs ranging from airplane mechanics to private secretaries. Later a large group of WACs were sent to Whitehorse and another to Fairbanks, after the WACs were taken into the Army after having been auxilliaries in the WAAC.

P-63s being pre-heated in frigid weather at Fort Nelson, British Columbia. AAC

Operations building at the Bismarck, North Dakota, detachment.
COURTESY 7th FERRYING GROUP ASSOCIATION

Flight Officer Andrew Traverso and his flight of Bell P-63 Kingcobras at Fort Nelson, British Columbia. AAC

On July 15, 1943, the 7th Ferrying Group established a detachment at the Bismarck, North Dakota, airport to service transient aircraft. Later this unit was taken over by the ferrying division in Cincinnati.

On October 15, 1943, East Base at Great Falls was transferred from the Second Air Force to the 34th Sub-Depot. Originally, processed aircraft left Gore Field, Great Falls, for the trip north. All activity was soon centered at East Base, insofar as arrivals, processing and departures were concerned.

On November 18, 1943, the 402nd Service Squadron was attached to Edmonton Air Base and the 405th Service Squadron to the Whitehorse Air Base. These units, together with the 6th Air Depot Group at Fairbanks and the 398th Service Squadron at Nome, provided the higher-echelon aircraft maintenance required at the major bases.

By December 1943, the Alaskan Wing had a strength of some 5,438 officers and enlisted men. The assigned personnel included 1,200 men who had passed through the Arctic Training School at Buckley Field, Colorado.

Flight Officer C.D. Markle flying a P-63 west of Canyon Creek, Yukon. AAC

With the organization in January 1944 of Search and Rescue Flights at Edmonton, Fort Nelson, Whitehorse, Fairbanks and Nome, the Alaskan Wing had in operation a systematic procedure for recovering missing personnel and aircraft. One hundred dollars reward was paid for information leading to the discovery of pilots or crew members forced down in the bush. Posters were printed to make this known to trappers, Indians, prospectors and other civilians.

The Arctic Training School, a satellite of Buckley Field, Denver, Colorado, was located at Echo Lake on the slope of Mount Evans, some 10,600 feet above sea level. This school prepared personnel for duty in Arctic areas. The training included practical instruction in personal gear, use of clothing and equipment and Arctic travel. Enlisted personnel assigned to the Alaskan Division, Air Transport Command, were all processed through a six-week course at the school.

Salvaging a crashed P-39 at Carpenter Lake, Yukon.
COURTESY 7th FERRYING GROUP ASSOCIATION

Later the Arctic Training School was transferred to the Alaskan Division, ATC, and moved to East Base, Great Falls, Montana, and then to Namao, Alberta. Small detachments were sent to Search and Rescue Flights and other personnel were used to brief northbound pilots. Maj. A.K. Innes-Taylor was director of the Arctic Training School, while the technical phase of the training school was under Maj. Elga M. Glendy at East Base.

An entry in the Alaskan Division's history states:

"All aircraft assigned to Search and Rescue Flights are equipped with skis and wheels; in the spring and summer, some are equipped with floats. Most S.&R. aircraft carry automatic compasses capable of picking up the 'Gibson Girl' radio. Power launches and allied equipment are available wherever they are needed. Fort Nelson, Whitehorse, Fairbanks, and Nome maintain pack and sledge dogs. These dogs and the men who handle them are experienced travelers and have proven their value in arctic rescue work. Seventeen of these dogs are used in the Canadian Sector and a comparable number in the Alaskan Sector. An additional 20 head are being requisitioned for the Canadian Sector for use between Fort Nelson and Whitehorse. These dogs, Siberian, Eskimo, Malemute and MacKenzie River huskies, have

been trained exclusively for pack and sled work at Camp Rimini, Montana. A 'practical experience' training program has been prescribed for the Arctic Search and Rescue Training unit."

As a result of numerous aircraft accidents over the route during February 1944, the Alaskan Wing operations officer complained in a radiogram to ATC headquarters:

"The majority of these accidents could have been prevented provided the pilots had sufficient time in type aircraft being flown over the route. It also points to a lack of flight discipline. This headquarters cannot continue to accept responsibility of accidents unless sufficient transition time is given to pilots departing over this route."

Accidents listed for the month were: a mid-air collision between two P-39s near Harding Lake, southeast of Fairbanks; the forced landing of an A-20, flown by Lt. A.J. Neal, which went down at Calgary, Alberta, due to partial engine failure; a forced landing near Fairbanks of a P-39, flown by Lt. Joseph Sulmeyer, caused by weather conditions and poor judgement on the part of a flight leader; and a C-64 crash at Carpenter Lake that killed Lt. W.L. Nodine and the plane's crew chief. Nine additional accidents occurred to ferried and assigned aircraft.

As of March 31, 1944, the installation at Gore Field became known as the 557th Army Air Forces Base Unit. Under this new set-up, it was not necessary to issue general orders to activate squadrons.

The movement of a typical ALSIB airplane from the factory to Fairbanks worked as follows. Ferrying Division control officers were stationed at the factories. These officers were advised of aircraft ready for delivery by air material command officers at the same factories. The aircraft distribution office in Dayton, Ohio, advised them of the destinations of these planes. At the same time, the control officers kept in close touch with the ferrying group which they represented.

A P-63 on a flight over the frozen north country. AAC

Whitehorse airport, October 1943. A-20s and P-39s being refueled for their final leg to Ladd Field and Marks Field.
RF

For example, when a P-63 was turned over to the AAF by Bell in Buffalo, New York, through the material command officer, he in turn contacted the control officer. The latter turned the plane over to a pilot, usually one from the 3rd Ferrying Group of Romulus, Michigan. This pilot would deliver the plane to East Base in Great Falls.

In May 1944, the 16th AACS Squadron, which supplied radio and teletype services to the Alaskan Wing from Edmonton to Nome, was designated the 60th AACS Group with two squadrons, the 122nd serving Canada and the 123rd Alaska.

As facilities on the route improved, the Soviet Union chose to have larger proportions of its lend-lease aircraft delivered over the route. In June 1944, Gen. Leonid G. Rudenko, chairman of the Soviet Purchasing Commission in Washington, requested that all aircraft to be delivered under the Fourth Protocol be sent by way of Fairbanks. On July 1, 1944, the Alaskan Wing ATC was redesignated the Alaskan Division ATC.

The last A-20 was accepted by the Russians in July 1944. However, this was not to be the last heard of the A-20s.

There were two classes of pilots assigned to ferrying aircraft in the Air Transport Command. The first was the graduate of the Army Flying Training Program who, upon graduation, received the aeronautical rating of "airplane pilot" and usually a commission as second lieutenant. Some were made flight officers. Flight officer rank was equal to warrant officer and was utilized only during World War II. The other class of pilot was the civilian trained pilot who was taken into the Army as a flight officer with the aeronautical rating of "service pilot." The service pilot wore the same silver wings as a regularly rated pilot except that there was a letter "S" on the shield of his wings.

On August 14, 1944, the 25th, 307th and 90th Ferrying Squadrons were inactivated and their personnel taken into

Russian ferry pilots arriving at Ladd Field. Soviet combat pilots were sent to Alaska to pick up lend-lease aircraft. It was regarded as a "rest from combat."
COURTESY 7th FERRYING GROUP ASSOCIATION

the 7th Ferrying Squadron. This put all the pilots and crews into one unit. The squadron strength became 559 officers and 39 enlisted men, a somewhat unusual type of squadron. By this time, ALSIB required a large number of pilots.

In August 1944, a record-breaking 423 aircraft arrived at Ladd Field. Two hundred thirty-seven were delivered in September and 186 in October. The 11th Air Force received nine replacement aircraft from September deliveries, while the Cold Weather Testing Detachment got nine.

On September 6, 1944, the new Red Air Force insignia was painted on aircraft for the first time. It was a red star with a narrow white border outline. This replaced the red star in a white globe or circle.

Russian officers quarters at Ladd Field. AAC

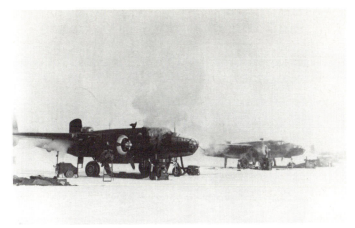

B-25s on the line at Ladd Field at 35° below zero F. AAC

Main hangar and tower at
Ladd Field. P-39s are lined up
on the ramp.
COURTESY 7th FERRYING GROUP
ASSOCIATION

P-39s on the ramp at Ladd
Field. AAC

On Sept. 10, 1944, ceremonies were conducted at Ladd Field to celebrate the delivery of the 5,000th lend-lease airplane over the ALSIB route. Left to right are: Col. Russell Keiller, Brig. Gen. Dale V. Gaffney and Soviet Col. P.S. Kisilov. Note that the display airplane has its tail number censored.

COURTESY 7th FERRYING GROUP ASSOCIATION

Weather services were provided for the ALSIB operation by the 16th Weather Squadron. Four weather and four AACS men were sent to Dease Lake on September 13, and the same numbers to Takla Landing on the 17th. The Takla Landing men moved into sumptuous quarters which had recently been abandoned by Pan American Airways. These quarters included two married couples' quarters and a dwelling for bachelors, in addition to an operations building and housing for the power plant. They had wood stoves and running water.

While the airbases needed for the ALSIB operation were relatively few in number, the sites required for weather and communications services were many. Many of these outposts provided nothing but discomfort, loneliness and hardships. There were only a few men at each post and most of the sites were very isolated. They were resupplied infrequently, usually by the UC-64s of the Search and Rescue Flights. The men that served at these outposts will never forget such places as Cape Wales, Point Spencer, Koyuk, Kokrines and Kaltag in Alaska; Trout Lake and Eskimo Point in the Canadian Northwest Territories; Takla, Dease Lake and Muncho Lake in British Columbia; Duck Lake, Manitoba and Island Falls in Saskatchewan; and Brooks Brook, Rancheria, Trout-Liard, Morely River, Flight Strip Eight, Canyon Creek and Swift River in the Yukon Territory. At their peak, there were over 60 of these stations covering western Canada and Alaska.

Life at the air bases was not always easy, either. Galena, long viewed by many division personnel as a place of exile for the visibly disaffected and flagrantly uncooperative, received a shot in the arm from Gen. Gaffney in September 1944. The general stated publicly that the assignment of a man to Galena was on the basis of a tough job to be done, and not as punishment for wrongdoing. The men at Galena were commended for having accomplished a difficult undertaking

with remarkably good spirit. Be that as it may, Galena was still considered the hell hole of the entire route stretching from Great Falls to Nome.

Life at Tanacross also became brighter on September 15, 1944, when the base theatre, rather appropriately named "The Parka Palace," opened to a capacity audience of 180 persons. During the month the Officers Club also opened, though it still lacked paint, and visiting officers were more comfortably cared for in a newly painted and decorated Stout house, left vacant by departing civilian employees. Baking, laundry and dry cleaning equipment, installed in July at Tok Junction, 10 miles south of Tanacross, was operated by the utility detachment at Tanacross aided by seven men from Northway.

A spacious, well-heated, Nissen hut-type building was completed at Whitehorse during September 1944, for use as a theatre or general recreation hall. During the first week of October, Whitehorse experienced a critical shortage of meat, potatoes and perishable food stuffs. The base had been without cheese for five months. Fresh meat and vegetables were being delivered by ship to Skagway and then transported on the White Pass & Yukon Railroad to Whitehorse. The WP&Y was out of service for a period of three weeks because of land slides. To relieve the situation, the Alaskan Division provided air transport and brought in 84,000 pounds of food to the Whitehorse base.

The 550th AAF Band was transferred to Edmonton from East Base, and morale was boosted at Whitehorse in October 1944 by the arrival of 125 WACs originally destined for Fairbanks. They were far from satisfied when they found out they were going to Whitehorse instead. After spending 15 days at Great Falls being processed, equipped and briefed, they began their plane trip. On October 15th, they left East Base, crossed the line into Canada, and upon arrival at Whitehorse, became the division's first "overseas" WACs.

Vice-president Henry A. Wallace, returning from a trip to China and Siberia, stopped at Ladd Field in 1944. He is dining with Col. N.S. Vasin, commanding officer of the Russian Air Force's first aviation ferrying regiment, who was stationed at Nome and Col. Russell Keiller, commanding officer of Ladd Field.
LC USW 33-53756-2C

Galena airbase during the 1945 Yukon River flood.
COURTESY 7th FERRYING GROUP ASSOCIATION

Conditions at Whitehorse were an eye opener for the girls. The notions of what the northland held for them were a combination of misinformation, popular legend, the poet, Robert Service and the stories they had heard of what the men in the AAF had experienced in the early days of the division.

Other problems experienced at the ALSIB bases included fires and floods. The occurence of two disastrous fires at Ladd Field, Fairbanks, in May and June 1945, drove division fire loss rates to a high level.

The first and most costly fire occurred shortly before 1800 hours in the evening of May 26 in Hangar 5, a birchwood building which housed those lend-lease aircraft in the course of processing. Though smoke was noticed at five minutes to six, the fire department was not called until about 20 minutes later. Though it appeared at one time that the fire was being brought under control, this hope was dashed as the main water supply failed. Investigation revealed that the water level in one well had fallen below the point at which it could be raised by the mobile pumping unit in use. The hangar was a total loss, with damage at well over a half million dollars. As well as could be determined, the cause appeared to be spontaneous, for the fire originated in a linseed oil soaked mop which was stored in a metal container in one of the classrooms.

The second costly fire took place the following month. Early in the afternoon of June 26, fire broke out in the WAC barracks. This building had been completed in February. Efforts to save the building were unavailing, and by the time the fire fighters succeeded in extinguishing the flames, the barracks was 95 percent destroyed. The damage was estimated at $230,000. One fatality occurred; a WAC, caught in the shower room, was unable to escape. Several others escaped by jumping from second story windows. All possessions, including clothing, were lost. Defective wiring was believed to be the cause of the fire, but the ineptness of the fire fighting personnel contributed to the completeness of the loss.

In the latter part of May 1945, Galena experienced its third flood in as many years. Each year the waters of the Yukon River had backed and flooded the airbase, only a stone's throw from the river. Efforts to prepare against the flood were of some value. Weather personnel studied data of years gone by in an attempt to anticipate the probable time and intensity of the 1945 flood. Stocks of bombs were made ready for the bombing of ice jams. Careful watch was kept on the river as far upstream as Fort Yukon, so that as much warning as possible could be given. Dikes were reinforced. These efforts proved relatively unavailing.

The ice broke at Fort Yukon on May 19. For the next few days, men worked feverishly as the water rose. On May 24, the waters began to rise rapidly, increasing in rate as evening

Marks Field, Nome, Alaska. Here the lend-lease aircraft took off for the flight to Siberia under operational control of the Russians. COURTESY 7th FERRYING GROUP ASSOCIATION

came on. All night long men worked with bulldozers, reinforcing the lowest and weakest places in the dike. In the morning, the water broke through and soon cut a gap of 25 feet in the dike. Work was abandoned, and personnel and supplies were moved out of danger. All activity ceased except radio communications, weather service and the work necessary to feed personnel.

Throughout the next two days, the water continued to rise until on the 27th, the level was seven feet above the 1944 level. By this time the field was completely inundated. Men slept on roofs, upper floors and in and under trucks parked on high ground. Many slept and ate on the gravel piles and dikes. Water purifiers were set up on the gravel pile. Drinking water was carried to men in the hangar. Sanitary facilities in the hangar consisted of buckets which were emptied out windows. The ice jams were bombed by the 11th Air Force to little avail. The Navy sent PBYs, in which a number of men were evacuated to Fairbanks and Nome. After reaching its peak on May 27, the water began to drop.

Discouraging is perhaps a moderate word to apply to the shambles which was left as the Yukon retreated from the base. Sixty-eight buildings were lost or unrepairable. Dozens of others needed repairs. Tons of supplies were lost or damaged. Personal belongings were lost. By the end of July, the main area within the dike had been cleaned up. Reconstruction went ahead. One hundred fifty men were placed on detached service at Galena from other stations, and they did not return to their home bases until August. All construction was ordered halted at Alaskan bases, including Galena, in August 1945.

Returning to the previous year, the 5,000th airplane was delivered to the Russians at Ladd Field on September 10, 1944. Deliveries declined after that date. This development was surprising, as the forecast had been that "this forecast will not change in the event that Germany is not defeated by 1 October, 1944."

September 1944 also marked the delivery of the last three P-39s and the final acceptance of the last 12 to the Russians.

Several periods of bad weather, one from September 15th to 19th and the other from October 24th to 28th, 1944, retarded deliveries of aircraft. These periods were reflected in an increased number of station stops and a lengthening of elapsed time between Great Falls and Fairbanks. For single-engine aircraft, the increase in the number of station stops was comparatively small, but for twin-engine planes it was appreciable. P-63s averaged one additional day to cover the route in September 1944 as compared with August; in October, the preceding month's median of 4.4 days jumped to 8.9. Twin-engine planes spent over twice as much time enroute in September as they had in August.

By October the figure was reduced, but it remained above the August median. Overall median elapsed time from departure at Great Falls to acceptance by the Russians amounted to eight and 13 days respectively for twin engine

-46-

The first Russian military mission to Alaska arrives at Nome in the late summer of 1942. AAC

Brig. Gen. Dale Gaffney, commanding general of the Alaskan Wing, Air Transport Command being welcomed by Col. N.S. Vasin, commander of the Russian detachment in Alaska. LC USW 33-53757-2C

A-20 bombers on the strip at Marks Field. Note the lettering on the near aircraft. LC USW 33-53755-2C

planes, and to 13 days during both months for the P-63s.

The Alaskan Division's first headquarters staff Search and Rescue officer, Maj. Joseph Westover, was appointed September 16, 1944. Prior to that date he served as Search and Rescue officer, sector A. He retained his former assignment along with assignment to the staff.

Flight A, which had centered its operations at Edmonton air base for many months, was transferred to Namao, the transfer being completed on September 28, 1944. This action was taken in anticipation of the imminent transfer of ferrying operations from Edmonton to Namao, and since ferried and tactical aircraft are Search and Rescue's primary concern,

it was considered appropriate that Flight A should be located at Namao as well.

The need for a long-range airplane for inland search and rescue involving extended flight had been noted by Brig. Gen. Francis M. Brady, ATC Air Inspector, in his report following an inspection of the Alaskan Division. Gen. Gaffney was able to report that a B-17 had been requested. Until it arrived, and it was not expected until late fall, it was proposed that two C-47s be assigned for long-range search and rescue, one to go to each Search and Rescue sector. In late October 1944, three pilots were sent to Gore Field, Great Falls, Montana, to take transition training in B-17s, so as to be prepared when the division planes arrived.

The desirability of relocating the Watson Lake radio range, a matter which had been considered for a year, was reemphasized in April 1945. The difficulty with the existing range location lay in the fact that the pilot, prior to his let-down, had to locate the cone and execute a sharp right turn toward the runway. A miscalculation in passing over the cone, at which time the plane is at 3,500 feet, would lead him directly into 3,000-foot mountains just ahead. The proposed relocation would provide a straight-in approach. Gen. Gaffney stated that at least three aircraft had been lost because of this installation. As the war ended in August, nothing had been done.

The Russians expected an early end to the war in Europe, as this Intelligence Report from Nome, written in April 1945, indicates:

"A large number of Russian aircraft have been parked at this base for several weeks. Ferrying from here to Siberian bases has been spasmodic due to weather conditions west of Nome, to a reported flooding of certain Russian bases in Siberia, and to what appears to be an increasing apathetic attitude by Russian personnel as to speed of delivery of aircraft to Siberian bases. Approximately six weeks ago a Russian non-com was reported to have told a small group of our enlisted men that he would return to his home by June 1st. During the past week, many Russian officers are reported to have made remarks, quite openly, that they would soon be packing and leaving Alaska, giving June 1 or July 1 as probable departure dates. Russian pilots display no interest in flying unless weather is CAVU, in contrast to past policy of flying in almost any weather. In short, the war necessity pressure appears to be removed and no longer engrosses the Russian personnel stationed or transient at Nome."

In May 1945, the Russians again started receiving A-20 light bombers over the route, of which 97 were delivered. During the same month, AT-6 advanced trainers started arriving and 54 of a projected 225 were delivered by the end of the ALSIB operation. With the close of the war in Europe, deliveries of lend-lease aircraft continued but were cut back sharply.

The close of the war in Europe, which also wrote "finis" to the need for ferrying planes to the Russians for use on the eastern front, brought about some abrupt revisions in ALSIB plans. The crux of the matter was, of course, Russian decisions regarding the war in the Pacific. It seemed perfectly obvious that if the U.S.S.R. entered the war against Japan, business over the northwest route would pick up tremendously. Air Transport Command was informed on May 22, 1945, that delivery of P-63s at the rate of 200 per month would continue for May and June. B-25s now en route or to be delivered from factories would complete the commitments for May and June and would proceed according to previous plans. The 225 AT-6s would be summarily

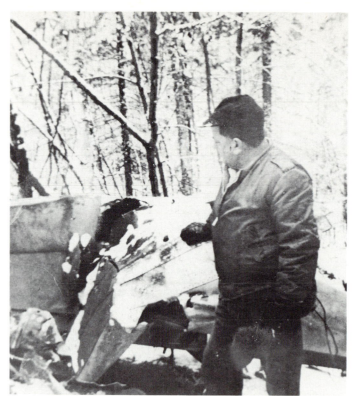

Deane Brandon, author of the ALSIB story, inspects the wreckage of a P-39 which crashed shortly after takeoff from Ladd Field in September 1944, killing its Russian pilot. Even in 1972, when this photo was taken, the wreckage was still visible in a wooded area off Badger Road, Fairbanks.
COURTESY 7th FERRYING GROUP ASSOCIATION

reduced to 55; C-47 assignments for May and June would continue as scheduled. After June 30, no deliveries were planned, with the exception of 240 C-47s delivered at the rate of 40 per month for the remainder of the year.

After June 30, the ferrying activity in the division consisted of the movement of previously allocated P-63s, A-20s, AT-6s and the new commitments of C-47s. One hundred fifty-seven planes were delivered in July; three types, 71 P-63s, 40 C-47s and 46 A-20s, made up the number. In August, the total fell to 37, of which 32 were C-47s. The remainder consisted of two P-63s, two A-20s and one AT-6. By this time, even the new commitments for C-47s had been cancelled.

By the end of August 1945, 7,971 planes had been delivered to the Russians at Fairbanks and 7,926 had been flown away from that base by Russian pilots. Of these, the Russians accepted 5,066 fighter aircraft, all of which, with the exception of 51, were either P-39s or P-63s. A-20 light bombers numbered 1,363. B-25s numbered 732, C-47s 710 and C-46 one.

In the final phase of the ALSIB movement, from November 1944 through August 1945, 2,447 planes were delivered to Fairbanks. During the same period, 180 other planes were delivered to the Ladd Field Cold Weather Testing Detachment and to the 11th Air Force.

There was no movement of aircraft to the Cold Weather Testing Detachment after April 1945. The detachment received its first B-29 in November 1944, and two more arrived in the next two months. Other unusual arrivals included a Bell P-59 jet fighter for which special fuel had been distributed over the route, a P-61 night fighter and two A-26 light bombers.

The 11th Air Force received 143 planes, the majority of which were P-38s. In mid-November, the division was advised that beginning in December, 50 B-24s would be delivered to the Russians each month until a total of 200 had been sent. In documents dealing with estimated foreign delivery, the B-24s continued to be mentioned as late as December. However, the subject was dropped eventually and no B-24s were ever delivered.

In May 1945 came the first two planes of a projected 100 A-20s, and in the months that followed, 97 were delivered. This was the first movement of A-20s since the preceding July and came as a surprise to the division, for advice had been to the effect that this model was to be discontinued. One C-46, the only one of its type ever to be delivered over

the route to the Russians, came through in April 1945. Advanced training planes, AT-6s, were newcomers in the ALSIB movement. These made their first appearance in May and although 225 were originally projected, the figure was reduced to 55 after VE Day.

By the end of September 1945, the ALSIB operation was finished. The last Russians departed Fairbanks in October.

From September 1942 until ALSIB ended in September 1945, the following numbers of aircraft were delivered over the route:

P-39	2,618
P-63	2,397
P-40	48
P-47	3
A-20	1,363
B-25	732
C-47	710
C-46	1
At-6	54
Total	7,926

Many planes crashed on the long flights from Great Falls to Fairbanks due to weather conditions, mechanical problems and sometimes pilot error. This A-29 Hudson III, came down near fort Nelson, British Columbia, in 1943. GA

Flight Officer

The rank of "Flight Officer" existed in the USAAF only during World War II. It was equal to the rank of "Warrant Officer" and only those awarded pilot or aircrew wings of the various kinds could be made Flight Officers. Many F/O later received commissions as Second Lieutenants.

The rating of "Service Pilot" was awarded to certain qualified civilian pilots who were taken into the service directly as

pilots. They wore a letter "S" on the shield of their wings as opposed to the regular wings. In 1944, due to over production of pilots in the Air Training Command, many civilian contract flying instructors were taken into the Ferrying Division of the Air Transport Command to ferry aircraft, being given "S" pilot wings and the rank of Flight Officer.

ROUTE INFORMATION
COASTAL ROUTE
SEATTLE TO ANNETTE

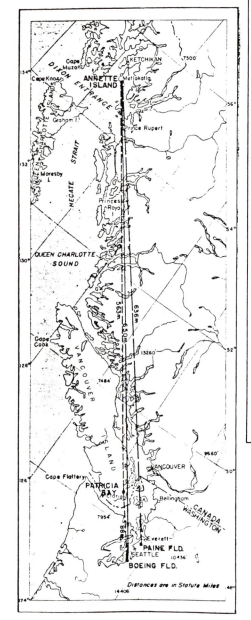

GREAT FALLS TO EDMONTON

All the major stops on this route are equipped with radio range stations and the route presents no major difficulties to flying.

From Great Falls to Lethbridge, the track is over sparsely settled, fairly low, rolling country averaging 4,000 feet in altitude and crossed by numerous streams. Lethbridge is located on the conspicuous Oldman River.

Flat plateau country between 3,000 and 3,500 feet in altitude, is typical between Lethbridge and Calgary. The Canadian Pacific Railroad runs between these two points and may be followed with little sacrifice in distance. Fifty-five miles out from Lethbridge, the course passes directly over Kirkcaldy. There are seven landing fields in the Calgary area, the best field lying to the northeast of the city. Calgary is located on the Bow River, which on the straight course is crossed 42 miles southeast of the airport. Most of these fields are training stations for the R.C.A.F. and due caution should be observed in this area because of the large number of planes in the air.

The railroad continues from Calgary to Edmonton, keeping to the west of the track for the first half of the distance, and to the east of the track for the latter half. Seventy-four miles from Calgary, Penhold Airport is 4 miles left abeam, and at 83 miles the large Red Deer River is crossed. The terrain is low, fairly level, and north of the Red Deer River a great many lakes are in evidence. Edmonton is very conspicuous from a distance and like the other large cities in this area, is situated on a large river, the Saskatchewan.

COURSES AND DISTANCES

FROM	TO	STATUTE MILES	NAUTICAL MILES	TRUE COURSE	MAGNETIC COURSE
GREAT FALLS	EDMONTON	431	374	343°	323° (143°)
GREAT FALLS	LETHBRIDGE	162	141	336°	315° (135°)
LETHBRIDGE	CALGARY	107	93	334°	311° (131°)
CALGARY	EDMONTON	172	149	07°	342° (162°)
CALGARY	PENHOLD	73	63	04°	339° (159°)
PENHOLD	EDMONTON	100	87	11°	346° (166°)

REGINA TO EDMONTON

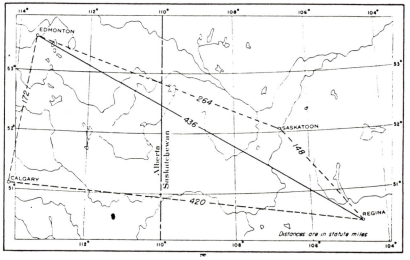

ROUTE INFORMATION

EDMONTON TO FORT ST. JOHN

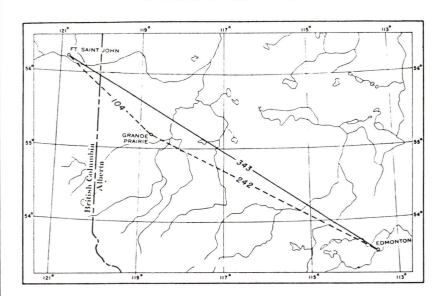

FLIGHT PROFILES

ON TRACK
---- 30 MILES EITHER SIDE OF TRACK
DISTANCES IN STATUTE MILES
FORT ST. JOHN TO EDMONTON

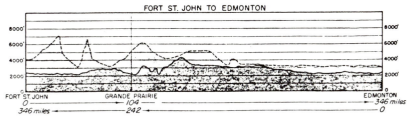

COURSES AND DISTANCES

FROM	TO	STATUTE MILES	NAUTICAL MILES	TRUE COURSE	MAGNETIC COURSE
EDMONTON	FORT ST. JOHN	343	298	302°	274° (94°)
EDMONTON	GRANDE PRAIRIE	242	210	300°	273° (93°)
GRANDE PRAIRIE	FORT ST. JOHN	104	90	320°	291° (111°)

EDMONTON TO GRANDE PRAIRIE

For the first fifty miles northwest of Edmonton, the terrain is flat to rolling, extensively cultivated, and with few small communities located throughout the area. The route follows closely the route of the Canadian Pacific Railroad to White Court, where it terminates at the junction of the Sarwataman and Athabasca Rivers. The next 150 miles, the country is uninhabited, and uncultivated, and no railroads or highways are observed. Emergency landings over this area would be extremely difficult and rescue parties would have considerable difficulty in getting to the site of the landing. Just prior to reaching Grande Prairie, the country flattens out and is extensively cultivated, with a few small communities located around the immediate vicinity at Grande Prairie. Emergency landings can be effected over this area safely. Charts of this area are not very accurate, and rivers indicated on these charts are not to be relied upon as landmarks for navigation purposes.

RADIO FACILITIES - The northwest leg of the Edmonton range is projected directly on this course and the southeast leg of the Grande Prairie range interlocks with the northwest leg of Edmonton. Under normal reception conditions, radio contact for navigation purposes can be maintained between these two points and it is recommended that pilots avail themselves of these facilities although flights may be proceeding contact. The range station at Grande Prairie is so located with the northwest leg projected directly over the field at Grande Prairie making low instrument approaches at these stations feasible.

INTERMEDIATE FIELDS - No intermediate fields are available for the entire distance between Edmonton and Grande Prairie.

NIGHT FLYING AIDS - With the exception of obstruction, boundary and beacon lights at Grande Prairie, no night flying aids are available on this leg of the route.

GRANDE PRAIRIE TO FORT ST. JOHN

For the first forty miles, the terrain is quite flat and extensively cultivated, with few small communities located in the immediate vicinity of Grande Prairie. Several large lakes can be observed from the course and serve as landmarks to the pilot over this area. Beyond this point, the terrain rises slightly and becomes uninhabited and quite heavily timbered with the average height of the hills about 3,000 feet above sea level. This uninhabited hilly and timbered country continues to Fort St. John and although numerous streams and rivers cross the route, due to the inaccuracy of present charts, they are not to be relied upon for navigation purposes. Within the immediate vicinity of Fort St. John, limited cultivation will be observed and few small communities are situated in the area. On this leg of the route, because of the rolling, hilly and timbered terrain, emergency landings would be difficult to effect safely.

RADIO FACILITIES - The northwest leg of the Grande Prairie range is projected along this course and the southwest leg of the Fort St. John range, although it is not interlocked with the northwest leg at Grande Prairie, is sufficiently close to the magnetic bearing of this route to be used in the approach to Fort St. John. Under normal radio conditions, contact can be maintained with these two stations for navigation purposes. The range site of the Fort St. John range is located to offer feasible low instrument approach.

INTERMEDIATE FIELDS - The only intermediate field available between Grande Prairie and Fort St. John is a flight strip under construction at Dawson Creek.

NIGHT FLYING AIDS - No night flying aids are available on this route with the exception of obstruction, boundary and beacon lights on the field at Fort St. John.

FORT ST. JOHN TO FORT NELSON

From Fort St. John to Fort Nelson, the terrain is chiefly hills, heavily timbered, averaging about 3,500 feet in height, with deep ravines and numerous streams and rivers. The territory is uncultivated and uninhabited with the exception of a few trappers and Indians trading with the Hudson Bay Company at Sikanni. There are few landmarks with the exception of the rivers crossed on the route, and charts for this area are unreliable. Because of the nature of the terrain, emergency landings over this area would be difficult.

RADIO FACILITIES - The northwest leg of the Fort St. John range is projected along this area and the southeast leg of the Fort Nelson range approximately interlocks. Under normal radio conditions, radio contact is easily maintained between these two stations and it is recommended that these two radio facilities be used even during contact flights. The range station at Fort Nelson is located southwest of the airport and the northeast leg is projected over the field, making low instrument approaches feasible at this station.

INTERMEDIATE FIELDS - No intermediate fields are available between Fort St. John and Fort Nelson. Several flight strips are under construction to the west of the route.

NIGHT FLYING AIDS - With the exception of obstruction, boundary and beacon lights at Fort Nelson, no intermediate night flying facilities are available.

FORT NELSON TO WATSON LAKE

Immediately upon leaving Fort Nelson, the terrain rises rapidly, becoming mountainous with high ranges of the Rocky Mountains plainly visible to the west. The route parallels this range the entire distance to Watson Lake with the average elevation between 7,000 and 8,000 feet above sea level. To the north and northeast, the terrain is much lower but the entire route over which this course is projected is rugged and mountainous. About 90 miles northwest of Fort Nelson, the route crosses the Liard River and follows closely to the grand canyon of the Liard for about 40 miles. The terrain over this area is high, averaging about 7,000 feet above sea level, offering few sites for emergency landing. Weather conditions over this area frequently are bad because of squall conditions due to the effect of the close proximity of the mountains. The charts for this area are unreliable; however, the course of the Liard River is quite accurately plotted. The Liard River offers an excellent landmark for pilots during contact flight and can be followed the entire distance into Watson Lake.

RADIO FACILITIES - The northwest leg of the Fort Nelson range is projected on a magnetic bearing of 261° and approximately interlocks with the east leg of Watson Lake range. Because of the distance between these two range stations, under normal radio conditions continuous radio contact is difficult. Therefore, heading should be established immediately upon leaving Fort Nelson and should be maintained until readable signals are heard from the Watson Lake station. The south leg of the Watson Lake range is projected directly over the field; however, it is not in line with the projection of the runway. Reasonable low instrument approaches are feasible at Watson Lake; however, extreme caution should be used in following this procedure.

INTERMEDIATE FIELDS - No intermediate fields are available between Fort Nelson and Watson Lake, but several flight strips are under construction along the route.

NIGHT FLYING AIDS - No intermediate night flying aids are in operation between these two points; however, beacon, obstruction and boundary lights are in operation at Watson Lake.

WATSON LAKE TO WHITEHORSE

For the first fifty miles, northwest of Watson Lake, the terrain directly on course is rolling, heavily timbered plateau, averaging an elevation of about 2,500 feet above sea level. As the course proceeds west, the mountains to the south form a horseshoe over the route and rise rapidly to an average elevation of about 8,000 feet above sea level. About 100 miles west of Watson Lake lies Wolf Lake, and just prior to reaching Wolf Lake, the terrain recedes, forming a wide valley running north and south, offering emergency landing within the immediate vicinity of Wolf Lake. Immediately after passing Wolf Lake, the mountains again rise rapidly to 7,000 feet with some peaks on the route extending to 8,000 feet above sea level. The mountains continue into Whitehorse, with Whitehorse lying in a narrow valley. Wolf Lake offers an excellent landmark for pilots as it is the largest lake in the area on the course. Teslin Lake lies to the south of the course and is plainly visible about 40 miles west of Wolf Lake. Numerous streams and rivers will be observed which are not plotted on the charts, and caution must be exercised in following these rivers during contact flight.

ROUTE INFORMATION

FORT ST. JOHN TO WHITEHORSE

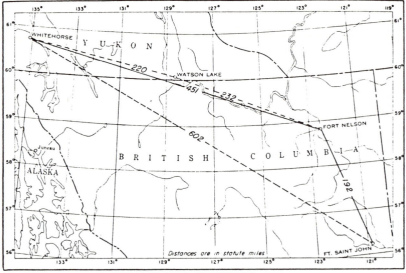

FLIGHT PROFILES

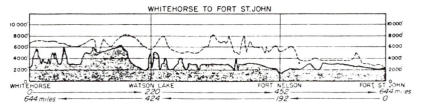

COURSES AND DISTANCES

FROM	TO	STATUTE MILES	NAUTICAL MILES	TRUE COURSE	MAGNETIC COURSE
FORT ST. JOHN	WHITEHORSE	602	523	301°	269° (89°)
FORT ST. JOHN	FORT NELSON	192	168	339°	307° (127°)
FORT NELSON	WHITEHORSE	451	392	287°	254° (74°)
FORT NELSON	WATSON LAKE	232	201	293°	259° (79°)
WATSON LAKE	WHITEHORSE	220	191	283°	249° (69°)

RADIO FACILITIES - The west leg of the Watson Lake range is projected on a magnetic bearing of 249 degrees and interlocks with the east leg of the Whitehorse range. Because of the great distance between these two stations, contact with these ranges is difficult to maintain, and the range at Teslin should be used as a check point. It is recommended that upon leaving Watson Lake, a heading be established on the west leg of this range and maintained until signals are readable from the Whitehorse station. Pilots should use these facilities even during contact flight.

INTERMEDIATE FIELDS - No intermediate fields are available between Watson Lake and Whitehorse except for several flight strips which are under construction.

NIGHT FLYING AIDS - With the exception of the beacon, obstruction and boundary lights at Whitehorse, no night flying aids are available over this leg of the route.

ROUTE INFORMATION

WHITEHORSE TO FAIRBANKS

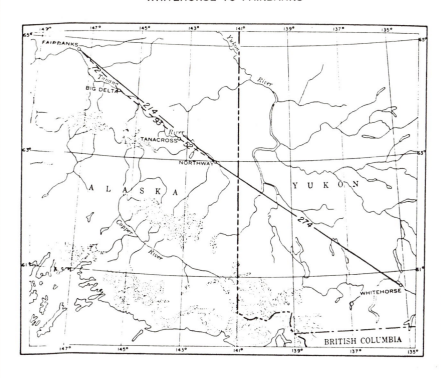

FLIGHT PROFILES

ON TRACK
30 MILES EITHER SIDE OF TRACK
DISTANCES IN STATUTE MILES
FAIRBANKS TO WHITEHORSE

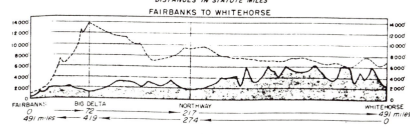

COURSES AND DISTANCES

FROM	TO	STATUTE MILES	NAUTICAL MILES	TRUE COURSE	MAGNETIC COURSE	
WHITEHORSE	FAIRBANKS	486	422	306°	275°	(95°)
WHITEHORSE	NORTHWAY	274	237	305°	270°	(90°)
NORTHWAY	FAIRBANKS	214	186	307°	276°	(96°)
NORTHWAY	BIG DELTA	145	126	303°	271°	(91°)
BIG DELTA	FAIRBANKS	72	63	312°	281°	(101°)
NORTHWAY	TANACROSS	52	45	304°	272°	(92°)
TANACROSS	BIG DELTA	93	81	306°	275°	(95°)

WHITEHORSE TO FAIRBANKS

The terrain between Whitehorse and Northway, a distance of 265 miles, is generally mountainous with numerous streams and rivers lying across the route. Immediately upon leaving Whitehorse, the terrain rises rapidly to an average elevation of 7,000 feet, making contact flight during adverse weather hazardous. About 70 miles northwest of Whitehorse, the route passes over Aishihik Lake, a long narrow lake easily distinguished by its shape. At the northwest end of the lake it is joined by a small stream with Sekulman Lake, another long lake, lying north and south, also easily identified from the route. Emergency landings could be effected with consequent damage, however, to aircraft in this area, and during freeze-up, flights could be landed safely on the ice. From Aishihik, for the next 75 miles, the route is extremely mountainous with no valleys and the average elevation of these mountains is 7,000 feet above sea level. Beyond this, the route crosses Wellesley Lake, which lies in a wide valley, to rolling plateau country with numerous valleys, rolling hills and intermittent mountains averaging 4,000 feet in height. Along the entire route from Whitehorse to Northway, the course parallels the St. Elias Mountains which lie approximately 50 miles to the southwest. These mountains are extremely high and rugged with peaks extending from 10,000 feet to 18,000 feet above sea level. Just prior to reaching Northway, the plateau flattens out into another large bowl with fewer rolling hills but with numerous scattered lakes. Contact flight from this point to Northway can be accomplished safely at low altitudes. The plateau continues in a northwesterly direction beyond Northway for about 40 miles; however, it narrows down into a wide valley and has a few hills rising to an elevation of about 3,000 feet. The course also approaches nearer to the St. Elias or Alaska range of mountains which now border the southwest side of the plateau. About 40 miles northwest of Northway, the terrain rises into rolling hills and mountains averaging in height about 3,000 to 4,000 feet above sea level. Upon reaching George Lake, the country again flattens out into a wide valley; however, the course follows within 20 miles of the Alaska mountain range. The range at this point averages about 8,000 feet in height, some peaks extending up to 9,000 and 10,000 feet above sea level.

At Big Delta, the valley broadens out, although Mt. Hayes, 13,740 feet in height, is only 35 miles south at this point. The terrain in the immediate vicinity of Big Delta is flat and marshy and contact flights at 3,000 feet can safely be made. At Salacher Lake, the valley widens further, and the Alaska range turns in a westerly direction leaving only a low range of hills to the west and northwest. For the entire distance from Northway to Fairbanks, the route follows closely the course of the Tanana River, which is an excellent landmark for pilots in contact flight. Caution is advised, however, in following the Tanana River with low visibility as frequent bends and turns are prevalent and the river at times approaches dangerously close to the higher mountains to the north.

RADIO FACILITIES - Between Whitehorse and Fairbanks, radio ranges in addition to the installations at Whitehorse and Fairbanks, are in operation at Northway and Big Delta. The northwest leg of the Whitehorse range approximately interlocks with the southeast leg of the Northway range and although it is difficult under normal radio conditions to maintain contact the entire distance, it is recommended that pilots establish heading on departure from Whitehorse. The range at Northway is located about 1½ miles northeast of Northway and the southwest leg projects directly over the runway. Because of the few obstructions in the immediate vicinity at Northway, low instrument approach is feasible however, caution is advised in following the procedure closely. Between Northway and Big Delta, the northwest leg of the Northway range and the southeast leg of the Big Delta range approximately interlock. Under normal conditions, continuous radio contact can be made over this leg of the route. At Big Delta also, the range station is located approximately 1½ miles northeast of the field and the southwest leg is projected along the NE./SW. runway. All approaches at this field are zero and this site makes low instrument approach feasible. From Big Delta to Fairbanks, the northwest leg of the Big Delta range is projected on a magnetic bearing of 281° and intersects the northwest leg of the Fairbanks range about 8 miles southwest of Fairbanks. Present identification procedure at Fairbanks requires pilots report at this intersection and contact the control tower at Ladd Field for approach and landing instructions.

INTERMEDIATE FIELDS - Intermediate fields are available between Whitehorse and Fairbanks at Northway, Tanacross and Big Delta, and all of these fields are adequate for large aircraft

NIGHT FLYING AIDS - With the exception of the lighted fields at Whitehorse, Northway, Big Delta and Fairbanks, and beacons installed at these points, no other night flying aids are in operation.

Russian merchant shipping in
Iliuliuk Bay, Unalaska Island,
Alaska, Aug. 10, 1945.
NA 80-G-354251

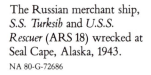

The first Russian freighter
unloads lumber at Adak. This
was a reverse lend-lease with
the Russians providing
lumber to American forces in
the Aleutians. NA 208-N-43517

The Russian merchant ship,
S.S. *Turksib* and *U.S.S.*
Rescuer (ARS 18) wrecked at
Seal Cape, Alaska, 1943.
NA 80-G-72686

These tugboats were transferred to Russia through lend-lease at Dutch Harbor, June 19, 1945. Note that both the American and Russian flags are flying on the boats.
NA 80-G-387036

Russian and United States sailors celebrating victory, August 1945. NA 80-G-354253

Officers of a Russian submarine which visited Dutch Harbor in October 1942.
NA 80-G-215250

A military convoy crosses the steel arch bridge over Deadhorse Canyon on its way north to the summit of White Pass on the White Pass & Yukon Route. YA. ERICKSON COLLECTION .

CHAPTER FOUR
TRANSPORTATION SYSTEMS

Canada's Armored Train

A very unusual train was put into service on Canadian National Railroad tracks in British Columbia during the early years of the war.

In early 1942, there was a real threat of Japanese sabotage against Canada's Pacific coast. There was a single railroad track linking the terminal port of Prince Rupert with the interior. For 80 miles this track ran alongside the navigable waters of the lower Skeena River.

There was a distinct possibility that a Japanese demolition party could be put ashore from a submarine to blow a bridge or block a tunnel; thus, effectively shutting off the port from the interior. Before the war Japanese fishing boats netted salmon up and down this wide estuary, so it was believed with some concern that the enemy already had maps of the area.

To provide a mobile defense along the railroad, No. 1 Armored Train was built at Winnipeg, Manitoba. It made its first operational trip from Terrace, British Columbia, to Prince Rupert, British Columbia, on July 29, 1942.

Its configuration was designed for defense. In front was a general purpose flat car equipped with one 75mm gun, together with a searchlight and diesel generator. The second car carried two 40mm Bofors anti-aircraft guns. A low steel parapet around each of these cars gave the gun crews some protection from the wind. The third car was a steel-covered coach carrying the headquarters and one platoon of infantry. Four 3-inch mortars and personal weapons were also carried. The locomotive was in the center of the train. It was followed by another all steel car, which served as a train office and first aid room. A third armored coach followed, carrying two infantry platoons. The final two cars of the train duplicated the first two.

Initially, the armored train made a return trip down and up the river each 24 hours. This schedule was discontinued in late 1943 after the Japanese were driven from the western Aleutians. The train was later used for training exercises with troops of the 8th Canadian Division and finally disbanded completely on July 31, 1944.

Overhead view of gondola cars showing anti-aircraft guns and searchlight. PAC

Interior view of the armored car. PAC

Front view showing gun position. PAC

Side view of gondola car showing anti-aircraft guns and searchlight. PAC

Bern gun position atop of train. PAC

Gun positions and searchlights. PAC

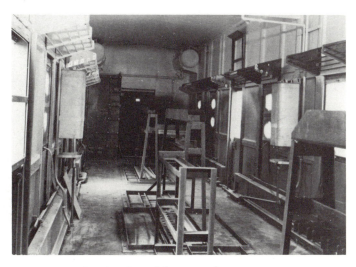

Interior view of the armored car. PAC

Running The Alaska Railroad

The Alaska Railroad, connecting tidewater Alaska at Seward to interior Alaska at Fairbanks, was opened to through traffic in 1923. It was built and operated by the federal government as Alaska's main transportation artery.

1941-1942

Immediately following the outbreak of war, civilian guards were placed at all principal bridges, trestles, terminal yards and at the Seward dock. The strategic Loop District on the Kenai Peninsula and freight trains carrying military supplies were given military guards.

Many restrictions also were introduced. These included a blackout, a requirement that switch lights be turned off, the banning of picture taking, the organization of civilian volunteer firefighting forces and a prohibition on train travel by aliens. All civilians heading for Alaska were screened by the Alaska Travel Control section of the Army in Seattle.

In addition, many extra precautions were taken. The extremely important Loop District had a switchback and shoo-fly constructed as alternate lines in case the existing line became inoperative. A short truck road was built to bypass the deep gully of Hurricane Gulch.

The labor shortage became increasingly acute, as many employees joined the military. Men were brought up from the States, but many went to other jobs upon their arrival in Alaska. By the fall of 1942, the Alaska Defense Command had to place some soldiers on temporary duty with the railroad to relieve the manpower shortage.

Freight tonnage in 1942 was the greatest in the history of the railroad. Most of the passenger traffic was the movement of troops. Also, river traffic on the Yukon River, supplying downriver towns and airfields, increased tremendously. In September 1943, the railroad purchased the river steamer *Yukon* and several barges.

During 1942, several locomotives were brought north to help with this increased traffic. Communication lines were upgraded along the railroad and work was started in June on a new dock at Seward.

On September 15, the new railroad depot and general office was opened near the old headquarters in the railroad yards. This building is still in use today. Two months later, the Whittier Cut-off project was completed, several months ahead of schedule. One month later, on December 13, the Fairbanks engine house was completely destroyed by fire. This caused an extreme hardship on train schedules during the winter months.

Troops of the 4th Infantry Regiment arrive in Anchorage on June 27, 1940, from Seward aboard the Alaska Railroad special. They were the vanguard of thousands of troops that were soon to pour into Alaska. AAC VIA RUSS DOW

1943

The second year of the war was the busiest yet for the Alaska Railroad. Thousands of soldiers were carried to Mt. McKinley for rest and relaxation. Civilian traffic increased later in the year after the Japanese were expelled from Alaska.

However, there was still a critical shortage of railroad workers, and men were recruited from the States. Women were also employed in certain non-strenuous jobs.

Improvements were made throughout the year, including new buildings and rolling stock, improved communications and a new engine house at Fairbanks.

To supplement the civilian work force, the 714th Railway Operating Battalion arrived in Alaska on April 3 and was immediately assigned to operate the railroad. The railroad reimbursed the War Department for the payroll and overhead expenses of the battalion. In addition, the Alaska Railroad took over operation of the McKinley Park Hotel as a recreational camp.

The Whittier Cut-off was placed in operation on June 1, 1943, and a mixed passenger and freight train ran daily, ex-

The old (left) and new (right) Alaska Railroad stations at Anchorage. The inadequate old station was replaced in 1942 by the new station, which is still in use today. AMHA

Otto F. Ohlson, general manager of the Alaska Railroad, poses in front of the Curry Hotel with his 1938 Dodge railmobile. Ohlson guided the railroad through much of its early development, including the difficult war years. His tenure ran from 1928 to 1945.
AMHA, ALASKA RAILROAD COLLECTION

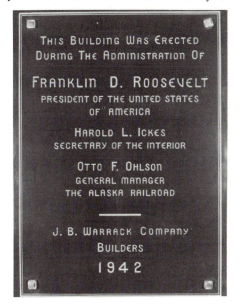

THIS BUILDING WAS ERECTED
DURING THE ADMINISTRATION OF

FRANKLIN D. ROOSEVELT
PRESIDENT OF THE UNITED STATES
OF AMERICA

HAROLD L. ICKES
SECRETARY OF THE INTERIOR

OTTO F. OHLSON
GENERAL MANAGER
THE ALASKA RAILROAD

———

J. B. WARRACK COMPANY
BUILDERS
1942

cept Sunday, between Anchorage and Whittier.

New rolling stock, including six Baldwin consolidation types, was received by the railroad. A head-on collision, the only one to occur during the war years, happened at Mile 112.5. Four people were slightly injured and one engine and several freight cars were severely damaged.

1944

Manpower shortages continued to plague the railroad in 1944. There was also a shortage of coal miners at the Eska mines and soldiers had to be transferred to the Enlisted Reserve Corps and sent to the mines to keep the trains running.

The winter of 1944 was severe and storms closed portions of the railroad for days in January. All of the Army's interior traffic was routed through Whittier, with only civilian ships docking at Seward. With the Whittier Cut-off in operation, approximately 75 percent more tonnage was handled than when Seward was the only port. Two diesel engines, the first on the railroad, were brought up in June for use on the Whittier run. This eliminated a forced draft ventilation system in the long Whittier tunnel which was necessary when steam engines were used.

Many improvements were made on the railroad to facilitate a smoother running operation, including a new turntable in Anchorage, an additional river steamer and two barges for the Yukon River traffic, a diesel locomotive shop in Anchorage and several large water stations at Eklutna and Cache.

On December 21, a passenger train leaving Fairbanks was derailed at Mile 424.9. Of 98 passengers on board, 38 were injured, along with five crewmen.

A troop sleeper used on the Alaska Railroad.
AMHA, ALASKA RAILROAD COLLECTION

1945

The war wound down fast for the railroad in 1945. With the increase of civilian workers in the early months of the year, the 714th Railway Operating Battalion was released on May 1. However, 97 men of the battalion remained until August for section work. Soldiers were released from the Eska mines in April.

In March, the McKinley Park Hotel was closed as an Army recreation center and returned to railroad control. The telephone and telegraph system on the railroad, which had been operated by the Alaska Communication System since 1943, was turned back to the railroad in October, and in December all operations at Whittier were returned to railroad operations.

In recognition of the battalion's service, the Alaska Command gave it the Meritorious Service Unit plaque. It was cited "for superior performance of duty in the execution of exceptionally difficult tasks during the period April 5, 1943 to April 1, 1945." Members of the battalion, the announcement said, "literally rolled up their sleeves when they arrived that April and supplies which lined the various loading docks began moving over the railroad once again."

The announcement of the receipt of the award was made by Lt. Col. Walter F. Hastedt, the unit's commander, at an assembly near Ft. Richardson on May 4, 1945.

Brig. Gen. Frank I. Whittaker, deputy commander of the Alaska Defense Command, seated on an Alaska Railroad rail car. In the background are: Lt. Col. John Carlton, Special Service officer; Lt. William Schiff, Jr., aide to Gen. Whittaker; and Lt. Ralph C. Hilton, driver of the car.
USA SC337874

IN APPRECIATION

The splendid cooperation, devotion to occupational duty and prevailing good fellowship among the officers and enlisted men of the

714th Railway Operating Battalion

and personnel of

The Alaska Railroad

We dedicate this occasion in commemorative observance on completion of

ONE YEAR'S SERVICE with The Alaska Railroad

When Victory with Peace returns our honored guests to their homes, may their Alaskan service and associations be an epochal event in their book of memories.

OTTO F. OHLSON
General Manager

Anniversary BALL

The Alaska Railroad
McKINLEY PARK ROUTE

IN HONOR OF

The 714th RAILWAY OPERATING BATTALION
U. S. ARMY

Sponsored by

The ALASKA RAILROAD
New Depot — Office Building   Anchorage, Alaska.
April 22, 1944   9:00 PM

Housing for the 714th Engineer Railway Operating Battalion at Anchorage, May 1943. The housing area was called the "Snake Ranch" by some. AMHA, U.S. ARMY COLLECTION

The Alaska Railroad station at Fairbanks during the war. It has since been replaced.
COURTESY HENRY HUNT, BAYTOWN, TEXAS

The Portage-Whittier Railroad Cutoff

As a World War II measure, in order to safeguard the flow of military supplies, equipment and personnel from tidewater to Anchorage and Fairbanks, a branch called the Whittier cutoff was constructed through the mountains to Passage Canal on Prince William Sound. The line is 12.4 miles long and includes two tunnels through the mountains, one 13,090 feet long and one 4,910 feet. The construction of this cut-off shortened the distance from tidewater to Fairbanks by 51.5 miles and gave the railroad two terminal ports where connections are made with ocean-going vessels—Seward and Whittier. The route from Whittier to Anchorage is at near sea-level grade.

In addition, by the fall of 1944, the project at Whittier included a receiving and classification yard, a 1,500-foot terminal wharf, a 1,200-man garrison of temporary design to house military port companies, railroad engine terminal facilities, cold storage plant, dock warehouse, and a two-story reinforced concrete communications building. The contractor also constructed support facilities for driving two-tunnel headings from the Portage end and one from the Whittier end, including 400-man and 200-man camps respectively.

This particular route of travel, across the bottleneck of the Kenai Peninsula is not new, nor is the idea of a tunnel under the bottleneck.

At the turn of the century, men were transporting supplies by back-pack and mule train from what was then known as Sullivan's Camp, (Identical in location to the then Whittier Main Camp) to Girdwood. Traces of the old Sullivan's trail are still in existence.

In 1913, F.H. Estabrook, locating Engineer for the Matanuska and Portage Bay R.R. Co., made a reconnaissance of a possible tunnel, and in 1914, R.J. Weir of the Alaska Engineering Commission went over Estabrook's line and made a more complete survey, changing the long tunnel very little but recommending the construction of the short tunnel through Turnagain Shoulder, which Estabrook had not. This short cut had been long advocated by the Alaska R.R.

The First World War caused these projects to be abandoned and the Second brought them to the light again as a measure to relieve the transportation situation to the interior and to provide a better and more easily protected harbor. Mr. Berryhill and Mr. Grammer of the Alaska Railroad made a reconnaissance in 1940 and from their information the project was definitely planned. The final location was made by Anton A. Anderson, F.A. Hanson and O.V. Kukkola, of the U.S.E.D. during the spring of 1941.

The original contract was let on June 13, 1941, to the West Construction Company of Boston, Massachusetts. It called for the construction of railroad grade to subgrade only from what was to be the terminus of the future permanent dock at Whittier to within 4,700 feet of the connection to the existent Alaska Railroad near Portage. This included the construction of two tunnels, one approximately 13,070 feet in length and the other approximately 4,960 feet. It included all minor structures along the grade, i.e., bridges and culverts and other drainage structures. This original contract was later supplemented by Supplemental Contracts for remainder of the work.

A large proportion of the delays of Alaska construction can be credited to shipping difficulties and to the weather. Both of these items were magnified at Whittier, the shipping difficulties by the war and the weather by the fact that the winter weather at Whittier probably has no parallel in Alaska.

Neither the original contract nor any one of the supplements thereto were timed to allow the construction during the good weather season. Every major item of construction either had to be started in the season of extreme weather prevailing from November to February, or it was so started that it overlapped into that season. The tunnel, of course, was relatively weather-proof once under ground, but the snowshed was built under conditions that would be understated if described as horrible.

When the contract for the construction of the tunnel was let, it was then apparent that eventually rail would be needed. Yet, the rail did not arrive until after the tunnel was completed, and until after the grade had been ready for steel for some weeks. It did not arrive until after the first snow. Had this rail arrived as little as two weeks earlier, the item of track-laying would have been completed at least two months earlier. Had some of it, a few-thousand track feet, arrived at least six months earlier, it would have made a marked difference in the procedure of making the final cuts and fills in one section; tunnel muck would have been used instead of truck-hauled borrow. On this item alone a thousand dollars per day for two weeks could have been saved.

Not all the material difficulties are attributable to the war and the lack of shipping. Loads were diverted, either to another job, or just diverted through misunderstanding. Material that was most needed was sometimes not ordered; the most spectacular effort of this kind being the ordering of material for the temporary dock and not for the 384′ of approach to the dock. A thousand tons of cargo were unloaded over a jerry-built approach before the material arrived. Sometimes material came in that was not expected and for which no provisions had been made. This happened in the case of the first shipment of materials for the Permanent Timber Dock; 1,200,000 board feet of lumber came in on the *S.S. Elna* with no warning beforehand and no facilities for handling this lumber provided. The contract for the dock had

Officers and civilians ride in Maj. Gen. Buckner's private railroad car to Whittier for an inspection trip. USA SC396826

Holing-through ceremonies on Nov. 20, 1942. Col. Otto F. Ohlson, left, shakes hands with Maj. Gen. S.B. Buckner.
AMHA, ALASKA RAILROAD COLLECTION

Climbing through debris after the blast. The explosion completed the tunnel, located on the Whittier Cutoff route.
AMHA, ALASKA RAILROAD COLLECTION

not been let at that time and, it was actually not the responsibility of the West Construction Company, but they were obliged to take men from all crews on the project, and in many cases complete crews, and spend five days unloading this boat.

Much of the weather delay could have been avoided with some forethought. Perhaps the only occasion where this could not have been foretold was when the access bridge at Station 33 + 00 was washed out in August 1942. The same flood took out part of the Wye fill and part of the yard fill, requiring the redriving of the access bridge. The same could not be said for the other weather delays. Had the permanent dock been started by April 15, 1942, it would have been safely completed by November 1 of the same year. Instead the construction was started in mid-July and was therefore extended into the winter weather which by conservative estimate doubled the cost of construction. This was accentuated by the lack of sufficient piling. No pilings were driven from September 22 to October 27 because there were none on hand.

The unskilled type and insufficient supply of labor which was experienced on this job delayed all projects considerably. This, however, probably was unavoidable because of the existing war conditions.

These difficulties were met on the job with patience and resourcefulness. Unavoidable bottlenecks were alleviated as best they could when they arose, as often as not requiring a complete change of plans. The best that could be done was done with the materials at hand. The progress of the tunnel was excellent and that of the grading was good.

Work on the tunnel began with the facing-off of the surface material from the Portal Area by tractor during the latter part of August 1941 and the actual work on the wallplate heading began in September. The main policy, along with expedited camp construction, was getting the tunnel underground as soon as possible. This allowed cover from the inclement weather for the tunnel crews, and although work was intermittent for the next several months due to the tunnel crew doing most everything but driving tunnel, i.e. longshoring, building snowsheds, carpentering, etc. the tunnel was 170 feet underground by the middle of January 1942, when actual steady progress began to be made.

The first work on the grade was done at approximately station 32 + 00 where fill was made from borrow taken from the diversion channel. This is excepting the centerline fill made at the tunnel portal when that area was filled to allow the construction of the tunnel service buildings.

The Passage Tunnel was holed through at 11:18 a.m. November 20, 1942, at station 183 + 04. The Whittier crew thus accounting for 7,795 feet of the total of 13,286 feet. By January 1943, the tunnel was ready for tracklaying. The elapsed time from January 15, 1942, when steady progress was begun, to November 20, 1942, when holing through

was accomplished, was 309 days.

The total solid rock cut (excavation and borrow under the feature of grading) amounted to 94,250 cubic yards of which 78,550 cubic yards were excavated by dynamite. The total amount of dynamite used was 107,000 lbs., or an average of 1.36 lbs. per cubic yard.

The grade, from the south portal of the Passage Tunnel to the dock was completed and ready for ballast on October 15, 1942.

All ballast was complete and the grade was ready for steel by November 1. However, steel could have been laid through the yards and at least on one half of the main line grade to the portal, before this date, had the steel and ties been at the job.

Tracklaying was started on December 31, 1942 in the tunnel.

The Terminal Dock, was started on July 10, 1942 and completed in the spring of 1943.

Diesel engine #1001 at Whittier. It was one of the first four diesels that were placed in service in June 1944.
AMHA, ALASKA RAILROAD COLLECTION

Marie Silverman

Program

8:00 a.m. Special guest train, furnished by the Alaska Railroad, leaves Anchorage.

9:30 a.m. Train arrives at Portage Junction.

Motor transportation takes guests to north end of Turnagain Tunnel.

Party proceeds through Turnagain Tunnel, across Bear Valley to the north portal of Whittier Tunnel.

General Buckner sets off the last charge, "holing through" the Whittier tunnel.

After the "holing through" the party proceeds through Whittier Tunnel to Whittier. An Alaskan banquet is served.

CEREMONIAL SPEAKERS

Mr. H. E. Carleton, Vice President, West Construction Company.
"The Contractor's Viewpoint of the Project."

Col. B. B. Talley, C.E., Officer in Charge, Alaska Construction (for Col. P. P. Goerz, District Engineer, Seattle)
"The Administration of the Project"

Maj. Gen. Simon B. Buckner, Jr., Commanding General, ADC.
"Defense Aspects of the Project."

Col. O. F. Ohlson, General Manager, Alaska Railroad.
"The Importance of the Project to the Territory of Alaska."

Mr. A. M. Coker, General Superintendent, West Construction Company.
"Interesting Features of the Project."

Holing Through Ceremony

WHITTIER TUNNEL
November 19, 1942

PASSAGE CANAL CONNECTION
ALASKA RAILROAD CUT-OFF

Guests

General Jesse A. Ladd
Col. E. D. Post
Col. T. M. Crawford
Col. P. W. Brown
Col. J. G. Nold
Col. D. McK. Ashton
Col. Chas. F. Baish
Col. C. M. Chamberlin
Lt. Col. V. L. Womeldorff
Major D. O. Givens
Major Craig Smyser
Major J. D. Bush, Jr.
Major Kermit Roosevelt
Major Rubin Smith
Captain J. Wark
Mr. Robert B. Atwood
Dr. George Chase
Mr. Earl Delaney
Mr. Winfield Ervin, Jr.
Judge Simon Hellenthal
Mr. E. Jacobsen
Mr. W. L. Kinsell
Mr. H. Leppich
Mr. John Manders
Mr. D. W. Metzdorf
Mr. R. Musser
Judge Thomas Price
Mr. L. V. Ray
Mr. V. Rivers
Mayor William Stolt

Menu

Hors d'eouvres

Fruit Cocktail   Cream of Clam Soup

Shrimp Salad

Entree'
Moose   Caribou   Goat

Mashed Potatoes

Green Asparagus   Whole Kernel Corn

Hot Rolls with Honey

Pumpkin Pie with Whipped Cream

Coffee

Fruit and Nuts

The Final Blast

Accompanied by colorful ceremonies, the last rock was blasted out of the Whittier tunnel at 11:12 o'clock the morning of November 20, 1942, and passage through the nation's fourth longest railroad tunnel became possible for the first time.

A large group of dignitaries and guests witnessed the blasting of the final curtain of rock and had the honor of being the first persons to travel through the glacier-ridden mountains between Portage Junction and the townsite of Whittier.

The event, which marks a milestone of great significance in the development of Alaska, took place with Maj. Gen. Simon B. Buckner, Jr., commanding general of the Alaska Defense Command, pulled the switch that set off 56 blasts.

The muffled roar of the series of explosions deep in the mountain was heard by the spectators who were standing in the Turnagain portal.

The party then boarded a "muck" train and rode to the scene of the blast. There they saw the rubble left by the explosion, climbed over it and were on the Whittier end for the first time.

Maj. C.B. Burgoyne, resident engineer who was later master of ceremonies at a banquet, announced that the two bores came together with discrepancies of only one-half inch in elevation, one and one-eighth inch in line and about one foot in distance.

These slight discrepancies were pointed to as a masterful job of engineering because of the extreme difficulties in surveying over the mountains. Computations were by triangulation because of the impossibility of running a line over the rough pinnacles and deep crevasses of a glacier three-quarters of a mile in width.

The party left Anchorage by special train at 8 o'clock, arriving at Portage Junction at 9:30 o'clock. Motor transportation carried the guests to the Turnagain portal of the long tunnel where General Buckner set off the final blast.

Helmets were worn by the guests as they went through the tunnel and as they climbed over the muck pile men were still scaling loose rock from the sides and top.

The dignitaries inspected the point where the two bores came together. It was approximately a mile and one-half from Whittier and one mile from the Turnagain portal.

Boarding a second muck train, the party went to Whittier where a wild game dinner was served in the camp messhall.

Speakers hailed the event as of greatest importance. Major Burgoyne was master of ceremonies.

Col. B.B. Talley, officer in charge of Alaska construction for the Engineer Department, invited an impartial auditor to inspect the records of the project and declared it would show that the best interests of the nation were served. He lauded the West Construction Company for cooperation and efficiency.

General Buckner pointed to the tunnel as "preventing the enemy from knocking out the most important piece of transportation in Alaska." He also commended the construction company, the Engineers, the railroad and the workers.

Col. O.F. Ohlson, general manager of the Alaska Railroad who has for many years favored construction of the tunnel, declared that the tunnel will pay for itself in less than five years under present business conditions.

A.M. Coker, general superintendent of the West Construction Company, said the real celebration will come "when the first train runs through the tunnel and we unload the first ship." He handed honors to the Engineers, the Alaska Railroad and his men for the performance.

Noting the precision with which the two bores came together, Mr. Coker said the credit for that "goes to Antone Anderson, civil engineer on the job, and his associates, J.M. Adams and Ole Kukkola."

He declared it was the closest he had ever seen a tunnel hole through when the engineering work was under such extreme difficulties.

Following the banquet the party returned to Portage Junction by way of the tunnel, making the second trip over the final muck pile. The special train arrived back in Anchorage at 7:30 o'clock.

from *Anchorage Daily Times*
November 21, 1942

Dock facilities at Whittier, June 1943. With the completion of the cutoff route in late 1942, Whittier provided a much shorter and safer route to Anchorage for the thousands of tons of cargo that were pouring into Alaska. AMHA, ALASKA RAILROAD COLLECTION

The McKinley Park Hotel was built by the National Park Service. At one time the Park Service was short of funds so Interior Secretary Harold Ickes asked Col. Otto F. Ohlson, manager of the Alaska Railroad, to take over operation of the hotel. The building had been poorly built and the railroad reluctantly complied. When war came the Alaska Defense Command asked to take over the building for use as a rest center for its troops. After the war the railroad took back the hotel, in somewhat better condition, and operated it until 1954 when the Interior Department took it back. The interior of the hotel was a nice respite from the far-flung outposts in the Alaska theater of war. AMHA

A variety of recreation opportunities were available for servicemen staying at Mt. McKinley.

Going back to the war zone after a stay at Mt. McKinley.

White Pass & Yukon Route: At War

The White Pass & Yukon Route played an historic role in the opening up and development of the vast Yukon Territory of Canada in the early 1900s. A global war put its 110 miles of rails in the spotlight of military strategy.

The road was a direct link from the inland waterways to the trackless and forested wilderness through which the Alaska Highway was being pushed. With its terminal at Skagway and Whitehorse, vital supplies and needed skills were transported quickly to the Alaska Highway and elsewhere for the construction and enlargement of airports guarding the far-flung outposts of the continent.

Lt. Gen. Brehon Somervell, Army Service Forces commander, who had first-hand knowledge of the situation and the terrain, recognized the strategic importance to the Allies of the White Pass & Yukon Route. Thus, plans were drawn up in his office for the lease of the railroad for the duration of the war and one year thereafter.

The United States Army took over the White Pass & Yukon Route at 12:01 a.m. on Oct. 1, 1942. It retained on the payroll all employees of the road except its president.

For the entire year of 1941, the White Pass & Yukon Route had carried 22,646 tons of supplies (freight) and 12,790 passengers. Its revenue from these sources was $466,489 for freight, $82,192 for passengers. The bulk of this freight went beyond Whitehorse by trans-shipment, chiefly to Dawson and Mayo. However, in the three-month period between taking over the road and the end of 1942, the Army transported 33,756 tons of supplies and 1,368 passengers.

Under the terms of the lease, the average cost of operating the road per month, including the pay of enlisted men of the 770th Railway Operating Battalion, was $192,467.12. The net cost of operating the road for the 11-month period of Jan. 1 through Nov. 30, 1943, was $2,177,138.29.

The cost of the lease for January 1943 was $27,708.33. The civilian payroll came to another $30,137.09. During that month, Army freight moved over the route amounted to 720 tons, while other government freight accounted for another 3,209 tons. Had the regular freight rates of $40 per ton been in effect, the cost to the Army for moving that freight would have been $157,160. So it saved almost $100,000 in that one month. In addition, the Army's revenue from the 1,525 tons of commercial freight moved during that 31-day period totaled $61,000.

From a total of 5,454 tons moved in January 1943, the volume of traffic rose to 38,531 tons in July and hit an all-time peak of 47,126 tons in August. Subtracting 2,561 tons of commercial traffic carried in August, the cost to the government of moving much needed stores, had regular freight rates been assessed, would have been $1,782,600 for that month alone.

Most important of all, and a fact which even adverse figures could not offset: the Army moved vital freight, troops, and civilian construction workers when and where they were most needed. The prompt and steady delivery of men and materials to Whitehorse, headquarters of the Northwest Service Command, from Skagway, headquarters of the 770th Railway Operating Battalion, made it possible to complete the Alaska Highway pioneer road in only nine months and, equally important, the Canol project was also completed.

770th Railway Operating Detachment/Battalion

Constituted and activated in the U.S. Army on August 29, 1942, as Engineer Railway Detachment 9646 at Camp William C. Reid, Clovis, NM. Authorized strength: 12 officers, 352 enlisted men.

Left for Alaska on Sept. 1, 1942, and redesignated the 770th Railway Operating Detachment, Transportation Corps, on November 16, 1942.

Redesignated on March 27, 1943, and reorganized as the 770th Railway Operating Battalion on April 14, 1943.

Left Alaska on Nov. 17, 1944 for its new station at Camp Claiborne, LA.

Transferred to Korea on Aug. 10, 1945, and inactivated there in 1946.

Engine 195 pulls a train toward Skagway, 1944. USA SC 323064

Winter travel on the White Pass & Yukon Route was very hazardous and long delays were experienced when it was necessary to clear the tracks or remove a wreck. Extreme temperatures occurred, especially during the harsh winter of 1944-45. This caused further delays in running the railroad. USA

Even the large rotary snowplows had a hard time operating during the 1944-45 winter. USA SC200220

The White Pass & Yukon Route passed some magnificent scenery on its 110-mile journey from Skagway to Whitehorse. USA SC 247709

Men are shown here shoveling snow away from a derailed train in the winter of 1944-45. Three reels of cable, en route to Whitehorse for use as an airbase telephone system, rolled into a canyon and were never recovered. USA SC247718

Taking on water at the Fraser stop in the British Columbia portion of the White Pass Route. USA SC 247720

A freight train heading north enters the tunnel on the Alaska side on its steep climb to the summit of White Pass, December 1942. USA SC163100-B

A White Pass train entering the Skagway terminal after a run from Whitehorse, December 1942. USA SC163111-B

Maj. John E. Auslund of Chicago, Illinois, formerly with the Burlington Route and military superintendent of the White Pass & Yukon Route, is shown talking to fireman, Pvt. Ross Weye of Havre, Montana, December, 1942. USA SC163090-B

Interior view of a White Pass passenger car, December 1942. Some of these coaches had been in use since the gold rush days of 1898-1900. Sgt. William H. Howard, Waycross, Georgia, a train conductor, takes the ticket from Miss Margaret Johnston of Skagway. USA SC163101

Sgt. Vaviour A. Athey examines credentials of Eddy W. Elliott, a passenger on board a White Pass train, December 1942. USA SC 163101

Bennett station on Lake Bennett, British Columbia, February 1943. During the 1897-98 Klondike Gold Rush, this site was the head of navigation for prospectors heading north down the Yukon River to Dawson City. RF

A three-inch pipeline was laid along the tracks of the White Pass & Yukon Route to Whitehorse to supply fuel to construction equipment along the Alaska Highway and Canol Project. RF

Carcross (Caribou Crossing), Yukon, was an important stop on the White Pass & Yukon Route in the early days and again took on importance as a transshipment point for highway and pipeline supplies. The old Caribou Hotel and church to the right are still standing, along with the original railroad bridge and long warehouse next to the lake. RF

Mishaps sometimes occurred even in the best of weather conditions. Engine #71 derailed just past the station at Whitehorse in 1943. RF

Loading supplies at Skagway for the journey to Whitehorse and the Alaska Highway, 1942. LC

The Skagway dock area was a busy place in 1942 and 1943 when the Alaska Highway and Çanol Pipeline projects were being built.
USA SC323262, SC163102-B, SC323312

Yakutat and Southern Railway

The Libby McNeil and Libby Canning Company built and owned at Yakutat a 10 mile standard gauge railroad. This railroad ran from the village of Situk to the Cannery at Yakutat.

When construction of the Yakutat air base and garrison was commenced by the Army Engineers in the latter part of 1940, an agreement was reached whereby the Army was allowed the operation of a portion of the rolling stock on this railway. The track was in fair condition, although it was necessary for the Army Engineers to perform a small amount of maintenance work. This agreement continued in effect until April 1941, by which time a highway from the dock to the garrison was completed.

Government worker, Robert Vent of Koyukuk, Alaska fastens sections of oil raft together in preparation for a trip down the Yukon River in August 1944. As many as 300 55 gallon barrels of fuel would be formed into a raft and floated down the Tanana and Yukon rivers. The Alaska Railroad bridge is in the background. USA SC-427955

Dock area at Nenana, Alaska, August 1945. Nenana was a major transshipping point for goods coming up the Alaska Railroad from Anchorage, then off loaded and reloaded on barges for shipment down the Tanana River to the Yukon River to remote sites. Note the ice pool tower on the extreme left. This is still a yearly tradition in Nenana—guessing the day, hour and minute that the winter ice breaks up on the Tanana River. USA SC-254428

View of U.S. Army vehicles being loaded onto barges at Dawson, Yukon. These were brought down the Yukon River after being brought up to Whitehorse from Skagway by rail. They were taken to Eagle, just over the Alaska border, and then driven over very rough roads to Fairbanks. The sternwheelers *Klondike* and *Whitehorse* are visible behind the barges. The *Klondike* is now on display at Whitehorse. Circa 1943. YA, C. HAINES COLLECTION

Steamer *Klondike* at Eagle, Alaska, in 1943 with a barge full of military equipment bound for the Alcan Highway.
NATIONAL ARCHIVES OF CANADA #C-4033

Airlines At War

The Civil Aeronautics Administration (CAA) initiated a program in 1940 to construct Defense Landing Areas (DLA) or emergency landing fields in Alaska. Eighteen million dollars was made available and in 1941 thirty million dollars was added to this.

The first fields were built at Nome and Naknek, the latter on the Alaska Peninsula, providing access to the Aleutians. Other fields were built at Galena, Northway, McGrath, Bethel, Big Delta and Gulkana.

When America entered World War II and the Japanese threatened Alaska the three airlines who serviced Alaska, Pan American, United and Western were pressed into wartime action to fly supplies and personnel to the far north country.

Movement of supplies by water to Alaska was increasingly menaced by possible enemy submarines and the length of time it took ships to make the northern journey. Speed was essential. An inland air route, far from the bad flying weather of the coast, was desperately needed. The landing fields through Canada, built in 1941 and eventually known as the Northwest Staging Route, were upgraded and the DLA's were put to maximum use.

Western Airlines had an important part in the Alaska operations. In three and one-quarter years the line flew, between Great Falls, Montana and Nome, Alaska by way of Edmonton, Alberta and Fairbanks, Alaska, 6,150 trips with a perfect safety record. In that period it transported more than 22,012,623 pounds of cargo in C-46s and C-47s, flying a total of 7,050,506 miles.

Pan American had been in Alaska for many years prior to the war through its subsidiary Pacific Alaska Airways. It pioneered many of the cold weather techniques and procedures used by all the airlines in the extreme cold temperatures and remote flying areas.

Pan Am entered into a contract in September 1942 to transfer its facilities to the U.S. Navy. The airline also attempted to continue regularly scheduled service to Alaska but wartime priorities interfered.

In its north contract Pan Am carried more than 3,170,000 pounds of cargo and 77,150 passengers to Alaska and out to the Aleutian Chain.

United Airlines chalked up more than 5,200,000 miles of flying between the United States and points in Alaska for the Air Transport Command from 1942 until mid-November 1944. In May 1942 the airline began transport service between Ohio and Anchorage by way of Chicago, Minneapolis, Fargo, Regina, Fort St. John, Whitehorse and Fairbanks, a total route of 3,489 miles. Additional service was established from Salt Lake City through Edmonton and from Seattle to Anchorage by way of Ketchikan, Juneau, Yakutat and Cordova, a distance of 1,541 miles.

Northwest Airlines signed a contract in February 1942 with the U.S. Army to conduct a survey for the installation of gas storage and to analyze communications and other needs at Alaska airfields. The airline abandoned part of its commercial flights in the lower 48 and rushed planes and pilots north. In the midst of an Alaskan winter a regular scheduled operation north started in March 1942. Edmonton, Alberta was the southern terminus of this route.

One of Pacific Alaska Airways Lockheed Electras that went into wartime service in late 1941.

COURTESY PAN AMERICAN WORLD AIRWAYS

ALBERTA DISTRICT

CANADIAN PACIFIC AIR LINES

Canadian Pacific
AIR LINES

AUGUST 1st, 1943

Wings for the World's Greatest Travel System...

Canadian Pacific AIR LINES

Half a century ago, the Canadian Pacific linked ocean to ocean across Canada by rail. Now it adds air transport to its rail and steamship facilities. Recently, it consolidated ten Canadian air transport companies running northward like arteries from the main east-west lines of communication...to the borders of the Yukon ...and the shores of the Arctic.

It now operates close to 100 planes, with a flying mileage of more than 5,000,000 plane miles a year. This makes it one of the world's largest commercial air operators. Its routes connect with Trans-Canada Air Lines and the leading American air lines.

Information, rates and reservations through any Canadian Pacific Railway agent.

PASSENGERS — MAIL — EXPRESS

CONNECTING SERVICES

WHITEHORSE - FAIRBANKS

Wed. Fri.	Tues. Sat.	Thur.	Pan American Airways	Thur Sat.	Sun. Thur
PM	PM	PM		AM	PM
6.15	6.30	5.05	Lv....Whitehorse 155 MWT....Ar.	9.45	1.15
6.35	3.40		Ar....Fairbanks 150 MWT....Lv.	5.30	9.00
PM	PM	PM		AM	AM

VANCOUVER - EDMONTON - LETHBRIDGE
WINNIPEG - TORONTO - NEW YORK

	Daily	Daily	Trans-Canada Air Lines	Daily	Daily
	PM	AM		AM	PM
MT	6.15	6.30	Lv....Edmonton....Ar.	11.45	11.05
	7.25	7.40	Ar....Calgary....Ar.	10.30	9.50
	8.20	8.35	Ar....Lethbridge....Lv.	9.40	9.00
PT MT	5.00 9.30	6.00 9.30	Lv....Vancouver....Ar. Ar.....Vancouver....Lv.	10.40 8.50	10.40 8.50
CT ET ET	AM 1.55 9.20 6.00 PM	PM 2.55 10.55 1.30 AM	Ar....Winnipeg....Lv. Ar....Toronto....Lv. Ar....New York....Lv.	PM 4.35 10.00 7.00 AM	PM 4.45 10.40 8.00 AM

VANCOUVER - SEATTLE - LOS ANGELES

Daily	Daily	United Air Lines	Daily	Daily
PM	AM		PM	PM
11.30	5.00	Lv....Vancouver....Ar.	4.46	10.46
12.46	6.16	Ar....Seattle....Ar.	3.30	9.30
	2.14	Ar....San Francisco....Lv.	9.15	
	5.31	Ar....Los Angeles....Lv.	7.00	
AM			AM	

EDMONTON - SALT LAKE CITY - LOS ANGELES

Daily	Daily	Trans-Canada Air Lines	Daily	Daily
PM	AM		PM	PM
6.15	6.30	Lv....Edmonton....Ar.	11.05	11.45
7.25	7.40	Ar....Calgary....Lv.	9.55	10.40
8.20	8.35	Ar....Lethbridge....Lv.	9.00	9.40
PM	AM		AM	AM
	PM	Western Air Lines	PM	
	1.30	Lv....Lethbridge....Ar.	12.40	
	7.05	Ar....Salt Lake City....Lv.	7.00	
	10.20	Ar....Los Angeles....Lv.	3.00	
	AM		PM	

YUKON DISTRICT

YUKON SOUTHERN AIR TRANSPORT LTD.

EDMONTON - WHITEHORSE

Miles	Trip 1		NORTHBOUND Read Down		Trip 2	Miles
					PM	
0	7.00 MT	Lv.	Edmonton	Ar.	5.00 MT	949
243	7.45 PT	Ar.	Grande Prairie	Lv.	2.15	
	8.00	Lv.	Grande Prairie	Ar.	2.00	706
350	N.G.	Ar.	Fort St. John	Lv.	1.15	
	9.00	Lv.	Fort St. John	Ar.	12.30	599
527	10.20	Ar.	Fort Nelson	Lv.	11.00	422
	10.35	Lv.	Fort Nelson	Ar.	10.45 PT	
748	11.00 YT	Ar.	Watson Lake	Lv.	8.00	201
	11.15	Lv.	Watson Lake	Ar.	7.45	
949	12.30	Ar.	Whitehorse	Lv.	6.00 YT	0
	PM				AM	

	Tues. & Fri.				Tues. & Fri.	
0	9.00	Lv.	Whitehorse	Ar.	3.15	295
	×		Carmacks	×		
	×		Selkirk	×		
193	10.30	Ar.	Mayo	Lv.	1.35	
	10.45	Lv.	Mayo	Ar.	1.20	
295	11.55	Ar.	Dawson	Lv.	12.30	0
			Read Up SOUTHBOUND			

VANCOUVER - WHITEHORSE

Miles	Trip 3		NORTHBOUND Read Down		Trip 4	Miles
					AM	
0	9.00 PT	Lv.	Vancouver	Ar.	4.45	1196
288	11.30	Ar.	Prince George	Lv.	2.15	
	11.45	Lv.	Prince George	Ar.	2.00	708
507	1.00	Ar.	Fort St. John	Lv.	12.45	
	1.30	Lv.	Fort St. John	Ar.	12.00	599
774	3.00	Ar.	Fort Nelson	Lv.	11.00	422
	3.15	Lv.	Fort Nelson	Ar.	10.45 PT	
995	4.00 YT	Ar.	Watson Lake	Lv.	8.00	201
	4.15	Lv.	Watson Lake	Ar.	N.G.	
1196	6.00	Ar.	Whitehorse	Lv.	6.30 YT	0
	PM				AM	

	Tues. & Fri.				Tues. & Fri.	
0	9.00	Lv.	Whitehorse	Ar.	3.15	295
	×		Carmacks	×		
	×		Selkirk	×		
193	10.30	Ar.	Mayo	Lv.	1.35	
	10.45	Lv.	Mayo	Ar.	1.20	
295	11.55	Ar.	Dawson	Lv.	12.30	0
			Read Up SOUTHBOUND			

OFF-LINE SERVICES

Peace River-Vermilion		Prince George-Fort St. James		Fort Nelson-Fort Liard		Prince George-Fort Ware	
Wed.	Thu.	Regular Charter Service from Fort St. James	Prince George	Leave Fort Nelson May 25 July 22 Oct. 14 Dec. 16	Prince George	Leave Prince George Every Second Saturday in Jan., July Feb., Aug. May, Oct. Dec. 28	Prince George
PM 5.30	PM 12.30		Fort St. James		Fort Nelson		Fort McLeod
7.15 AM	10.00 AM	Lv. Peace River Ar. Ar. Fort Vermilion Lv.	Takla Landing		Nelson Forks		Finlay Forks
			Germansen		Fort Liard		Fort Grahame
							Fort Ware

EXPLANATION OF SYMBOLS

× Flag Stop.
† Black Faced Sunday.
‡ Complimentary Meals Served: Midi.
PM Black Faced Type.
AM Light Faced Type.

PT Pacific Time.
MT Mountain Time.
YT Yukon Time.

Time used is Standard. Time as Established in Canada Feb. 9, 1942.

There is a time spread of 2 hours between Yukon Time and Mountain Time and of one hour between Yukon Time and Pacific Time and between Pacific Time and Mountain Time. That is 12 Noon Yukon Time is 1.00 P.M. Pacific Time and 2.00 P.M. Mountain Time.

FARES & EXPRESS RATES

KEY TO RATES

One Way Light Face Type
Return Trip Black Face Type.
(In Dollars)

Express Rate, per lb.
(in Cents)

Fares in Canadian Funds not including tax.

	Edmonton	Grande Prairie	Fort St. John	Fort Nelson	Watson Lake	Teslin	Whitehorse	Prince George
Grande Prairie	20. 38. .13							
Fort St. John	36. 15. 72. 18. 05.	30. 58. 08.						
Fort Nelson	76. 143. 38.	55. 103. 29.	40. 72. 12.					
Watson Lake	83. 150. 41.	81. 146. 40.	76. 117. 29.	45. 85. 20.				
Teslin	85. 153. 43.	83. 150. 42.	80. 144. 40.	75. 117. 33.	25. 45. 14.			
Whitehorse	85. 153. 43.	83. 150. 42.	80. 144. 40.	75. 117. 33.	40. 72. 20.	10. 18. 05.		
Prince George	55. 14.	50. 26.	98. 46.	99. 48.	175. 49.	175. 49.	97. 49.	
Vancouver	185. 23.	175. 41.	177. 49.	180.	180. 64.		54.	30.

OTHER FARES

	One Way	Return	Express
FROM PRINCE GEORGE TO —			
Fort St. James	$10.00	$18.00	.05
Fort McLeod	16.00	29.00	.08
Finlay Forks	30.00	54.00	.15
Fort Grahame	42.00	76.00	.21
Fort Ware	57.00	103.00	.28
FROM FORT ST. JAMES TO —			
Manson	20.00	36.00	.08
Germansen	20.00	36.00	.08
Takla Landing	20.00	36.00	.08
FROM FORT NELSON TO —			
Nelson Forks	20.00	36.00	.10
Fort Liard	40.00	72.00	.20
FROM WHITEHORSE TO —			
Mayo	50.00	90.00	.20
Dawson City	60.00	108.00	.25
FROM PEACE RIVER TO —			
Carcajou	30.00	56.00	.10
Ft. Vermillion	30.00	54.00	.15

GENERAL INFORMATION

BAGGAGE: Forty pounds of baggage will be carried free, on ticket. Bulky baggage by special arrangement with company. Fifty-five pounds of baggage will be carried free on ticket from Vancouver or Edmonton to Whitehorse, and Whitehorse to Vancouver or Edmonton.

GROUND TRANSPORTATION: Ground taxi-cab service charges between airports and urban centres are independent of Air Lines fare and therefore at passenger's option.

SCHEDULES: The schedules, Fares and Rates are subject to change without notice to the public. Canadian Pacific Air Lines reserves the right to delay departures and postpone or cancel flights. Arrival time and connections with other transportation services cannot be guaranteed.

CANCELLATION By The Company: The Company reserves the right, at its sole discretion, to cancel bookings before passage or en route whenever it deems such action advisable or necessary, in all such cases the passenger's sole recourse shall be the recovery of the value of the unused portion of the fare paid.

EXPRESS: A minimum charge of $1.00 will be made for each package carried. See tables above for rates.

Chilkoot Barracks and the town of Haines from the top of Mt. Rapinski, 1942. COURTESY WILLIAM LATTIN JR.

CHAPTER FIVE
ALASKA
NATIONAL
GUARD

Co. B., 297th Infantry stand inspection at Chilkoot Barracks, 1942.
COURTESY WILLIAM LATTIN JR.

Officers of Co. B, 297th Infantry at Chilkoot Barracks, 1942. From left: Lt. Soholt, Lt. Friedman, Lt. McIsaacs, Capt. VanGilder, Lt. Cochran and Lt. Beck.
COURTESY WILLIAM LATTIN JR.

Troops of the Alaska National Guard qualify on the firing range in 1941 before their induction into federal service.
COURTESY WILLIAM LATTIN JR.

Barracks buildings of Co. A
(left) and Co. B (right), 297th
Infantry, 1941. The barracks
on the right was destroyed by
fire in 1982.
COURTESY WILLIAM LATTIN JR.

Officers Row and parade
grounds at Chilkoot Barracks,
1941.
COURTESY WILLIAM LATTIN JR.

Co. B., 297th Infantry troops
land on Pennock Island opposite Ketchikan in 1941 on a
training exercise. U.S. Coast
Guard boats participated in
this exercise.
COURTESY WILLIAM LATTIN JR.

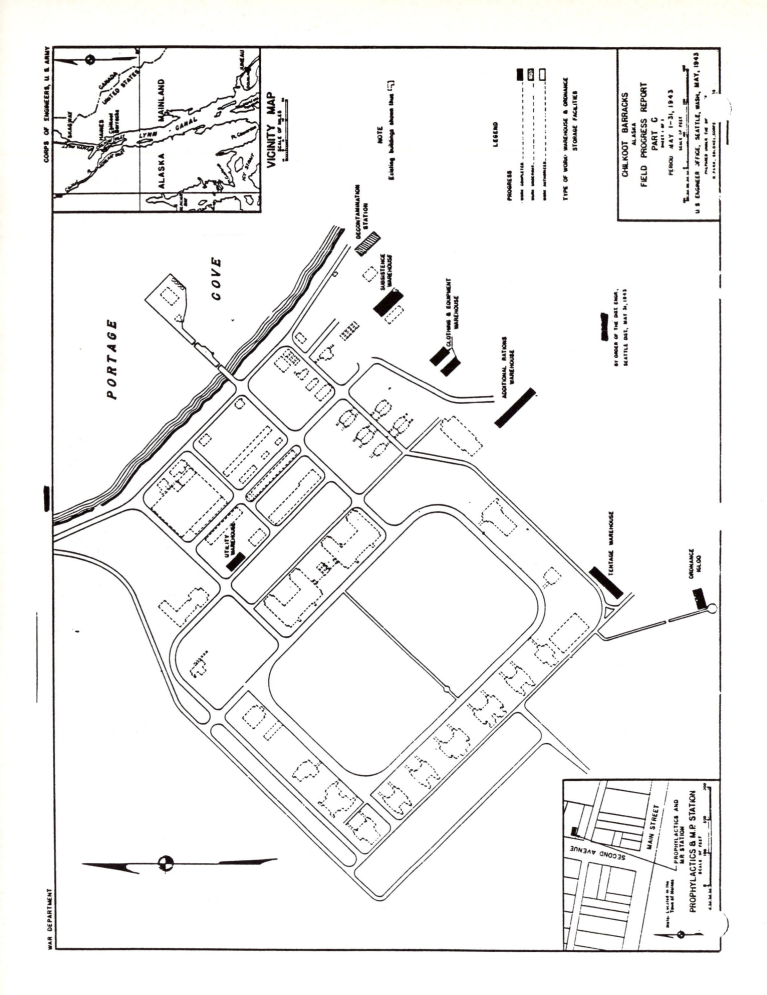

Army Construction in Valdez, Alaska, 1941-1944

During World War II, a garrison of the Alaska Army National Guard was established in Valdez. The 297th Infantry Battalion worked at the Port of Valdez and on the Richardson Highway. Their duties also included unloading freightships carrying materials for military construction in Alaska's interior and building their own facilities.

The Valdez garrison's housing site was located on a glacial moraine approximately one and one-half miles west of the original Valdez townsite near today's Zook Subdivision.

The facilities included housing for 15 officers and 250 enlisted men, a 25-bed hospital, motor repair shop and 20,000 square feet of storage space. Later, a dry cleaning plant and a small laundry building were built.

The 297th Infantry worked on the construction "between boats." Preparation of the ground and foundation work was done in April 1943 when two feet of snow was still present and was finished before the end of October. Project cost: $392,000 (in 1943 dollars).

The unit also conducted ski patrols on the Valdez Glacier. One such patrol in February 1943 ended in tragedy with 20 members of the unit requiring hospitalization; one member of the patrol—a Corporal Birdwell—was lost in a crevasse.

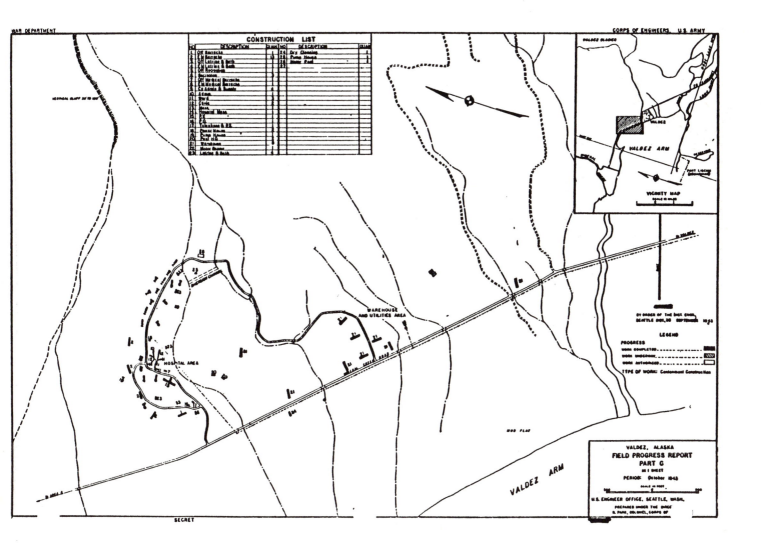

The 297th in the Valdez area

Hq. & Hq. Det. and Medical Det. departed Fort Richardson on July 6, 1942, to a permanent station at Valdez. These units remained at Valdez until ordered back to Fort Richardson on October 23, 1943.

Company C, less 3rd platoon, was sent to Valdez on June 30, 1942. It was transferred to Ladd Field on September 22, 1943.

Company D, 2nd platoon was sent to Valdez on July 6, 1942, and transferred to Whittier on December 21, 1943.

In January 1943 several officers and men from Hq. Company, Companies C & D, were transferred to Portage, Whittier and Chitina.

Valdez was an important ice-free port and gateway to interior Alaska via the Richardson Highway. Supplies for Ladd Field and construction of the Alaska Highway came through this port. The 297th acted as the Valdez port operating company, unloading boats at the dock. In between they worked on housing construction at the garrison camp, one and a half miles west of Valdez.

Company D living conditions in December 1943.
COURTESY CHUCK MIDDLETON

A makeshift setup for washing dishes. Notice the weather station in the background. COURTESY WILLIAM LATTIN, JR.

Training exercise by troops in the Valdez Harbor. Notice that the troops are still wearing World War I issue helmets.
COURTESY WILLIAM LATTIN, JR.

On the Valdez Glacier. COURTESY WILLIAM LATTIN, JR.

297th Infantry Battalion Headquarters, Valdez, December 1943. COURTESY CHUCK MIDDLETON

Training exercises on the Valdez Glacier by men of Company D.

Associated Press releases glacier story

With a banner line of "One Soldier in Alaskan Ice Tomb" the *Cordova Times* carried an Associated Press story of a recent tragedy on the Valdez Glacier.

This was the first official press release of the event and though it differs somewhat from actual happenings, it is reprinted here as it appeared:

VALDEZ, Alaska March 25, 1943—
Died in the line of Duty.

"That's the War Departments requiem for a brave young soldier who sleeps deep in a crevasse of Valdez Glacier, famed trail to the gold camps of '98. Snow seals his tomb and towering mountains are his monument.

Twenty companions barely escaped the same fate when a hurricane of winds and avalanches caught them on a training trip.

It was five days after the storm broke and while the gales still howled that the first survivor staggered and crawled back into camp.

It had taken the speediest of them five days to cover sixteen miles.

That was six weeks ago and none of 20 is yet able to return to active duty.

The army declines to make public the soldiers names now.

This story concerns three who still are missing when all apparent survivors were brought into camp.

They were given up for dead and a new party set out to find their bodies.

The strongest, caught in the shallow edge of an avalanche, struggled out and crawled and staggered back to town on the morning of the seventh day, a Sunday.

Rescuers heard faint crys for help and before them in the snow, too weak to stand, and frozen, they found the almost unrecognizable figure of the 20th survivor.

On the Valdez Glacier. COURTESY WILLIAM LATTIN, JR.

"Kid" Cantrell and Ed Atkinson from Metlakatla on St. George Island, 1942. The island was guarded by one platoon (heavy weapons) Co. B, 297th Infantry and three machine guns.
COURTESY JOHN GRAINGER

Pvt. Jackinsky awarded the Soldiers Medal

Private Edward Jackinsky, a local soldier, who was with a party on the Valdez Glacier in December 1942, was awarded the Soldiers Medal for heroism. In making the award, the Alaska Defense Command stated:

"Private Edward Jackinsky, who entered the United States Army from Anchorage, Alaska, was awarded the Soldiers Medal by the Commanding General, Alaska Defense Command for heroism in Alaska today, Feb. 5, 1943 it was announced today.

Private Jackinsky, on a training trip with two other soldiers had dug a snow house to await the cessation of a severe blizzard. During the night he went outside to clear away the snow from the entrance but was only a short distance away when a snowslide buried the snowhouse and the two men inside with about 30 feet of snow. Lightly clothed and in an extremely severe blizzard and in constant danger of another snowslide, he stayed on the scene all night digging for his companions.

Having found no trace of the two others by morning, Private Jackinsky travelled over 16 miles of dangerous ice with the blizzard still raging to get help.

The two men buried alive, by working constantly for 24 hours, finally managed to dig themselves out."

Men of Co. D, 297th Infantry in front of their sparse living quarters on St. Paul Island, 1943.
COURTESY WILLIAM LATTIN JR.

Troops of Co. B, 297th Infantry gather firewood on the beach at Moses Point, 1942. COURTESY WILLIAM LATTIN JR.

Alaska National Guard

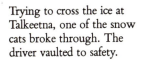
Alaska Scouts break trail.

Late in 1943, 300 members of the 297th Infantry volunteered to test winter equipment for the army. Snowcats and D-8 tractors were a part of the unit as well as men on sleds. With temperatures ranging from 0 to 40 below zero, the troops spent six weeks trekking up the Susitna River from Fort Richardson to Mt. McKinley National Park. None of the snowcats or tractors completed the trip, but all the troops made the trip with a casualty list of less than one percent. At the outset of the trip the casualty list was expected to be 20 percent.

COURTESY CHUCK MIDDLETON

Heavy snow and cold weather made the going tough.

Trying to cross the ice at Talkeetna, one of the snow cats broke through. The driver vaulted to safety.

German POWs at Excursion Inlet, November 1945. AAC

CHAPTER SIX
EXCURSION INLET

Excursion Inlet

An unusual story emerged some years ago about a $17 million Army construction project in Southeast Alaska and the method of dismantling it at the end of the war.

After war broke out in December 1941, the possibility of a Japanese attack in the Alaskan area prompted an Army engineer to suggest that a barge terminal be built someplace in Southeast Alaska so that barges could be towed up the Inside Passage from Seattle or Prince Rupert. Then the military cargo could be transferred to ocean going vessels which would take it across the water to the mainland area and down the Aleutian chain. This system would decrease the demand on the already critically short supply of vessels and reduce the threat of submarine sinkings in the open Gulf of Alaska.

A site 38 miles northwest of Juneau in the eight-mile-long estuary off Icy Straits was selected for this facility. It was known as Excursion Inlet. The Astoria & Puget Sound Canning Company was near the site, along with a small village.

The Army Corps of Engineers contracted with the Guy F. Atkinson Company of San Francisco to construct the barge facility. Work started in August 1942, and at the peak of construction more than 2,700 civilian workers were on the job, along with 850 men of the 331st Engineer General Service Regiment. The contract involved the construction of three docks (to accommodate up to nine ships), sheds, oil docks, cold storage buildings, a water reservoir, warehouse, a large gasoline tank farm, a marine repair facility and many other buildings to house a potential garrison of 4,000.

By the time the construction was complete in November 1943, at a cost of over $17 million, the threat of Japanese incursion into Alaska had long vanished. Very few people knew of the existence of this port, and it sat virtually idle until the end of the war in Europe.

Without a post-war need for such a large port, isolated in the Alaska wilderness, the Army decided to dismantle it and salvage as much material as possible. As there was a temporary shortage of men in the Alaska area at the time, or so the Army perceived, it was decided to bring up about 700 German POWs who were doing the same kind of work at Camp Hale, Colorado. These men had been found to be good workers, and as they were still POWs would not cost the Army much in wages.

In June 1945, the POWs were transported from Camp Hale to Fort Lawton, Washington, and then to Alaska in early July. The 1933rd Service Command Unit, consisting of 17 officers and 34 men, was formed to act as a guard unit.

The prisoners were housed in an old small boat repair facility and set up their camp with a mess hall, tailor shop, barber shop, canteen (Kantine in German) and other amenities of camp life. Due to the isolated area of the terminal,

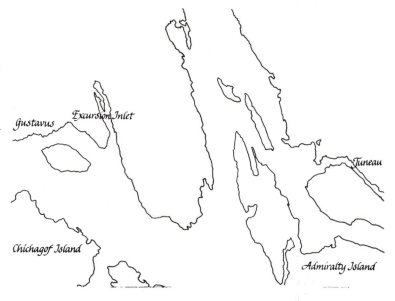

Gustavus   Excursion Inlet   Juneau

Chichagof Island   Admiralty Island

Excursion Inlet off of Icy Strait.

there were only a few attempted escapes, or as some have said, "a few men got lost in the surrounding woods." There was no place for the men to go if they did get far from the camp. Under the circumstances it was, for the most part, a pleasant experience for the POWs.

By early January 1946, all the POWs were gone from Alaska and returned to Germany. There were still about 15 structures intact at Excursion Inlet, which were later sold.

Guards examine each prisoners possessions prior to their departure from the inlet Nov. 29, 1945. ASL

A former warehouse and boat repair shop was made over to a barracks to house the POWs. COURTESY LYMAN WOODMAN

Top: Shed used for mail call, pay and hiring by civilian contractors. Note the hiring sign in front. Bottom: Vandenberg at the Indian village near the construction site.
COURTESY LEONARD VANDENBERG, KALAMAZOO, MICHIGAN

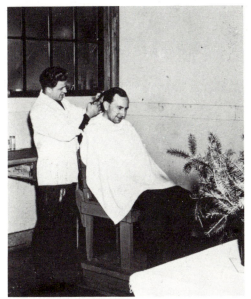

Sgt. Herbert Thrun, a POW, getting his hair cut. Thrun was captured in Italy and sent to Alaska after stays in North Africa, Virginia, Nebraska and Colorado. He still lives in Wiesbaden, West Germany and has stayed in touch with Maj. John C. Hales, retired sergeant major of the camp.
COURTESY LYMAN WOODMAN

Living quarters. ASL

Shoe repair shop. The camp was set up to be as self-sufficient as possible. ASL

Tailor shop. The prisoners were responsible for maintaining their own uniforms. ASL

The blackboard in the camp office accounted for the whereabouts of each prisoner daily.
COURTESY LYMAN WOODMAN

Fuel tanks dismantled from the Excursion Inlet complex.
COURTESY LYMAN WOODMAN

Line-up to receive clothing at a warehouse. ASL

Mess Hall. COURTESY LYMAN WOODMAN

The Kantine (Canteen) was a popular spot for prisoners to buy their tobacco and personal items. USA SC-269364

Dismantling the POW compound at the end of their stay at the Inlet, late November 1945. ASL

Dismantling of the large buildings in November.
COURTESY LYMAN WOODMAN

POWs boarding a transport ship leaving Excursion Inlet on Nov. 29, 1945. ASL

Elmendorf Field, taken by Flight F, 1st Photo Squadron, July 1941. AAC, COL. FRANK O'BRIEN COLLECTION

CHAPTER SEVEN
AIRFIELDS

Elmendorf Field

```
GENERAL ORDERS  )                          WAR DEPARTMENT
    NO. 9       )  .          WASHINGTON. December 12, 1940

                                                      Section
Designation of military reservation as Fort Richardson--  I
Designation of flying fields ---------------------------II
* * * * * * * * * * * * * * * * * * * * * * * * * * * *

    I.--Designation of military reservation as Fort Richardson.
The military reservation located at Anchorage, Alaska, is
announced as a permanent military post under the provisions
of paragraph 2c, AR 210-10, and is designated Fort Richardson
in honor of Brigadier General WILDS P. RICHARDSON, United
States Army.  Post Office address:  Anchorage, Alaska.

    II.--1. * * * * * * * * * * * * * * * * * * * * * *

    2. The flying field at Fort Richardson, Alaska, is
designated "Elmendorf Field" in honor of Captain HUGH M.
ELMENDORF, A.C.  Captain Elmendorf was killed in an airplane
accident at Wright Field, Ohio, on January 13, 1933.

    * * * * * * * * * * * * * * * * * * * * * * * * * *


    By order of the Secretary of War:



                              G. C. MARSHALL,
                              Chief of Staff


OFFICIAL:
        E. S. ADAMS,
         Major General
          The Adjutant General
```

Early photo of headquarters at Elmendorf. AAC, JOHN BURT COLLECTION

P-36s of the 18th Pursuit Squadron, summer 1941. AAC

Early views of Fort Richardson, probably in the spring of 1941. It was still a tent base at this time. AMHA

P-36s waiting to be assembled in March 1941. They were crated and shipped to Anchorage by steamer. AAC, TED SPENCER COLLECTION

Construction of one of the large hangars, spring 1941. AAC

ELMENDORF FIELD, ANCHORAGE, ALASKA

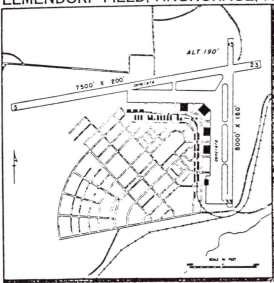

DESCRIPTION

DIMENSIONS - E./W. (5-23) 7,500' x 200',
  N./S. (15-33) 5,000' x 150'.
SURFACE - Concrete runways and parking areas.
  Runways only usable.
MARKINGS - Wind indicator, runway markers.
LIGHTING - Portable floodlights, boundary and
  obstruction lights. Flashing beacon on re-
  quest.
OBSTRUCTIONS - Hangars, water tower and building
  area to SW. High mountains to E. 60' trees
  1/4 mile to W. and 1/2 mile to E.

FACILITIES

HANGARS - Three permanent, one temporary, max.
  300' x 275'. Revetments for 40 bombers and
  80 fighters.
REPAIR FACILITIES - Sub-depot, 24th Air Base
  Squadron. Major repairs.
FUEL AND OIL - 100 octane gasoline available in
  underground storage. Tank trucks for servic-
  ing.
COMMUNICATIONS - Radio range, control tower,
  radio, teletype, telephone, telegraph.
WEATHER REPORTS - AAF Station, hourly reports.
TRANSPORTATION - Bus or taxi to town, railroad
  to Seward and Fairbanks, steamers to United
  States.
ACCOMMODATIONS - Extensive barracks and messing;
  hotels in town.

NAME AND LOCATION

ELMENDORF FIELD, located 4 miles NE. of
  Anchorage, N. of the Alaska Railroad.
POSITION - Lat. 61° 15' N., Long. 149° 48' W.
MAGNETIC VARIATION - 27° E.
ALTITUDE - 190 feet.
LANDMARKS - Alaska Railroad to the S., military
  barracks, city of Anchorage.

GENERAL INFORMATION

OPERATED BY - U.S. AAF, Hdq. 11th Air Force.
REMARKS - Field and facilities practically
  complete. Several dispersal fields in the
  area, namely Lake Spenard, Merrill, Campbell
  Creek, Goose Bay, Birchwood and Willow.

WEATHER

PREVAILING WINDS - North. Maximum velocity 58
  m.p.h. Average velocity 5 m.p.h.
PRECIPITATION - Rain 15" per year, snow 77" per
  year.
TEMPERATURE - Extreme range: 75° F. to -9° F.
VISIBILITY - Fog about 30 days per year.

CHARTS - Kenai (Alaska Aeronautical Charts)

B-18A bomber at the Juneau Airport on its way north, 1941.
This outdated bomber belonged to the 36th Bombardment
Squadron. AAC

B-18As at the Nome field, 1941. AAC

EDMONTON, ALBERTA, CANADA

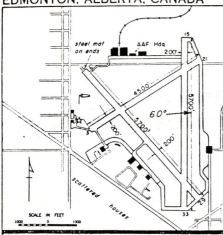

NAME AND LOCATION

EDMONTON MUNICIPAL AIRPORT, 2½ miles NW. of center of Edmonton, within city limits.
POSITION - Lat. 53° 34' N., Long. 113° 31' W.
MAGNETIC VARIATION - 25° E.
ALTITUDE - 2,185 feet.
LANDMARKS - Canadian Nat. RR. yards to N. Grain elevator 1 mile NW. Yellow arrow on roof of Armory in city points toward airport. A concrete boulevard extends N. from the city to the airport.

GENERAL INFORMATION

OPERATED BY - Dept. of Transport and R.C.A.F.
REMARKS - Field practically complete. Areas around field and temporary housing facilities very muddy after rains.

DESCRIPTION

DIMENSIONS - NW./SE. (11-29) 5,700' x 200'
  N./S. (15-33) 5,700' x 200'
  NE./SW. (3-21) 4,500' x 200'
SURFACE - Runways hard, concrete and asphalt. Remainder of field sod, can be used except in wet weather. Level, poor drainage.
MARKINGS - Wind cone on hangar, W. side of field. White runways strips, white circle, boundary markers.
LIGHTING - Boundary, contact, obstruction and floodlights. Rotating beacon flashing "EN" 6 times per minute.
OBSTRUCTIONS - Do not circle under low overcast due to radio towers, grain elevators and city buildings. NE. - radio towers 5½ miles. NW. - grain elevator 4,800' distant, coal dock and water tower 2,300' distant, house 500' from end of runway. SE. - chimney 3,000' distant. SW. - power line 1,000' from end of runway. W. - Tele. poles along edge of field.

FACILITIES

HANGARS - Two C.P.A. Three R.C.A.F. One TCA. Two Aircraft Repair Ltd. One A.T.C.
REPAIR FACILITIES - Complete. Major rebuilding.
FUEL AND OIL - Bulk storage large quantity high octane gas.
COMMUNICATIONS - Telephone, telegraph, teletype. Radio and radio range.
WEATHER REPORTS - Complete. Army Weather Service.
TRANSPORTATION - By taxi or motor transport.
ACCOMMODATIONS - Quarters and mess at field. Numerous hotels in town.

WEATHER

PREVAILING WINDS - SW. in winter, NW. in summer.
PRECIPITATION - 18" of rain and 43" of snow per year. Winter operations O.K.
TEMPERATURE - Extremes: 98° max., -57° min.
VISIBILITY - Fog rare, 5 days annually.

CHARTS - Red Deer-Edmonton (Canada Air Navigation); North Saskatchewan Regional.

A C-54 Skymaster flying over the Parliament Building, Edmonton, Alberta, 1944.
AAC

GRANDE PRAIRIE, ALBERTA, CANADA

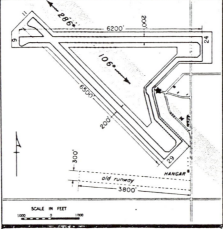

NAME AND LOCATION

GRANDE PRAIRIE MUNICIPAL AIRPORT, 3 miles W. of town, on Edmonton - Dawson Creek Highway.
POSITION - Lat. 55° 10' N., Long. 118° 53' W.
MAGNETIC VARIATION - 28° 30' E.
ALTITUDE - 2,200 feet.
LANDMARKS - Town of Grande Prairie, Bear Lake to NE.

GENERAL INFORMATION

OPERATED BY - Dept. of Transport and R.C.A.F.
REMARKS - Old field borders airport on S. and consists of one dirt and sod rough runway, marked with red and white wooden runway markers. Fueling from one pit at passenger station at SE. corner of field. CPA (Lockheed Lodestars), NWA (C53) and Army (all types) use the new field.

DESCRIPTION

DIMENSIONS - NW./SE. (11-29) 6,500' x 200'
  E./W. (6-24) 6,200' x 200'.
SURFACE - Hard surfaced runways. Remainder of field sod. Natural drainage.
MARKINGS - Wind cone at old hangar.
LIGHTING - Rotating beacons. Obstruction and contact lights. Lanterns for emergency lighting.
OBSTRUCTIONS - Trees 800' to E. Farm buildings 1,500' to S. Trees 50' high to W. and NW. Tele. lines parallel to S. side of field.

FACILITIES

HANGARS - One frame hangar, 30' x 36'.
REPAIR FACILITIES - None.
FUEL AND OIL - Quantity of 100 octane gas. One fueling pit at E. end of old field.
COMMUNICATIONS - Telephone. Radio and radio range facilities.
WEATHER REPORTS - Hourly weather service available.
TRANSPORTATION - By auto. Railroad to Edmonton.
ACCOMMODATIONS - Small hotel in town. Staff quarters. Rest room at E. end of field. Small hospital in town. Population - 400.

WEATHER

PREVAILING WINDS - W. all year, secondary winds NW. and E. Maximum 30 to 35 m.p.h.
PRECIPITATION - 15" of rain and 65" of snow per year.
TEMPERATURE -
VISIBILITY -

CHARTS - Grande Prairie-Peace River (Canada Air Navigation)
  North Saskatchewan Regional.

FORT ST. JOHN, BRITISH COLUMBIA, CANADA

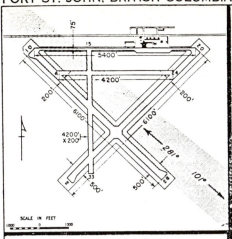

NAME AND LOCATION

FORT ST. JOHN AIRPORT (NEW) located 4 miles E.
of town, on S. side of main highway.
POSITION - Lat. 56°14'30" N., Long. 120°46'00" W.
MAGNETIC VARIATION - 30° E.
ALTITUDE - 2,400 feet.
LANDMARKS - Town of Fort St. John. Peace River
to S., Charlie Lake to NW.

GENERAL INFORMATION

OPERATED BY - Dept. of Transport and R.C.A.F.
REMARKS - Old field 5 miles W. used during construction, 4,000' x 400', fueling from pit.
Field under construction. When tower is
inoperative, contact range.

DESCRIPTION

DIMENSIONS - NE./SW. (2-20) 6,100' x 200'
E./W. (6-24) 4,200' x 150', graded (closed)
NW./SE. (10-28) 6,100' x 200'
N./S. (15-33) 4,200' x 200' under construc-
tion.
SURFACE - NE./SW. and NW./SE. runways asphalt,
with concrete turning circles. Other runways
sod, under construction.
MARKINGS - Cones and flags outline usable area.
Wind cone.
LIGHTING - Rotating beacon and flares on re-
quest. Obstruction and boundary lights.
Contact lights planned.
OBSTRUCTIONS - Timber on NE. approaches. Radio
masts 1,000 yards E. and S. of field, build-
ings to N.

FACILITIES

HANGARS - Planned. One small hangar 75' x 75'
not suitable for C-53, owned by C.P.A.
REPAIR FACILITIES - One mechanic, minor repairs.
FUEL AND OIL - Unlimited supply from railhead
at Dawson Creek. One tank truck. Bulk stor-
age for approximately 250,000 gallons gas.
COMMUNICATIONS - Radio and radio range. Tele-
phone, teletype and control tower.
WEATHER SERVICE - Available from D. of T.
TRANSPORTATION - Served by Northwest Airlines
(C-53), Canadian Pacific Airways (Lockheed
Lodestars). Road to RR. at Dawson Creek.
ACCOMMODATIONS - Practically nil in town.
Staff quarters at field. Limited quarters
nearing completion, more planned.

WEATHER

PREVAILING WINDS - SW., maximum 35 m.p.h.
PRECIPITATION - Approximately 18" of rain and
62" of snow per year.
TEMPERATURE - Annual range: 90° F. to -38° F.
VISIBILITY - Subject to smoke conditions.
Ground fog late summer and fall.

CHARTS - Peace River Regional.

FORT NELSON, BRITISH COLUMBIA, CANADA

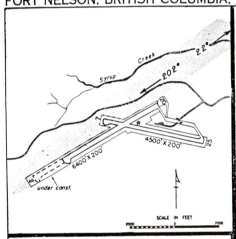

NAME AND LOCATION

FORT NELSON AIRPORT, 3 miles WNW. of town, along
road and just N. of Muskwa River.
POSITION - Lat. 58° 50' N., Long. 122° 40' W.
MAGNETIC VARIATION - 33° E.
ALTITUDE - 1,300 feet.
LANDMARKS - Town and Ft. Nelson River to E.
Muskwa River to S.

GENERAL INFORMATION

OPERATED BY - Dept. of Transport and R.C.A.F.
REMARKS - Snow controlled by rolling. Nelson
River Canyon is 300 - 400 feet deep. Affords
depth perception.

DESCRIPTION

DIMENSIONS - NE./SW. (2-20) 6,400' x 200' under
construction. NW./SE. (7-25) 4,500' x 200'
graded and under construction.
SURFACE - NE./SW. runway asphalt on 4,800'.
Remainder of field clay and gravel.
MARKINGS - Wind cone at runway intersection.
Red and white runway markers indicate area on
which to land.
LIGHTING - Rotating beacon and flares on request. Obstruction, contact and boundary
lights.
OBSTRUCTIONS - Approaches clear. Building area
at runway intersection. Trees all around
field. Hills 2,000' S. and W. of field.

FACILITIES

HANGARS - One large nose hangar.
REPAIR FACILITIES - Minor.
FUEL AND OIL - Bulk storage under construction.
Large quantity high octane fuel. Gas tanks,
one pit and one truck.
COMMUNICATIONS - Radio and radio range.
WEATHER REPORTS - Hourly weather reports from
Department of Transport.
TRANSPORTATION - By auto. Served by Canadian
Pacific Airways (Lockheed Lodestars) and
Northwest Airlines (C-53). Small boat.
ACCOMMODATIONS - Staff quarters and temporary
barracks.

WEATHER

PREVAILING WINDS - E. and W.
PRECIPITATION - Average 12½" of rain and 65" of
snow per year.
TEMPERATURE - Extremes: 88° F. to -39° F.
VISIBILITY - Often restricted in summer and
fall. Subject to considerable ground fog.

CHARTS - Peace River Regional.

A C-54 Skymaster at the Fort
Nelson, British Columbia
field.
EARL BARTLETT COLLECTION
VIA EARL BROWN

Fort Nelson,
British Columbia Airfield

ALL PHOTOS FROM THE EARL BARTLETT COLLECTION
VIA EARL BROWN

WATSON LAKE, YUKON TERRITORY, CANADA

DESCRIPTION

DIMENSIONS - Strip WNW./ESE. (7-25) 5,500' x 500' with runway 5,500' x 200'. NE./SW. (1-19) 4,700' x 200' (available when required) of crushed compacted gravel.

SURFACE - Runway blacktop, remainder of strip dirt and gravel. Gravel taxi strip and standing in front of administration building. Blacktop turning areas on ends. Gravel as good as blacktop.

MARKINGS - Wooden runway markers. Wind indicator at SE. end of strip. Red flags, flares.

LIGHTING - Rotating beacon. Flares at ends of runway. Boundary lights along edge of strip. Contact lights.

OBSTRUCTIONS - Approaches clear except for trees close to E. end of runway. Hills to N. and E. Runway 16' higher than lake.

FACILITIES

HANGARS - Small nose hangar, 2 hangars planned.

REPAIR FACILITIES - Minor, some mechanics.

FUEL AND OIL - No planes will be refueled at Watson Lake unless absolutely necessary. Plan to gas at Whitehorse or Fort Nelson. Bulk storage under construction.

COMMUNICATIONS - Radio and radio range.

WEATHER REPORTS - Available from D. of T.

TRANSPORTATION - Army motor transport. Alcan Highway.

ACCOMMODATIONS - Staff quarters and temporary barracks; permanent under construction. Meals are excellent.

WEATHER

PREVAILING WINDS - Summer W. and WSW. Winter W. and WSW. with occasional wind from NE. Maximum in summer - 30 m.p.h.

PRECIPITATION - Quite frequent instability showers. Average 15" rain and 68" snow per year.

TEMPERATURE - Annual range: 90° F. to -40° F.

VISIBILITY - Ground fogs in fall until freezeup.

CHARTS - Whitehorse-Watson Lake (Canada Air Navigation); Whitehorse Regional.

NAME AND LOCATION

WATSON LAKE AIRPORT, located on N. shore of Watson Lake, 20 miles NW. of Lower Post.

POSITION - Lat. 60° 07' N., Long. 128° 46' W.

MAGNETIC VARIATION - 33° E.

ALTITUDE - 2,245 feet.

LANDMARKS - Confluence of Liard and Dease Rivers, 20 miles S. Watson Lake S. of airport.

GENERAL INFORMATION

OPERATED BY - Dept. of Transport and R.C.A.F.

REMARKS - Snow controlled by rolling. Subject to icing conditions all year. Icing level approximately 10,000' in summer.

Watson Lake, Yukon Airport, January 1944. USA SC 323088

WHITEHORSE, YUKON TERRITORY, CANADA

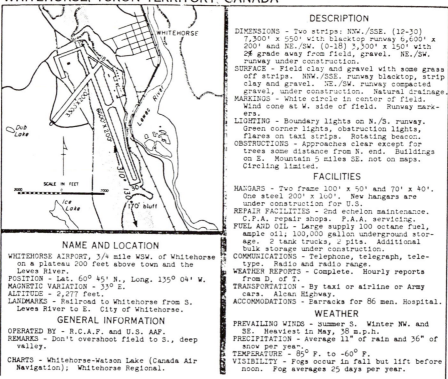

DESCRIPTION

DIMENSIONS - Two strips: NNW./SSE. (12-30) 7,300' x 550' with blacktop runway 6,600' x 200' and NE./SW. (0-18) 3,300' x 150' with 2% grade away from field, gravel. NE./SW. runway under construction.

SURFACE - Field clay and gravel with some grass off strips. NNW./SSE. runway blacktop, strip clay and gravel. NE./SW. runway compacted gravel, under construction. Natural drainage.

MARKINGS - White circle in center of field. Wind cone at W. side of field. Runway markers.

LIGHTING - Boundary lights on N./S. runway. Green corner lights, obstruction lights, flares on taxi strips. Rotating beacon.

OBSTRUCTIONS - Approaches clear except for trees some distance from N. end. Buildings on E. Mountain 5 miles SE. not on maps. Circling limited.

FACILITIES

HANGARS - Two frame 100' x 50' and 70' x 40'. One steel 200' x 100'. New hangars are under construction for U.S.

REPAIR FACILITIES - 2nd echelon maintenance. C.P.A. repair shops. P.A.A. servicing.

FUEL AND OIL - Large supply 100 octane fuel, ample oil; 100,000 gallon underground storage. 2 tank trucks, 2 pits. Additional bulk storage under construction.

COMMUNICATIONS - Telephone, telegraph, teletype. Radio and radio range.

WEATHER REPORTS - Complete. Hourly reports from D. of T.

TRANSPORTATION - By taxi or airline or Army cars. Alcan Highway.

ACCOMMODATIONS - Barracks for 86 men. Hospital.

WEATHER

PREVAILING WINDS - Summer S. Winter NW. and SE. Heaviest in May, 38 m.p.h.

PRECIPITATION - Average 11" of rain and 36" of snow per year.

TEMPERATURE - 85° F. to -60° F.

VISIBILITY - Fogs occur in fall but lift before noon. Fog averages 25 days per year.

NAME AND LOCATION

WHITEHORSE AIRPORT, 3/4 mile WSW. of Whitehorse on a plateau 200 feet above town and the Lewes River.

POSITION - Lat. 60° 45' N., Long. 135° 04' W.

MAGNETIC VARIATION - 33° E.

ALTITUDE - 2,277 feet.

LANDMARKS - Railroad to Whitehorse from S. Lewes River to E. City of Whitehorse.

GENERAL INFORMATION

OPERATED BY - R.C.A.F. and U.S. AAF.

REMARKS - Don't overshoot field to S., deep valley.

CHARTS - Whitehorse-Watson Lake (Canada Air Navigation); Whitehorse Regional.

The airport at Whitehorse was situated on a bench above the town. It was the major stopping point on the route between Edmonton, Alberta and Fairbanks, Alaska. AAC

TANACROSS, ALASKA

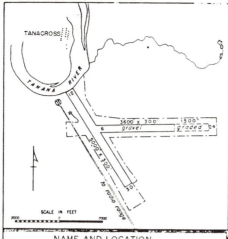

NAME AND LOCATION

TANACROSS CAA FIELD, 1/4 mile S. of Tanacross, on S. bank of Tanana River, across river from town of Tanacross, 1½ miles N. of Alcan Highway.

POSITION - Lat. 63° 23' N., Long. 143° 21' W.

MAGNETIC VARIATION - 31° 30' E.

ALTITUDE - 1,516 feet.

LANDMARKS - Tanana River and Tanacross village, Alcan Highway 1½ miles to S.

GENERAL INFORMATION

OPERATED BY - U.S. AAF.

REMARKS - Ski landings can be made on river between November and April.

DESCRIPTION

DIMENSIONS - NW./SE. (12-30) 5,000' x 300'. E./W. (6-24) 5,100' x 300'.

SURFACE - Both strips gravel, level grade, natural drainage except for ditches on each side of runway. Adequate for ordinary weather.

MARKINGS - Wind sock on beacon tower, W. side of NW./SE. strip.

LIGHTING - Boundary lights on NW./SE. strip. E./W. strip 70% lighted. Beacon, range lights.

OBSTRUCTIONS - Low bush surrounds field, ditches along edge of runways. Poles 60' high 1,000' NNE. Antennae at NW. corner. Mountain range 5 miles S. reaching 6,000' to 16,000'.

FACILITIES

HANGARS - Nose hangar.

REPAIR FACILITIES - First echelon repairs.

FUEL AND OIL - Ample supply of 100 octane gas and 98 and 120 oil.

COMMUNICATIONS - PAA radio.

WEATHER REPORTS - U.S. Weather Bureau station.

TRANSPORTATION - Served by Wien Alaska (Stinson and small ships), PAA (DC-3's, Lockheed 14), and Reeves (small ships).

ACCOMMODATIONS - Quarters and meals at PAA station. CAA staff quarters. Accommodations for 12 officers and 50 enlisted men. Population of Tanacross - 162 (1/41).

WEATHER

PREVAILING WINDS - Summer SE. Winter SE. Highest winds in summer from S.

PRECIPITATION - 12" of rain per year, considerable snowfall.

TEMPERATURE - Extremes: 93° maximum, -55° minimum.

VISIBILITY - Fogs occur frequently during freezeup for two month period, occasionally during winter.

CHARTS - Fairbanks (Alaska Aeronautical Charts).

COURTESY STACY DOBRZENSKY

Hangar under construction at Tanacross, fall 1943.
COURTESY LEONARD VANDENBERG, KALAMAZOO, MICH.

The Tanacross hangar in 1966. It was later taken apart piece by piece and re-erected in Fairbanks for a recreation center.
ACC

Nome Air Base. COURTESY STACY DOBRZENSKY

NORTHWAY, ALASKA

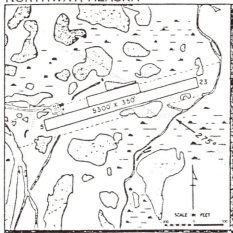

DESCRIPTION

DIMENSIONS - E./W. (5-23) 5,300' x 500' with emulsion stabilization on 5,300' x 350' and 1,800' x 300' parking area on N. side. Stabilization to be extended to 500' on runway.

SURFACE - Strip asphalt emulsion. Artificial and natural drainage. May not be usable during the spring when water level is high.

MARKINGS - White corner and boundary markers. Illuminated wind cone on beacon tower.

LIGHTING - Rotating beacon in building area, boundary, obstruction lights, two 18" floodlights.

OBSTRUCTIONS - Approaches clear. Buildings, beacon and radio masts on N. side of field. Radio range station 1.1 miles NW. of field. 50' trees in area.

FACILITIES

HANGARS - Nose hangar.

REPAIR FACILITIES - Very limited.

FUEL AND OIL - Large quantity in drums. Bulk storage under construction. Supplied by air from Fairbanks at the present time.

COMMUNICATIONS - Radio and radio range.

WEATHER REPORTS - Available.

TRANSPORTATION - Served by NWA (C-53), Pollack (Stinson and Waco). Truck and jeeps.

ACCOMMODATIONS - Staff quarters. Barracks for limited number. Small tent camp.

WEATHER

PREVAILING WINDS - NE. and SW.

PRECIPITATION - Rain 12" per year, snowfall 2 to 3 feet per year.

TEMPERATURE - Extremes: 93° maximum and -70° minimum.

VISIBILITY - Morning fogs during fall months. Ceiling usually very good.

CHARTS - Fairbanks (Alaska Aeronautical Charts).

NAME AND LOCATION

NORTHWAY STAGING FIELD, located 6 miles S. of junction of Nabesna and Tanana Rivers.

POSITION - Lat. 62° 58' N., Long. 141° 58' W.

MAGNETIC VARIATION - 32° E.

ALTITUDE - 1,803 feet (approximate).

LANDMARKS - Nabesna and Tanana Rivers. Field is difficult to discern from a distance due to numerous small lakes in area. Alcan Highway 17 miles NE.

GENERAL INFORMATION

OPERATED BY - C.A.A. and A.A.F.

REMARKS - This field has had the following names in the order given: Nabesna Village, Boundary, Moose Creek, Tetlin and Scotty. It should not be confused with the emergency field at Tetlin.

COURTESY STACY DOBRZENSKY

BIG DELTA, ALASKA

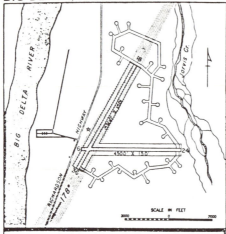

NAME AND LOCATION

BIG DELTA CAA FIELD, located 11 miles SSE. of Big Delta and E. of Richardson Highway, between Big Delta River and Jarvis Creek.

POSITION - Lat. 64° 00' N., Long. 145° 44' W.

MAGNETIC VARIATION - 31° E.

ALTITUDE - 1,266 feet

LANDMARKS - Richardson Highway, Tanana and Big Delta Rivers. Donnelly's Dome 15 miles S.

GENERAL INFORMATION

OPERATED BY - C.A.A. and A.A.F.

REMARKS - This is one of the best fields in Alaska. There is an old field located at Big Delta town which is still in use by private operators. Population of Big Delta - 25. Wing covers and heating units available in quantity.

DESCRIPTION

DIMENSIONS - NE./SW. (18-36) 5,300' x 500' strip with 5,300' x 150' runway. E./W. (6-24) 4,500' x 500' strip with 4,500' x 150' runway. 2,700' parking area on NE./SW. strip with tie-down cable for 60 planes.

SURFACE - Gravel with 150' asphalt strips on each. Parking areas and hardstands to be asphalted.

MARKINGS - Sock on tower at W. side of runway.

LIGHTING - Boundary, range, approach and obstruction lights. Rotating beacon.

OBSTRUCTIONS - Building at W. end of E./W. runway. Radio towers (135') 1.8 miles to NE. Beacon (51') 150' W. of NE./SW. runway. Mountain range reaching 13,740' to the S. with foothills 15 miles distant.

FACILITIES

HANGARS - Two nose hangars.

REPAIR FACILITIES - None.

FUEL AND OIL - Large quantity 100 octane fuel and oil available. Bulk storage under construction.

COMMUNICATIONS - Telegraph. Telephone to Valdez and Fairbanks. Radio and radio range. Control tower.

WEATHER REPORTS - Available

ACCOMMODATIONS - Quonset huts for Army Staff. Barracks and messing for 200. CAA quarters.

WEATHER

PREVAILING WINDS - Summer N. Winter N. and NW.

PRECIPITATION - Rain 20" per year, snow 60" per year.

TEMPERATURE - Extremes: 90° F. maximum to -50° F. minimum.

VISIBILITY - Occasional fog during winter Clouds average 175 days per year.

NOTE: Wind conditions troublesome to pilots the majority of the year. Only drawback to field.

CHARTS - Fairbanks (Alaska Aeronautical Charts)

COURTESY STACY DOBRZENSKY

BIG DELTA

LADD FIELD, FAIRBANKS, ALASKA

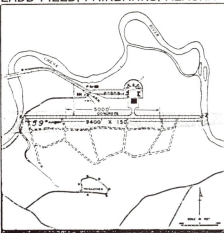

NAME AND LOCATION

LADD FIELD, located 4 miles E. of town, on S. shore of Chena River.
POSITION - Lat. 64° 49' N., Long. 147° 38' W.
MAGNETIC VARIATION - 30° E.
ALTITUDE - 448 feet.
LANDMARKS - City of Fairbanks. Building layout at field. Railroad to Fairbanks.

GENERAL INFORMATION

OPERATED BY - U.S. A.A.F.
REMARKS - Field nearly complete. Dispersal hardstands under construction. Use procedure approach. No civil operations except emergency. Snow compacted or removed in winter. Seaplane anchorage in Chena River just W. of highway bridge.

DESCRIPTION

DIMENSIONS - E./W. (6-24) 9,400' x 150' with 5,000' center section paved and gravel strips 2,100' and 2,185' long at each end. Earth-gravel taxi strip to both ends from hangar.
SURFACE - Land heavy ships on concrete runway only. Field overgrown with thick brush, trees.
MARKINGS - Wind indicators N. of and at both ends of runway.
LIGHTING - Beacon, approach, flood and runway lighting on both sides.
OBSTRUCTIONS - Hill across river at E. end of runway, 130' above field level. Hangar and buildings on N. side of runway. 500' hill 2½ miles N. of field. Beacon 150' high N. of W. end of runway.

FACILITIES

HANGARS - One steel and concrete, 320' x 270'.
REPAIR FACILITIES - Complete repair depot.
FUEL AND OIL - Bulk storage; when completed will be 800,000 gallons. Trailer trucks and underground tanks at field. Additional bulk storage in town.
COMMUNICATIONS - Telephone, telegraph, teletype. Radio and radio range.
WEATHER SERVICE - U.S. Weather Bureau, Army Weather Service combined. Hourly service.
TRANSPORTATION - Taxi or regular bus service.
ACCOMMODATIONS - Barracks. Hotels in town, very expensive. Housing limited.

WEATHER

PREVAILING WINDS - Annual N. Summer S. Winter N.
PRECIPITATION - Rain 16" per year, snow 108" per year.
TEMPERATURE - Extremes: 99° F. maximum, -65° F. minimum.
VISIBILITY - Light fog 80 days per year, dense fog 10 days per year. Fog prevails when less than 40° F.

CHARTS - Fairbanks (Alaska Aeronautical Charts).

Ladd Field, 1941, taken by Flight F, 1st Photo Squadron. AAC, FRANK O'BRIEN COLLECTION

Hangar, Ladd Field, 1941. AAC

Ladd Field control tower. COURTESY STACY DOBRZENSKY

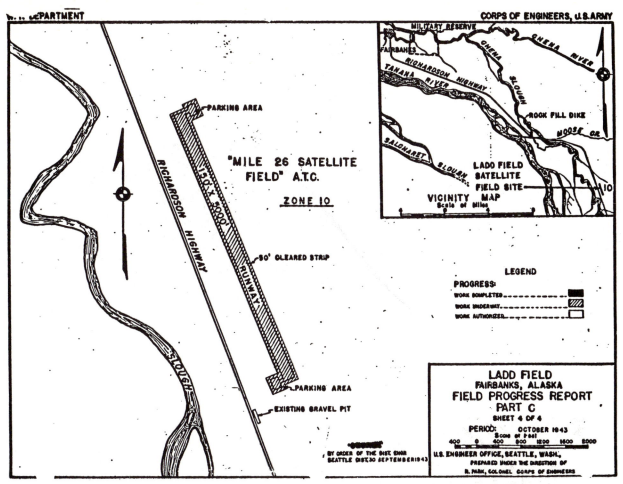

PARKING AREA

"MILE 26 SATELLITE FIELD" A.T.C.

ZONE 10

130' X 5000'

RICHARDSON HIGHWAY

RUNWAY

80' CLEARED STRIP

PARKING AREA

EXISTING GRAVEL PIT

SLOUGH

MILITARY RESERVE

FAIRBANKS

RICHARDSON HIGHWAY

CHENA RIVER

CHENA SLOUGH

TANANA RIVER

ROCK FILL DIKE

MOOSE CR.

SALCHAKET SLOUGH

LADD FIELD SATELLITE FIELD SITE

VICINITY MAP
Scale of Miles

10

LEGEND

PROGRESS:

WORK COMPLETED

WORK UNDERWAY

WORK AUTHORIZED

LADD FIELD
FAIRBANKS, ALASKA
FIELD PROGRESS REPORT
PART C
SHEET 4 OF 4

PERIOD: OCTOBER 1943
Scale of Feet
400 0 400 800 1200 1600 2000

U.S. ENGINEER OFFICE, SEATTLE, WASH.,
PREPARED UNDER THE DIRECTION OF
R. PARK, COLONEL CORPS OF ENGINEERS

BY ORDER OF THE DIST. ENGR.
SEATTLE DIST. 30 SEPTEMBER 1943

COURTESY STACY DOBRZENSKY

-117-

Control tower, Galena Field. COURTESY STACY DOBRZENSKY

Galena Airport was constructed adjacent to the Yukon River by the Civil Aeronautics Authority in late 1941. The field was turned over to the military on July 1, 1943, and became a satellite of Ladd Field. It served as a refueling stop for ALSID aircraft on the way to Nome. Today the airport is the home of the 21st Tactical Fighter Wing. COURTESY STACY DOBRZENSKY

Galena Field Flood,
May 25-29, 1945

A major flood hit Galena Field when an earthen dam across the Yukon River washed out on May 25, 1945. The hangar pictured is still intact, the only World War II building left. It is used for storage and operations.

PHOTOS COURTESY LT. COL. ROBERT D. FLEER, GALENA, ALASKA

Floating ice endangers hangar.

Ice flows in a strong current.

Army river boat in hangar.

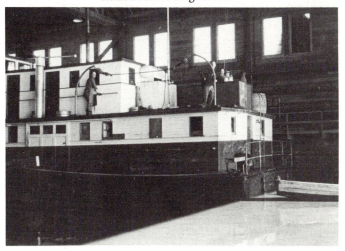

Hazel B steams into hangar.

1609 1468 BU 28 May 45 Floating Ice in Barracks Area

1108 G 1468 BU 28 May 45 The Hangar in Rising Water

1539 G 1468 BU 28 May 45 Typical Roof Scene at Flood

1895 G 1468 BU 29 May 45 View of Base From Yukon

AACS Station, Prince George, B.C. (1943-44)

Prior to the time that the Aleutian campaign was concluded, it was planned to develop an alternate route from U.S. airplane factories to Fairbanks, particularly for the ferrying of aircraft but also for cargo and administrative flights, etc. Two new "service stations" were thus planned, one at Kamloops, British Columbia, the other at Prince George, British Columbia. With these two there would be a third alternative air route: One was the "coastal route" from Seattle; the other was the "Alcan Route," through Minneapolis/Great Falls, to Edmonton, northwesterly up through Whitehorse. This third route would permit flights from various U.S. points, via Kamloops and Prince George and then either straight up to Watson Lake or westerly over to the coast. As the Aleutian campaign wound down, Kamloops was abandoned as a plan, Prince George, however, was commissioned, although it served mainly as a weather data gathering point (one of the AACS missions). There were a few visitors, including Canadian Hurricanes, and Bolingbrokes bombers. There was a small crew of aircraft mechanics, Weather Service and AACS station personnel and the RCAF-operated control tower. Other visitors included Pam Am passenger flights, and a U.S. Navy operation, which used the base as an alternate when the coastal weather was bad.

A further "mission" of this station was that of an AACS "NCOIC School." As men came and went from the various stations in Alaska and Western Canada, there was always the need to promote operators (radio) to "Non-Commissioned Officer in Charge." Further, the Alaskan Defense Command, faced with insufficient transport to rotate its forces home on leave, issued orders sharply curtailing leaves and furloughs. Meanwhile, the Air Corps could manage its own transport. Since we were not terribly busy at Prince George, I suggested the "NCOIC" school, based on my own observations that the transition from "Radio Operator" to "NCOIC" was not easy (hard to find oneself in a position of authority over one's buddies), and that we could assign eligible men to my "school," which was in Canada and outside of the ADC, and give them furloughs coupled with what I felt was a fairly decent "curriculum" that I devised and ran. Further, men not eligible for leave were assigned for the training and for duty "near civilization," Prince George being a small city, unlike Galena, Northway, Big Delta, Tanacross, Barrow, even Nome.

My initial assignment was, predicated on my experience at Whitehorse, to assist in the construction, equipping and commissioning of the Prince George AACS station, working with the civilian engineer who had been sent up to supervise the construction, etc. (a former "Ham" from eastern U.S., Bruce H. Hart).

Stacy Dobrzensky
Oakland, CA

Administration Building at the Prince George, British Columbia airfield, March 1944. COURTESY STACY DOBRZENSKY

RCAF transmitter sites at Prince George, March 1944. COURTESY STACY DOBRZENSKY

ANNETTE ISLAND, ALASKA

DESCRIPTION

DIMENSIONS - NW./SE. (12-30) 7,500' x 300';
NE./SW. (3-21) 6,000' x 300'.
SURFACE - Water-bound macadam.
MARKINGS - Standard markings.
LIGHTING - Emergency lighting.
OBSTRUCTIONS - Trees and brush. Mountains
some distance to NE. and E. Radio masts in
camp area.

FACILITIES

HANGARS - One hangar 200' x 160', under construction. Revetments available.
REPAIR FACILITIES - Limited repair facilities
available.
FUEL AND OIL - 100 octane gasoline available.
COMMUNICATIONS - Radio range, radio, control
tower.
WEATHER REPORTS - First order weather station.
TRANSPORTATION - Roads to Metlakatla and to
small docks in Tamgas Harbor where supplies
are unloaded.
ACCOMMODATIONS - Barracks and extensive
quarters.

WEATHER

PREVAILING WINDS - SE. winds above 30 m.p.h.
occur 11% of the time during January and
February, decreasing during remainder of
year.
PRECIPITATION - Rain 157" per year, snow
infrequent.
TEMPERATURE - Extreme range: 96° F. to -80° F.
VISIBILITY - Frequent fogs and low ceilings.
Cloudy days average 240 days per year.
Ceilings average 1,500 feet. Rain and
drizzle reduce visibilities during the
autumn months. Fog occurs 2 days per month
in June, July and August, less than 1 day
per month during remainder of year.

CHARTS - Fraser River Regional Chart.

NAME AND LOCATION

ANNETTE ISLAND AIR BASE, located 6 miles S. of
Metlakatla, on the SW. peninsula of Annette
Island.
POSITION - Lat. 55° 03' N., Long. 131° 35' W.
MAGNETIC VARIATION - 29° E.
ALTITUDE - 50 to 100 feet.
LANDMARKS - Military barracks, extinct volcano
crater nearby.

GENERAL INFORMATION

OPERATED BY - U. S. Army Air Forces.
REMARKS - Annette Island is a restricted area.
Use anti-aircraft procedure approach.
Seaplane facilities in Tamgas Harbor.

AACS control tower at Annette Island Air Base, 1943. AAC

P-39s on a stopover flight at Annette Island Air Base. GA

JUNEAU, ALASKA

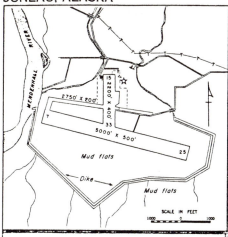

DESCRIPTION

DIMENSIONS - WNW./ESE. (7-25) 5,000' x 500'.
N./S. (15-33) 2,200' x 400' taxi strip. Old
field: E./W. 2,750' x 200' parking area.
SURFACE - Runway asphalt. E./W. strip is old
field, sod and gravel on silt.
MARKINGS - Wind cone.
LIGHTING - Beacon and boundary lights.
OBSTRUCTIONS - Hills and trees to the NE.
Radio masts and buildings to the N. Mountain
ranges surround field. Approaches clear.

FACILITIES

HANGARS - Three small hangars; largest 60' x 40'
Revetments under construction.
REPAIR FACILITIES - P.A.A. repairs available.
FUEL AND OIL - Large quantity available. Bulk
storage for 58,000 gallons.
COMMUNICATIONS - Radio range, radio. Telegraph
in town.
WEATHER REPORTS - Available.
TRANSPORTATION - P.A.A. and other airlines,
highway to Juneau, steamships.
ACCOMMODATIONS - Extensive housing and messing
facilities at field. Hotels in town.
Population - 5,650'.

WEATHER

PREVAILING WINDS - Summer S. Winter SE.
Maximum 58 m.p.h. in winter.
PRECIPITATION - Rain 82" per year, snow 114"
per year.
TEMPERATURE - Extreme range: 89° F. to -15° F.
VISIBILITY - Dense fog about 6 days per year.
Morning fog in winter, usually lifts during
the day. Maximum fog from August to December.

CHARTS - Whitehorse Regional Chart.

NAME AND LOCATION

JUNEAU AIRPORT, located 9½ miles NW. of Juneau
on mud flats near base of Mendenhall Glacier.
POSITION - Lat. 58° 22' N., Long. 134° 35' W.
MAGNETIC VARIATION - 31° E.
ALTITUDE - 23 feet.
LANDMARKS - Mendenhall Glacier, docks and radio
towers at Juneau.

GENERAL INFORMATION

OPERATED BY - C.A.A.

Remote Flight Strips/Stations in Alaska

Cape Wales, 1944. COURTESY STACY DOBRZENSKY

Point Spencer, 1944. COURTESY STACY DOBRZENSKY

Tanana, 1944. COURTESY STACY DOBRZENSKY

Akulurak, 1944. COURTESY STACY DOBRZENSKY

Kokrines, 1944. COURTESY STACY DOBRZENSKY

Manley Hot Springs, 1944. COURTESY STACY DOBRZENSKY

Point Hope, 1944. COURTESY STACY DOBRZENSKY

Koyuk, 1944. COURTESY STACY DOBRZENSKY

American River, 1944. COURTESY STACY DOBRZENSKY

Kaltag, 1944. COURTESY STACY DOBRZENSKY

Mountain Village, 1944. COURTESY STACY DOBRZENSKY

Middle Right: The secret airstrip at Otter Point on Umnak Island. This strip was built prior to the attack on Dutch Harbor and by its position, unknown to the Japanese at the time, forced them to change their battle plans for the Aleutian campaign. AAC

Moses Point, 1944. COURTESY STACY DOBRZENSKY

Northwest Service Command buildings at Whitehorse, fall 1942.

A P-40 en route to the Aleutians made a stop at Whitehorse in the fall of 1942. The landing gear collapsed upon landing.

RCAF tower and facility at Whitehorse, winter 1942-43.

Air Corps compound, later used by the 7th Ferrying Command and later by the ATC, Whitehorse, August 1942.

ALL PHOTOS COURTESY STACY DOBRZENSKY

MERRY CHRISTMAS

1942

to the

Men of the

Whitehorse

Detachment

383rd Base Headquarters

and

Air Base Squadron

Bomb hit on the *Northwestern*, June 4, 1942. NA 80-G-206192

CHAPTER EIGHT
DUTCH HARBOR

American Armed Forces and Unalaska

The U.S. Navy first became interested in Dutch Harbor at Amaknak Island in 1902, when a presidential executive order set aside 23 acres for use as a coaling station. This scheme was never realized and the navy did not arrive on Amaknak until 1911, when it established a radio communication station there. Initially, personnel were housed in a frame building, but well before World War II a handsome brick structure—the only brick structure in all the Aleutians—became the permanent quarters. In July 1939, the navy established an aerology station at Dutch Harbor, and in October 1940, a navy medical detachment and a detachment of the Marine Defense Force (four officers and 101 enlisted men) arrived, occupying a new 125-man barracks. By early 1941, however, the marines were reduced to a strength of 46 personnel with the mission of guarding the naval installations. Their armament consisted of machine guns and four 155mm guns on Panama mounts. Across Iliuliuk Bay, in Unalaska village, the U.S. Coast Guard maintained a station consisting of a 60-man bunkhouse, an administration building, one small seaplane hangar and shops.

Back in 1922, the United States and Japan had reached an agreement wherein Japan promised not to construct defenses in its newly-acquired mandate of Micronesia, and the United States agreed not to fortify the Aleutians or any Pacific islands west of Hawaii. During the 1930s, however, Japan embarked on a policy of expansion in eastern Asia by invading Manchuria, then a part of China. In 1935, Japan closed Micronesia to outsiders, and it was generally believed that the islands were being fortified. Although the 1922 agreement expired in 1936, the United States did not look to its Pacific defenses beyond Hawaii until 1938. That year, Congress directed the U.S. Navy to appoint a board of officers to investigate the need for additional bases in the Pacific. The board, chaired by Rear Adm. A.J. Hepburn, recommended the establishment of seaplane and submarine bases at Dutch Harbor, Kodiak, Midway and Wake, and patrol plane bases at Sitka and Oahu. Congress approved the recommendations in 1939.

A civilian contractor, Siems Drake Puget Sound, began construction of the naval facilities at Dutch Harbor in July 1940. Inasmuch as the U.S. Army had the assigned mission of defending naval installations, it was decided that the navy's contractor would construct the army facilities as well. At first, it was thought that Amaknak Island, only 4.3 miles in length, did not have enough level land for both bases, but after reconsideration the army base was erected at Margaret Bay, south of Dutch Harbor.

The naval section base was commissioned at Dutch Harbor in January 1941, and the naval air station in September.

The first army troops arrived on Amaknak on May 8, 1941. Until their barracks were completed, these soldiers lived in the marine barracks, most of the original marine detachment leaving Unalaska at this time. The village of Unalaska on the main island, had a population of 50 whites and 250 Aleuts. On September 10, 1941, the army post was named Fort Mears in honor of Col. Frederick J. Mears, who had been instrumental in surveying and building the Alaska Railroad earlier in the century.

Dutch Harbor looking north from the naval radio tower, 1936. NA 80-G-344352

Dutch Harbor and the naval radio unit, 1929. NA 80-G-344350

The old Russian Orthodox Church in the Unalaska townsite was erected in 1820 and is still standing.
AUTHOR'S COLLECTION

Siems Drake Puget Sound

The history of construction under Siems Drake Puget Sound is the chronology of an industrial achievement undertaken in peace and completed in war against some of the most difficult conditions ever encountered.

Certain notices in trade papers in April of 1939 gave the sign that the Navy Department was cognizant of the turbulence of tides running beneath international affairs. The Bureau of Yards and Docks told contractors that it would accept bids from those interested on construction projects on a cost-plus-fixed-fee basis for projects in Alaska, some Pacific islands, and Puerto Rico.

The Alaska invitation caught the attention of 108 contractors who filed applications. The work was so diversified that combinations of firms with experience needed for building a city were in order. One of the groups responding with applications and with letters of intent to combine facilities for the Alaskan venture comprised three companies.

The Siems Spokane Company of Spokane, Washington, had grown from a mail-hauling beginning in North Dakota in 1875 to a major general contracting concern. Johnson, Drake & Piper, Inc., of Minneapolis, Minneapolis, had a record of construction that blanketed the nation. Puget Sound Bridge & Dredging Company of Seattle, Washington, had spent more than a half-century in varied upbuilding of the Pacific Northwest and its home city particularly.

Having examined the financial condition and experience of each applicant, the Navy narrowed the field from a hundred-odd down to three groups, then invited their representatives to Washington, D.C., for consultation. Eight days of continuous negotiations followed. Meetings went into the night as naval officials questioned the firms represented as to experience, organization and finance. The trend of discussion disclosed that previous experience in Alaska would weigh heavily in the decision. The result was Contract NOy-3570 for construction of the air bases, awarded to the companies named above. It then called for the building of two major bases, at Sitka and Kodiak. Anticipated cost was $12,000,000.

On August 30, 1939, the contract was signed by President Roosevelt. Terms called for completion within three years. Two years were to elapse before Japan struck. There was no delay in action on the work, however. Organizational progress was swift. Headquarters for the co-venture, operating under the new name of "Siems Drake Puget Sound," were established at Harbor Island in Seattle. In 30 days crews were landing at Alaskan locations and the organization was in operation.

From the moment of signing, progress was so rapid that even against great odds of lack of transportation, communication and the harrowing weather conditions, an amazing record of industrial achievement was written. It evolved despite the climax of war. The contract deadline of three years was met. That contract expanded in that time from $12,000,000 to $20,000,000. At Dutch Harbor a third air center was near completion. Various section bases had been added. A listening post was installed at Kiska.

In four and a half years the construction contract mushroomed to the second largest in the Navy's history. Finished construction topped the $138,000,000 mark. These operations ranged more than 2,000 miles from Seattle, toward Tokyo. Every type of construction was included in stations whose combined area was as great as the total land and water space of a metropolis the size of Seattle.

All transportation was by water, because neither highways nor railroads existed to serve the coastal areas of Alaska. Except for a minor amount of airplane travel, steamships carried men and materials to the region, making enough trips to girdle the world at the equator 25 times.

The SS *Northwestern* shown upon its arrival at Dutch Harbor in 1941. It was used as a barracks for construction crews and produced power for the constuction projects. The steamer was built in 1889 as the *Orizaba* and sailed on the New York-Cuba run for several years. She was then purchased by the Northwestern Steamship Company in 1906 and operated in the Alaska area until being retired in 1938, when it was tied up at a Seattle pier. In late 1940 she was reconditioned and bought by Siems Drake and towed back to familiar waters in Alaska. In early 1941, while at anchor at Dutch Harbor, she blew ashore, where she was at the time of the attack. The ship lay in the bay until later, when it was towed south for scrap. AP

Dutch Harbor, U.S. Navy

In 1940, the Northern Commercial Company owned 127 acres at Dutch Harbor, where it had a dock, oil tanks and a water system. The remainder of Amaknak was public domain. The Navy purchased the company's interests for $78,973. The Navy's contractor, Siems Drake Puget Sound, took over an old steamer—the 3,000-ton S.S. *Northwestern*, which had beached adjacent to the dock during a storm—and modified it to serve as a barracks for civilian construction workers. Work on the naval facilities began in July of that year and continued through 1944.

Two concrete seaplane ramps, one north of the Dutch Harbor dock and the other across the island on Unalaska Bay, and a concrete parking area were completed. A 5,000-foot water runway for PBY patrol planes was marked off in Iliuliuk Bay. Other early structures at the naval air station included a semipermanent, steel-frame, Kodiak-type hangar (now gone), a repair shop and ammunition storage. Housing, administration, fueling and recreational facilities, all of frame construction, were erected at Dutch Harbor. A second pier, at the foot of Mount Ballyhoo in Dutch Harbor, was completed in March 1942. In May 1942, the navy approved construction of a small runway near the seaplane hangar for the emergency use of fighters—so small that arresting and catapult gear, similar to an aircraft carrier's, was installed. When the Japanese bombed Dutch Harbor in June 1942, work was underway on carving a gravel runway, 500 feet by 4,358 feet, along the south foot of Mount Ballyhoo. The first plane landing occurred on July 3, 1942. This runway, subject to severe crosswinds, continues to serve commercial aircraft. Also constructed were several aircraft revetments along the north side of the new runway and a permanent, blast-pen-type hangar, 115 feet by 310 feet, the latter completed in late summer 1943.

The summer of 1942 saw the beginning of work on an anti-submarine net and boom depot, marine railroad and shops, aerology building, air operations building, fire station and several warehouses. The original construction scheme called for the building of a number of cottages for naval family housing. Although the cottages were built, the coming of war prohibited families from coming to Unalaska and the houses served as officers' quarters.

Naval facilities continued to expand until, on January 1, 1943, the Dutch Harbor Naval Operating Base was commissioned. Its components were the air station, submarine base, marine barracks, radio station, section base, a fueling depot on nearby Akutan Island, and other naval shore activities. The 250-ton marine railroad, a 3,000-ton floating drydock, ammunition storage facilities and ship repair shops also served the fleet. A huge bombproof structure housed the main power plant.

By the time the naval base was complete in 1944, additional facilities included 17 office buildings, a 200-bed hospital, net depot and a facility for provisioning fleet units. A total of seven docks were in operation: Dutch Harbor dock, 50 feet by 500 feet, purchased in 1940; advance base depot dock, 58 feet by 575 feet; Ballyhoo dock, 60 feet by 900 feet, built in 1942; fuel oil dock, 50 feet by 500 feet; YP dock, 60 feet by 240 feet; submarine base dock; and several small boat and finger piers. Housing, mess and recreation facilities were completed for 281 officers and 5,444 enlisted men. The total estimated cost for Dutch Harbor Naval Operating Base was $44 million.

In the fall of 1942, the first of several naval construction battalions (Seabees) arrived at Unalaska to take over from the civilian contractor all construction work at both Dutch Harbor and Fort Mears. An unusual accomplishment of the Seabees was the salvage of the *Northwestern*. The Japanese bombed the barracks ship and set it on fire in 1942, and the burned hulk lay on the beach at Dutch Harbor. The Seabees

NAVAL AIR STATION

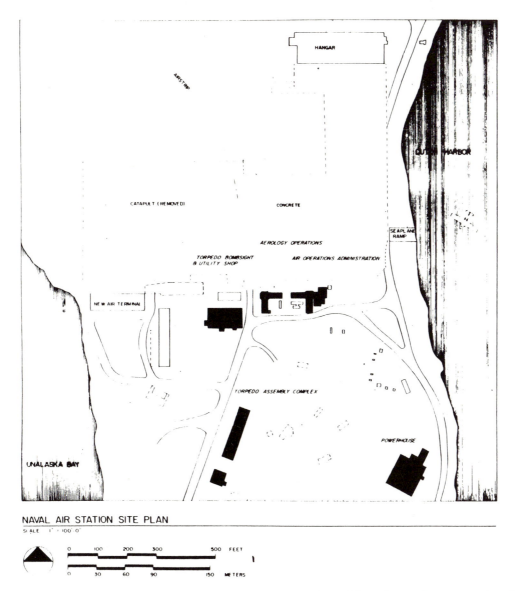

HANGAR

AIRSTRIP

DUTCH HARBOR

CATAPULT (REMOVED)   CONCRETE

SEAPLANE RAMP

AEROLOGY OPERATIONS

TORPEDO BOMBSIGHT
& UTILITY SHOP   AIR OPERATIONS ADMINISTRATION

NEW AIR TERMINAL

TORPEDO ASSEMBLY COMPLEX

POWERHOUSE

UNALASKA BAY

NAVAL AIR STATION SITE PLAN
SCALE 1" = 100'-0"

0   100   200   300   500 FEET

0   30   60   90   150 METERS

set to and made her seaworthy. The Navy had the vessel towed to Seattle where she was cut up, yielding 2,700 tons of scrap steel. (Today, the bow of a sunken ship sticks up from the water at the head of Captain's Bay. Many residents of Unalaska believe this to be the *Northwestern*.)

When lend-lease to the Soviet Union got into full swing, Soviet ships traveling from Siberian ports to the United States sailed through Unimak Pass east of Dutch Harbor. Eastbound ships were required to enter the harbor, where they picked up recognition signals and were boarded and interviewed. They also received fuel and underwent any necessary repairs. By the fall of 1942, this traffic had become so heavy that the U.S. Navy decided to build a fueling station on nearby Akutan Island. An abandoned whaling station was selected and Soviet ships were using the new facility in

November, although much construction lay ahead. Oil tanks were erected, coal yards constructed, and the pier rehabilitated. U.S. Naval Fueling Station Akutan remained in operation until April 1945, when it was decommissioned and Soviet ships again put into Dutch Harbor.

Throughout the war, the Navy operated the ferry that ran between Amaknak Island and Unalaska. The area containing the ferry slip on Amaknak was known as Agnes Beach. Today, a modern steel bridge spans the channel.

As World War II drew to a close, activity decreased at Dutch Harbor. The submarine facility was decommissioned in May 1945, and the air station was reduced to a naval air facility in June. The last Navy personnel left Dutch Harbor in 1947, and the naval operating base was decommissioned at that time.

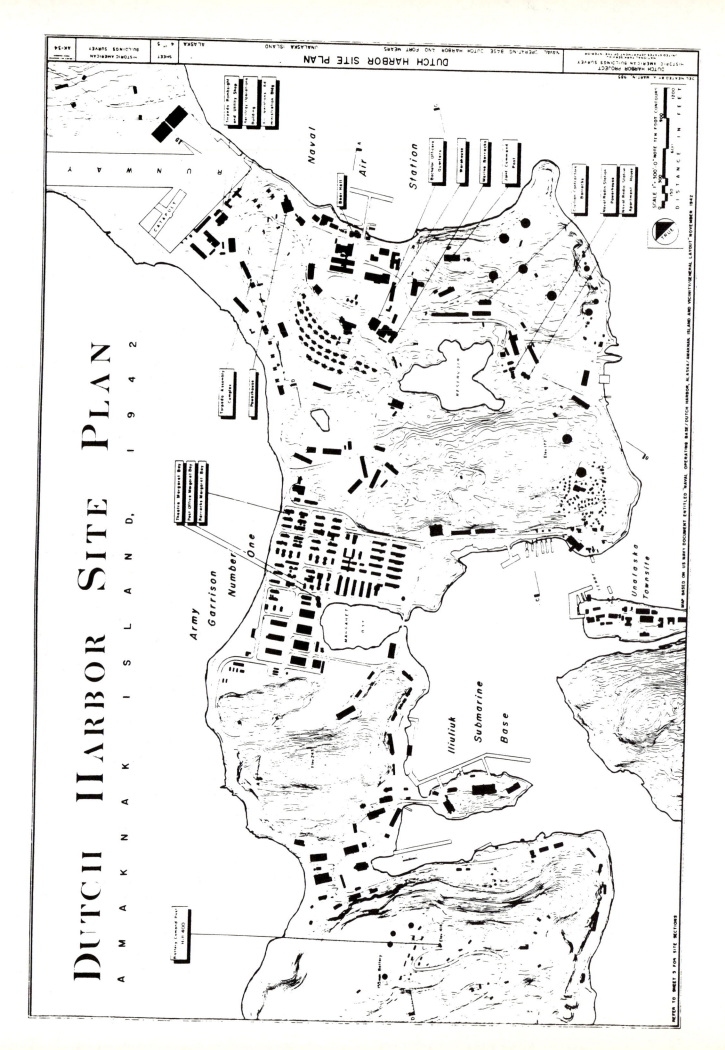

Fort Mears, U.S. Army

Because Siems Drake Puget Sound had already begun construction of naval facilities on Amaknak Island, the ½bvy let a contract to the firm in January 1941 to construct the ½amy defense installations, which principally consisted of an infantry garrison and coastal artillery positions. The garrison complex at Margaret Bay was mobilization-type in design. This consisted of wood frame buildings closely spaced, the barracks having two stories and the administrative, recreational, warehouse and mess structures having only one story. During World War II, this type of construction, designed for large cantonments in rear areas, was found at Army posts throughout the United States. Mobilization-type was probably chosen for Fort Mears because the small amount of land available had to provide quarters for 393 officers and 9,729 enlisted men. The cost was originally estimated at $12 million.

The initial Army garrison arrived on Amaknak on May 8, 1941, and occupied the Marine barracks at Dutch Harbor. Twelve days later, Lt. Gen. John L. De Witt, commanding the Western Defense Command with headquarters at San Francisco, arrived at Unalaska on a tour of inspection. A week later, the troops moved into their new quarters, the installation then known simply as "U.S. Army Troops," Unalaska. Although the United States was at peace, the troops received their first alert on July 4, 1941, when it seemed that the Russian front was about to collapse and Germany would be in a position to march through Siberia. By that time the Army garrison had grown to 225 officers and 5,200 enlisted men.

Along with the infantry garrison, coastal and anti-aircraft batteries were established at Unalaska. On Amaknak, coastal defenses were established at Ulatka Head (Eagles' Nest) at the north end of the island and at Hill 400 (Bunker Hill or Little South America) at the south end. The installations at Ulatka Head were eventually named Fort Schwatka. They consisted of a battery of two 8-inch coastal guns supported by three artillery fire control stations; a battery of two 90mm antimotor torpedo boat (and anti-aircraft) guns; a 3-inch anti-aircraft battery; an underground plotting-spotting-switchboard building; and 10 concrete or steel ammunition magazines. A combination harbor entrance control post/defense command post was also constructed; it was jointly operated by the Army and the Navy. On Hill 400 a battery of four 155mm guns were emplaced on Panama mounts. Nearby were a two-story, concrete artillery fire control station, a wood frame fire control station and nine steel magazines of various sizes.

At Summer Bay (Humpy Cove), eventually named Fort Brumback, on Unalaska Island, a battery of four 155mm guns on Panama mounts were emplaced, together with 12 steel magazines, a two-story concrete fire control station, and a second fire control station designed to resemble a cottage. A second coastal defense installation on Unalaska, Fort Leonard, was erected at Eider Point on the west side of Unalaska Bay. It consisted of a battery of two 6-inch guns with three fire control stations, a radar set and eight magazines; and a 90mm gun battery having a fire control station, magazine and 60-inch searchlight.

On tiny Hog Island, west of Amaknak, a 3-inch anti-aircraft gun battery was mounted to protect a naval radio range station already installed there. Other 3-inch batteries were installed at several locations in the vicinity of Unalaska Bay. A difficult construction project was the building of an aircraft warning station at Cape Winslow. Although less than 15 miles from Dutch Harbor, the cape could be reached only by sea. Begun in the spring of 1942, the station was not completed until that fall, well after the Japanese air raids. Its facilities included a small dock, 1,200-foot tramway, 2.5 miles of road, housing and utilities for 50 men, and the radar installation. Much later, in 1944, another aircraft warning station was built on Tigalda Island, 60 miles east of Unalaska. It, too, had a garrison of 50 men.

While construction of coastal and anti-aircraft defenses was underway, the army turned its attention to land defense. The most likely overland approach to Unalaska Bay was from the east, where an enemy force could land along Beaver Inlet, cross low passes in the mountains, then drop down Unalaska Valley. To guard against a surprise landing in the east, three infantry outposts were constructed in the vicinity of Beaver Inlet in January 1942: Fishermans Point at English Bay, Agamgik Bay and Ugadaga. Another potential approach was through Makushin Bay, southwest of Unalaska Bay. Here the infantry established an outpost in Makushin village. In April, every individual at Fort Mears was ordered to construct a slit trench. Also, the army had two-foot-thick concrete pillboxes installed at every road junction, a few of which remain.

Following the Japanese raids in June 1942, the tempo of construction increased. The belief was prevalent that Japan would invade Unalaska before winter. Work began on a tactical road net running around Unalaska Bay from Morris Cove to Eider Point, with lateral roads linking up Summer Run, Unalaska Valley and Pyramid Valley. To further the land defenses, the Iron Ring was established. It consisted of a semicircle of infantry positions along the ridges and peaks from Captains Bay to Summer Bay. The line passed through Pyramid Peak, Lookout Mountain, Sugarloaf Mountain, Raven Peak, Razorback, Ghost Ridge, Gateway Peak, Mount Coxcomb, and the low hills above Summer Bay. At Ugadaga Bay, the infantry outpost was reinforced with three batteries of 105mm field pieces and an anti-aircraft battery of 20mm guns. A battery of 75mm guns was placed in

Raven Pass, and another one at the west end of the runway at Dutch Harbor.

Fort Schwatka received a battery of two 155mm guns in addition to its other weapons. Several additional 3-inch antiaircraft gun batteries were installed, including sites on Artillery Hill and on the southern edge of Fort Mears. The peak of army construction came in June 1942, when there was a total of 1,655 contract employees and troop laborers involved. Fort Mears reached its peak strength on October 20, 1942, with 9,976 officers and men on its morning report.

Well before that date, it had become evident that Amaknak Island was not large enough for both Dutch Harbor and Fort Mears. The Army had filled the last available space at Mears with a complex of quonset huts south of the frame buildings. The coast artillery had moved into a permanent garrison in the saddle between Ulatka Head and Mount Ballyhoo. Over on Unalaska Island, a large complex of quonset huts had been completed east of the village on June 1, 1942. Still, Amaknak was near the bursting point. Finally, on August 11, 1942, the Army decided to turn Fort Mears over to the Navy and the latter agreed to have its Seabees construct new facilities for the Army on Unalaska. Construction took time, and the last of the Army personnel did not leave Amaknak until March 1944. The new Fort Mears post headquarters was constructed on Valley View, a plateau 200 feet up Unalaska Ridge on the south side of Unalaska Valley. It consisted of two two-story buildings for administration and command post operations, officers' quarters and mess, enlisted mess and cabanas for enlisted housing, and, on the edge of the plateau, a two-story quarters for the commanding general.

Pyramid Valley was chosen for a 500-bed Army hospital, a dock and housing for two infantry companies. In June 1943, when Fort Mears' strength was declining because of action farther west in the Aleutians, Pyramid Valley was abandoned except for the hospital. At Captain's Bay, an Army dock, warehouses, sheds and storage areas were completed in June 1943. The new dock was 760 feet in length and could handle two five-hold ships simultaneously. This facility reflected Unalaska's new role as a supply base for installations farther west. By the time American troops invaded Attu in May 1943, Fort Mears' troop strength had declined to 6,600 personnel, of whom only one battalion was infantry.

In preparation for the invasion of Kiska in August 1943, a training area was established in a bowl 750 feet above the floor of Unalaska Valley, and a switchback road was built to it. That summer, 1,000 casuals were trained there in techniques to combat Aleutian terrain and climate. They formed a composite regiment that served as a floating reserve during the invasion. After the conclusion of the Aleutian Campaign, the camp was abandoned. Another school was established at Fort Mears in May 1944. Called the North Pacific Combat School, it gave instruction to infantry troops sta-

tioned in Alaska in amphibious, mountain and muskeg combat techniques. Meanwhile, Fort Mears' troop strength continued to decline. The last figures available showed a garrison strength of 178 officers and 3,146 enlisted men on June 15, 1944.

Chernofski Harbor, Unalaska

In 1941, the site farthest west in Alaska at which fighter aircraft were stationed was Kodiak Island. Dutch Harbor was 600 miles farther west, beyond the range of the fighters. The Army sent Capt. Benjamin B. Talley to Unalaska in September 1941 to scout a suitable location for an airfield. At Dutch Harbor he rented a fishing boat and visited Umnak Island, five miles west of Unalaska Island. Talley reported that Otter Point at the east end of Umnak was suited for an airfield. Engineer troops landed at Umnak in January 1942 to begin the construction of Fort Glenn and its two airfields, Cape and Berry. Because Otter Point possessed no bay or harbor suitable for the docking of ships, Chernofski Harbor near the west end of Unalaska was chosen to be Umnak's harbor. At that time, the harbor had no facilities; supplies were unloaded from ships to barges and ferried to Otter Point. Eventually, Chernofski boasted a main pier, 72 by 402 feet, three barge docks and a repair dock. At Otter Point, three barge docks and a tanker discharge facility were constructed. The existence of Fort Glenn was kept a secret, and when Japanese planes roared over Unalaska in June 1942, American fighters rose to meet them.

By the summer of 1944, the war had moved far from Unalaska. Dutch Harbor continued to monitor Soviet ships and to dispatch air and sea patrols in the North Pacific. For Fort Mears, however, its original missions had been fulfilled. No longer was there a threat of an enemy attack. In August, the post was placed in a housekeeping status.

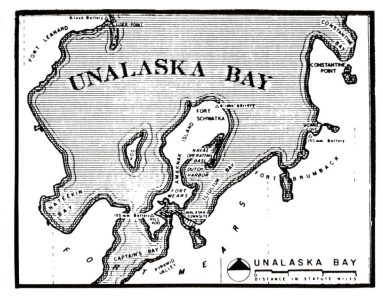

Company "A" 37th Infantry

by Robert E. Israel
Capt., Inf. Ret.

The "push" to get troops to the Aleutian Islands was because Germany and Russia signed a Non-Aggression Pact early in 1940 and it appeared that the two were dividing up areas of conquest. This put the west coast and our island possessions in jeopardy from the Japanese.

Company "A" of the 37th Infantry, a regular Army outfit, was formed and sent to Camp Clatsop on the Oregon coast and were outfitted with tropical gear, as we were scheduled to go to Guam. Suddenly in early May 1941 all this tropical gear was withdrawn and we were issued all types of winter uniforms. We did not get rid of the tropical huts which were sent to Dutch Harbor with screen doors, no insulation and doors that opened out. This caused us a lot of trouble when snow blocked the doors while in the Aleutians.

Major General DeWitt, of 5th Army, decided that "A" Company could proceed to Dutch Harbor in May 1941, to "protect the Naval base." When we arrived we found this consisted of a 90-foot dock and one YP boat commanded by a wonderful old Aleutian hand by the name of "Squeaky" Anderson. He had been commissioned a Lt. Commander by the Navy only a few months before but he did know the islands and this was a great help to us.

Since no one knew we were coming, we ended up living in tents for quite a few months until our tropical huts arrived. The Siems-Drake Construction Company was building barracks for some outfits that were to come up much later. Our commanding officer, Lt. Colonel Hollowell, was able to get us into their barracks for a short time. These were constructed in a line and rather close together, as were the ones in the states, and were not the best in case of enemy attack, as we found later.

Colonel Hollowell had us make many patrols over parts of the island since no one knew what lay beyond what could be seen by boats from the coastline. He was concerned by what routes an invading force could take through the "back door" of Dutch Harbor since that seemed to be the way the Japanese had been doing in the Far East. There was an outpost on Fisherman's Point, another one at the entrance of Ugudaga Bay on Beaver Inlet, and "A" Company took an outpost at Cathedral Point over on Makushin Bay so that we would have advance notice of any invasion at these points.

We dug foxholes and patrolled from May to the end of 1941, receiving the same information direct from the War Department in Washington as the people in Pearl Harbor. When, on December 7, 1941, it turned out to be the real thing we were prepared to do what we could. From Dec. 7, 1941 until June 1942, we did our best to put up some sort of defense. One discouraging note was when we asked General Buckner to send up some mules to pack supplies and ammunition to the outposts, over the mountains, we were told by Alaska Defense Command that they were not committed to defend anything west of Kodiak, some 800 miles back towards the mainland. This was a low point for all of us but we realized the problem of not enough troops and supplies plus a lack of shipping.

Now we come to June 1942. Colonel Hollowell and most all of us knew the Japanese made attacks on weekends and especially Sundays when the usual let down came to most American forces. We were all assembled in a mess hall at Dutch Harbor with guards at the doors for a special meeting. The colonel decided that we would change the days around so that a *real* Sunday would be our GI Wednesday and we would all be at work full force. Now what happened was on our "GI Sunday," which was a *real* Wednesday, the troops were not at full force in the field and many were sleeping in. How the Japanese knew this is still a mystery but this is the day they chose to bomb Dutch Harbor.

The outpost at Fisherman's Point sent in a message very early on the morning of June 3rd that there were "many planes heading for Dutch Harbor," and appeared to be Japanese. By this time the 206th Anti-Aircraft from Arkansas had just arrived on the *President Fillmore* and they were hard pressed to put up any defense from the bombing.

There were 11 to 15 planes involved, high level and dive bombers. They also employed quite a number of Zero Fighters that took low level runs at gun positions and personnel. There was a company of Engineers who fell out of their barracks in formation as they had been in the habit of doing, and a bomb hit the street in front of their barracks and about 22 were killed by that one bomb.

U.S. Marines shopping for
souvenirs in the Unalaska
townsite, 1940. USMC

U.S. Marines, decked out in
heavy water repellent
clothing, start out on a march
and maneuvers in the Dutch
Harbor area. USMC

Commissioning ceremonies at
NAS Dutch Harbor, Sept. 1,
1941, with a large contingent
of Navy and Army officers in
attendance. NA, 80-G-386668

The 51st NCB band at
Captain's Bay, Unalaska, 1942.
AP, ROBERT MERRICK COLLECTION

The first troops that arrived in
1941 had to put up with sparse
living conditions.
AP, ROBERT MERRICK
COLLECTION

Construction continued on
the runway at the Naval Air
Station in May 1942. This
runway, slightly re-aligned, is
still in use today. The
revetments remain today as
they were dug out in 1942.
NA 80-G-70455

The completed Fort Mears in May 1942, looking southeast with the town of Unalaska in the background. The fort would come under attack a month after this photo was taken. In recent years there has been a major cleanup in the area and much of Fort Mears has been removed, but many of the more stable buildings remain as a reminder of the importance of Dutch Harbor during the war. NA 80-G-70443

Panoramic view of NAS Dutch Harbor, March 1942. The SS *Northwestern* is moored in the bay and construction work continues on the large power plant and hangar in the background. NA 80-G-206182

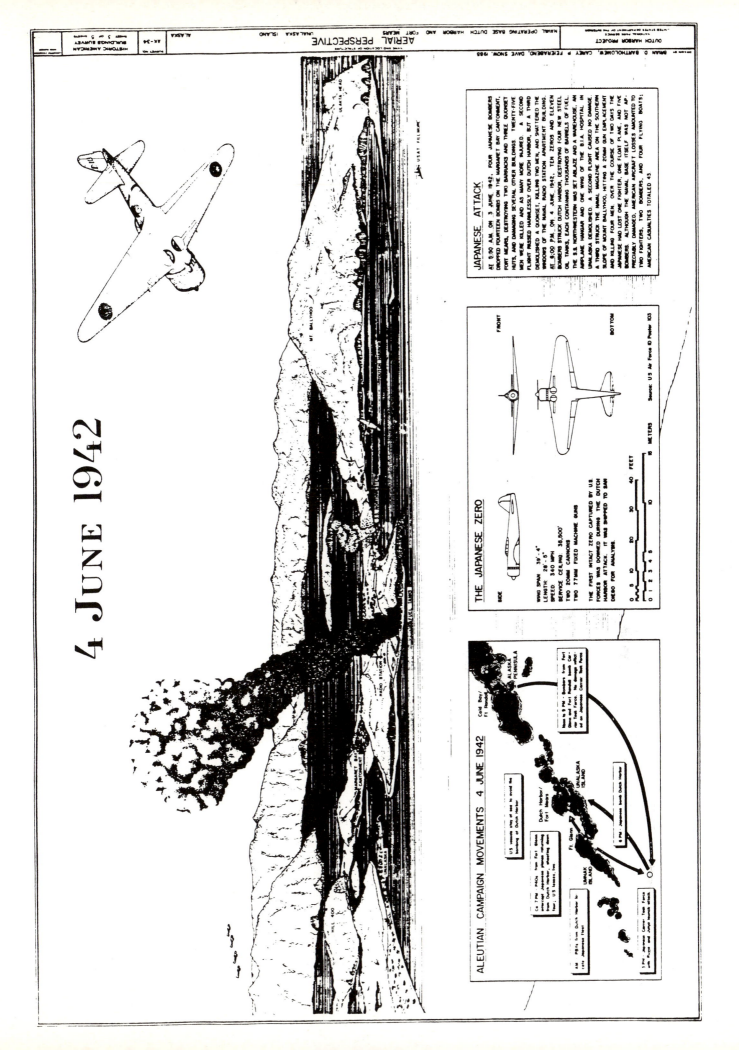

The Japanese Attacks, June 3 and 4, 1942

In the spring of 1942, the Japanese Imperial Navy prepared for a major strike against Midway with the goals of capturing that atoll and destroying the balance of the American Pacific Fleet. The plans called for a strike against the Aleutian Islands as they would be an anchor in Japan's advanced line—a great arc reaching from the Aleutians, passing through Midway, and extending to New Guinea in the south. In addition, control of the Aleutians would prohibit the United States from establishing a bombing shuttle route to Siberia should the Soviet Union enter the Pacific war.

The Japanese operations plan was issued on May 5, 1942. Vice Adm. Boshiro Hosogaya commanded the Northern Area Force with its 34 vessels ranging from aircraft carriers to troop transports. Three task forces were assigned to the Northern Area Force:

> Attu Occupation Force under Rear Adm. Sentaro Omori. One light cruiser, four destroyers and two transports with 1,200 army troops. Mission: First, to occupy Adak temporarily, then to occupy Attu.
>
> Kiska Occupation Force under Capt. Takeji Ono. One light cruiser, two destroyers, one transport with 1,250 naval troops. Mission: To occupy Kiska.
>
> Second Mobile Force under Rear Adm. Kakuji Kakuta. Two light carriers, *Ryujo* and *Junyo*, two heavy cruisers, one seaplane tender and four destroyers. Mission: To strike Unalaska from the air, then to support the temporary occupation of Adak (which the Japanese erroneously believed the Americans had defended).

At the end of May, Japanese submarines reported sightings of American warships at Dutch Harbor, Kodiak and southeast of Kodiak. All was set.

Unknown to the Japanese, Adm. Chester W. Nimitz's intelligence units at Pearl Harbor had broken major Japanese codes and had ferreted out the details of the coming attack. On May 17, 1942, Unalaska received word that the Japanese would attack the Aleutians sometime between June 1 and 10. American forces in the North Pacific included Rear Adm. Robert A. Theobald's North Pacific Force (formerly Task Force 8), composed of two heavy cruisers, three light cruisers and four destroyers. (Theobald and his ships took position south of Kodiak, far from the action and out of contact with his other forces because of the need for radio silence.) Also under Theobald were Task Group 8.2, Surface Reconnaissance Force, which consisted of small vessels including five U.S. Coast Guard cutters; Task Group 8.4, nine destroyers of which at least five were in Makushin Bay, Unalaska; and Task Group 8.5, with six submarines. The seaplane tender *Gillis* was stationed at Dutch Harbor, as were two old destroyers, *Talbot* and *King*, submarine S-27, Coast Guard cutter *Onondaga*, and two army transports, *President Fillmore* and *Morlen*.

Under Capt. Leslie E. Gehres, USN, eight radar-equipped PBY patrol planes operated out of Dutch Harbor. Daily search flights began on May 28. The Army Air Force had reinforced its two secret bases, Fort Randall at Cold Bay (six medium bombers and 16 fighters) and Fort Glenn on Umnak (one heavy bomber, six medium bombers and 17 fighters). Additional Army and Navy aircraft were stationed at Kodiak and Anchorage. Ground forces included 6,000 Army troops at Fort Mears and 639 sailors and Marines at Dutch Harbor. On June 2, a naval patrol plane spotted a Japanese fleet 400 miles south of Kiska.

At 2:43 a.m., June 3, 1942, Adm. Kakuta's Second Mobile Force stood 180 miles southwest of Unalaska. Despite a heavy fog and nasty seas, *Ryujo* launched 11 bombers and six fighters, and *Junyo* launched 15 bombers and 13 fighters. One of *Ryujo*'s bombers crashed into the sea and all of *Junyo*'s aircraft were forced to return to the carrier, unable to locate Unalaska because of the weather. At 5:40 a.m., the radar on seaplane tender *Gillis* detected the ap-

The HIJM *Ryojo* (top), flagship of the Aleutian invading force and the HIJM *Junyo* (bottom). JRC

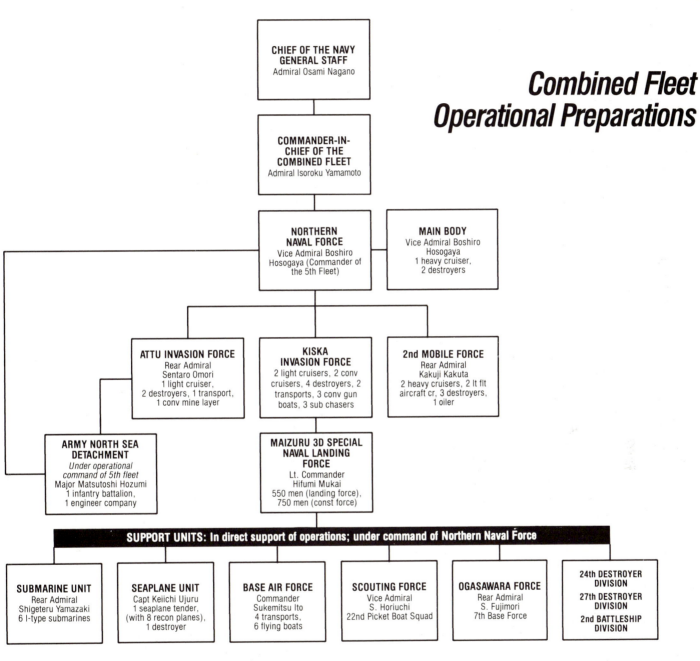

Combined Fleet Operational Preparations

CHIEF OF THE NAVY GENERAL STAFF
Admiral Osami Nagano

COMMANDER-IN-CHIEF OF THE COMBINED FLEET
Admiral Isoroku Yamamoto

NORTHERN NAVAL FORCE
Vice Admiral Boshiro Hosogaya (Commander of the 5th Fleet)

MAIN BODY
Vice Admiral Boshiro Hosogaya
1 heavy cruiser, 2 destroyers

ATTU INVASION FORCE
Rear Admiral Sentaro Omori
1 light cruiser, 2 destroyers, 1 transport, 1 conv mine layer

KISKA INVASION FORCE
2 light cruisers, 2 conv cruisers, 4 destroyers, 2 transports, 3 conv gun boats, 3 sub chasers

2nd MOBILE FORCE
Rear Admiral Kakuji Kakuta
2 heavy cruisers, 2 lt flt aircraft cr, 3 destroyers, 1 oiler

ARMY NORTH SEA DETACHMENT
Under operational command of 5th fleet
Major Matsutoshi Hozumi
1 infantry battalion, 1 engineer company

MAIZURU 3D SPECIAL NAVAL LANDING FORCE
Lt. Commander Hifumi Mukai
550 men (landing force), 750 men (const force)

SUPPORT UNITS: In direct support of operations; under command of Northern Naval Force

SUBMARINE UNIT
Rear Admiral Shigeteru Yamazaki
6 I-type submarines

SEAPLANE UNIT
Capt Keiichi Ujuru
1 seaplane tender, (with 8 recon planes), 1 destroyer

BASE AIR FORCE
Commander Sukemitsu Ito
4 transports, 6 flying boats

SCOUTING FORCE
Vice Admiral S. Horiuchi
22nd Picket Boat Squad

OGASAWARA FORCE
Rear Admiral S. Fujimori
7th Base Force

24th DESTROYER DIVISION
27th DESTROYER DIVISION
2nd BATTLESHIP DIVISION

*To support the operation if the situation requires.

The Nakajima B5N "Kate" torpedo bomber as used in the Dutch Harbor attack. JRC

Type 99 "Val" dive bomber as used in the Dutch Harbor attack. JRC

The five senior officers at Dutch Harbor the day it was bombed, June 3, 1942. "Squeaky" Anderson is in the center.
REEVE ALEUTIAN AIRWAYS

proaching Japanese planes. Immediately, all vessels at Dutch Harbor weighed anchors and stood out, but were still in Unalaska Bay when the first enemy planes arrived. Five minutes later, the Japanese, finding an opening in the clouds, began bombing and strafing Fort Mears and Dutch Harbor. At 5:50 a.m., four Japanese bombers dropped 14 bombs on Fort Mears, destroying two barracks and three quonset huts and damaging several other buildings, including the hospital. About 25 men were killed and an equal number wounded. A second flight of bombers caused no damage, but a third flight of three aircraft damaged the naval radio station and demolished a quonset, killing a sailor and an Army truck driver. Meanwhile, the Japanese fighters strafed likely targets, including a PBY on the water. The American ships joined the shore batteries in delivering anti-aircraft fire and resulting in knocking down one enemy plane and damaging another. Alerted, P-40 fighters from Fort Randall rushed to Unalaska, only to arrive 10 minutes after the last Japanese had left. Faulty radio communications with Fort Glenn prevented that base from learning of the attack until too late.

The Japanese planes spotted five American destroyers in Makushin Bay and, at 9 a.m., Adm. Kakuta launched a second strike. Fog, however, protected the ships and the weather forced most of the planes to return to their carriers. Also, the Japanese cruisers launched their four seaplanes. The P-40s at Fort Glenn did discover these planes and attacked, destroying two. Again, fog concealed the Umnak field. Although the Japanese now knew the Americans had an airfield somewhere near Dutch Harbor, they did not discover it until the next day.

Meanwhile, Navy patrol planes and Army bombers searched the waters for the Japanese ships without much success. In the south, Adm. Nimitz was fully prepared to meet the Imperial Fleet off Midway on the morrow. At Unalaska, the raid was over; the damage minimal. The Japanese lack of success stemmed, in part, from Aleutian weather, a condition that would affect both nations in the months ahead. During the night of June 3 and 4, Adm. Kakuta steamed through the stormy sea toward Adak to allow his planes to support the landing on that island.

June 4, 1942: During the stormy night of June 3 and 4, Adm. Kakuta led his carriers toward Adak. The heavy seas increased to the point that he decided to give up on Adak and to turn back to deliver a second raid on Unalaska. (Later, the Attu Occupation Force also cancelled its strike on Adak.) At 5:40 p.m. on June 4, American radar at Unalaska picked up the approaching planes. At 6 p.m., 10 Japanese fighters and 11 dive-bombers struck at Dutch Harbor. The principal damage was the destruction of four new, steel oil tanks, each containing 6,666 barrels of fuel. The barracks ship *Northwestern* was set on fire, while other bombs hit a warehouse and a hangar. A second flight of three horizontal bombers roared over the naval base at 6:21, all their bombs hitting the water. Four minutes later, five aircraft pounded the naval magazine area on the south foot of Mount Ballyhoo. One bomb hit a 20mm gun emplacement, killing four sailors.

On the return flight to their carriers, *Junyo*'s planes encountered P-40s over Umnak and sighted the new airfield below. In the two days, the Japanese lost one fighter, one float plane and five light bombers. American aircraft losses amounted to two fighters, one medium bomber, one heavy bomber and four flying boats. Total American ground casualties amounted to 43 killed (33 Army, eight Navy, one Marine, and one civilian) and 50 wounded.

While the raids were in progress, American bombers and patrol planes spotted and attacked the Japanese ships. Although the aircraft delivered a few near misses, no hits were made on the enemy vessels. No sooner had the carriers recovered their aircraft when Kakuta received a signal from Adm. Isoroku Yamamoto, commander in chief of the Com-

bined Fleet, whose great navy was suffering a disastrous defeat off Midway, canceling the Aleutian operations and ordering Kakuta south to rendezvous with the crippled force. A short time later, Yamamoto changed his mind and ordered the Attu and Kiska landings to proceed. Kakuta's ships retired to a point 600 miles south of Kiska from where they screened the landing forces, then returned to Japan.

The Japanese attack on Dutch Harbor created near hysteria in Alaska and a loud uproar in the United States, where citizens regarded it as comparable to Pearl Harbor. American honor was insulted and revenge was demanded. The Japanese occupation of Attu and Kiska resulted, a year later, in the only land battle of World War II on the North American continent. The air raids on Unalaska accomplished nothing for the Japanese, but they did increase American resolve to get on with the war. Dutch Harbor and Fort Mears continued to perform their wartime missions.

Tank farm afire after the June 3 attack. The reservoir is in the foreground, the radio station in the background. USN

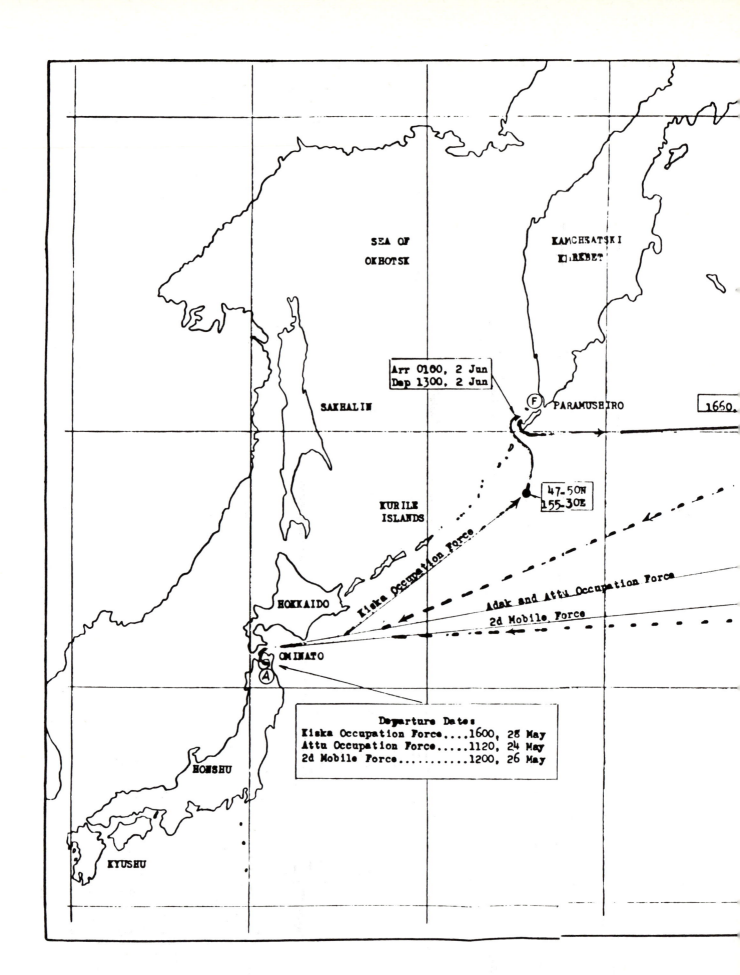

SEA OF
OKHOTSK

KAMCHSATSKI
KURKBET

SAKHALIN

Arr 0160, 2 Jun
Dep 1300, 2 Jun

(F) PARAMUSHIRO

1660.

47-50N
155-30E

KURILE
ISLANDS

Kiska Occupation Force

HOKKAIDO

Adak and Attu Occupation Force

2d Mobile Force

OMINATO
(G)
(A)

Departure Dates
Kiska Occupation Force....1600, 28 May
Attu Occupation Force.....1120, 24 May
2d Mobile Force..........1200, 26 May

HONSHU

KYUSHU

-146-

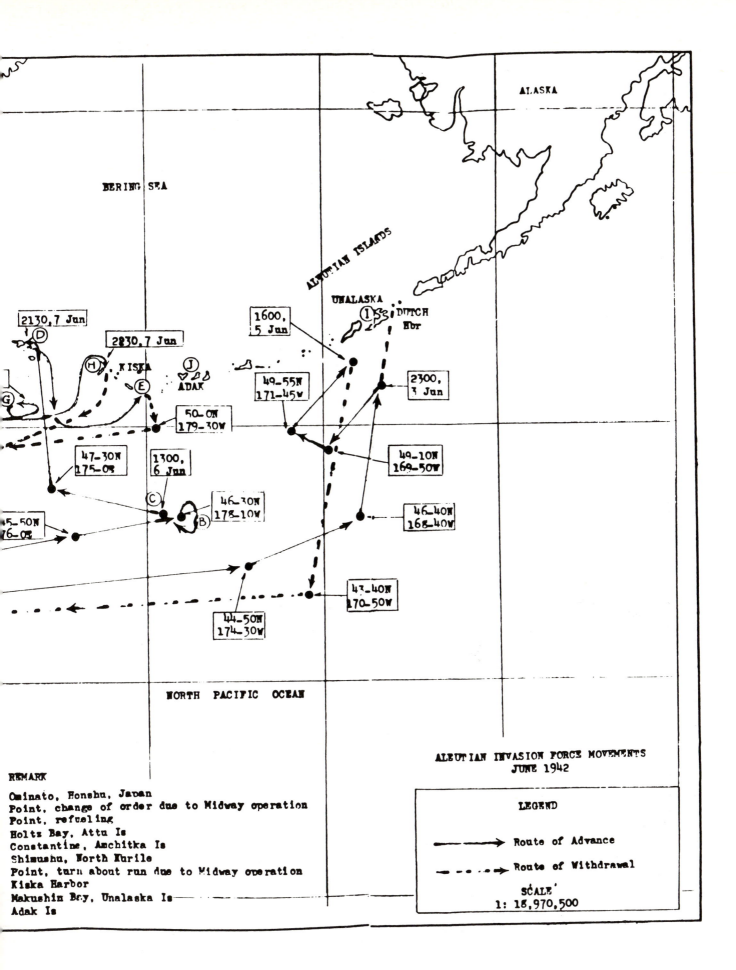

ALEUTIAN ISLANDS

ALASKA

BERING SEA

UNALASKA

DUTCH
Hbr

① I

2130, 7 Jun
① D

2330, 7 Jun
① H

KISKA
① E

J ①
ADAK

1600,
5 Jun

49-55N
171-45W

2300,
3 Jun

G

50-0N
179-30W

47-30N
175-0W

1300,
6 Jun

49-10N
169-50W

C

46-30N
178-10W

46-40N
168-40W

B

5-50N
76-0W

43-40N
170-50W

44-50N
174-30W

NORTH PACIFIC OCEAN

ALEUTIAN INVASION FORCE MOVEMENTS
JUNE 1942

REMARK

Ominato, Honshu, Japan
Point, change of order due to Midway operation
Point, refueling
Holtz Bay, Attu Is
Constantine, Amchitka Is
Shimushu, North Kurile
Point, turn about run due to Midway operation
Kiska Harbor
Makushin Bay, Unalaska Is
Adak Is

LEGEND

⟶ Route of Advance

⟶ Route of Withdrawal

SCALE
1: 18,970,500

Fires at Fort Mears immediately following the June 3 attack. Looking west with the officers mess in the foreground. NA 80-G-215465

Japanese bombs explode harmlessly in Dutch Harbor. NA 208-AA- 121C-1

One of the first photos of the attack on June 3. Note an enemy dive bomber directly over the radio tower. USN

Hit on the SS *Northwestern*. Debris can be seen in the air through the smoke. USAT *Fillmore* is seen in the right background maneuvering to evade the enemy attack, 6 to 7 p.m., June 4. NA 80-G-12075

Troops on alert during the attack near the radio towers. NA 208-AA-5P-1

Three weeks after the attack much of the damage has been cleaned up. The gutted *Northwestern* is mute evidence to the Japanese attack. NA 80-G-215442

Damage to the hospital in the Unalaska townsite in the center of the photo. Building construction appears to be taking place to the right. NA 80-G-12039

The Navy barracks and new recreation hall in the background, June 6, 1942. A bomb crater can be seen next to the road just above the barracks. NA 80-G-12042

Remains of four buildings at Fort Mears that were destroyed by enemy bombs. Margaret Bay is in the upper center. NA 80-G-12041

The Northwestern and the destroyed Siems Drake warehouse. The oil tanks have been partially camouflaged, June 6. NA -80-G-12045

The destroyed *Northwestern* on June 6. NA 80-G-11695

Damage to the *Northwestern* looking forward after the fire, June 6. NA 80-G-11701

Remains of a truck hit by a fragmentation bomb, June 4. NA 80-G-11755

Remains of burnt tanks, still smouldering several days after the June 3 attack. USN

A pillbox showing the effects of a bomb burst. NA 80-G-11758

Direct bomb hit on a Quonset hut, June 3. NA 80-G-12034

Burned barge-launching dock, left, and small craft dock, right. Fire was caused by burning oil from the onshore oil tanks. NA 80-G-11708

Remains of the Siems Drake warehouse and camouflaged oil tanks, June 7. NA 80-G-12036

Dutch Harbor, 1942-45

Test landing of a J2F observation plane on the new runway at NAS Dutch Harbor in July 1942. Notice the PBYs parked in the revetments.
NA 80-G-206162

Rocky Point Section Base, southwest of Unalaska, August 1942. NA 80-G-16422

The ramp, runway and revetments with Mt. Ballyhoo in the background. Note the seaplane on the mobile carrier to the left, August 1942.
NA 80-G-22522

Japanese prisoners, probably from sunken ships, were brought to Dutch Harbor in September 1942. NA 80-G-215362

PBYs on runway at the Naval Air Station, September 1942. NA 80-G-215262

Marine railway at Dutch Harbor, April 29, 1943. NA 80-G-72726

Ballast being taken off a submarine by crane at the Dutch Harbor sub pen. Old, obsolete S-type subs were stationed in the Aleutian Islands, March 1944. NA 80-G-386649

Arrival of the first DC-3 at NAS Dutch Harbor, April 6, 1943. NA 80-G-72732

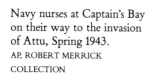

Navy nurses at Captain's Bay on their way to the invasion of Attu, Spring 1943.
AP, ROBERT MERRICK COLLECTION

On June 9, 1945, the U.S. Navy turned over 17 vessels to Russian sailors at Dutch Harbor. It was anticipated that Russia would eventually join the Allies in the war against Japan. NA 80-G-387086

Buildings and Facilities

Tunnel leading to confidential paper vault on Rocky Point. Interior fork of Tunnel No. 2 opening to the northeast. Tunnels were dug all over the Dutch Harbor area for defense purposes during the war years. NA 80-G-16390

Looking toward Dutch Harbor from within the entrance to Tunnel No. 1 under Rocky Point. NA 80-G-32091

NAVAL RADIO STATION

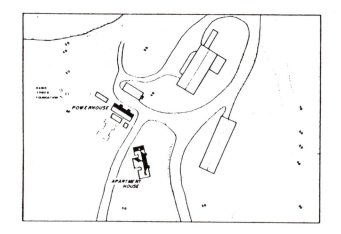

NAVAL RADIO STATION

A 1912 EXECUTIVE ORDER SET ASIDE 70 70 ACRES OF LAND ON AMAKNAK ISLAND IN UNALASKA BAY TO SERVE AS A NAVAL WIRELESS STATION. THE SITE BECAME A NAVAL RADIO STATION IN 1930 AND WAS INCORPORATED INTO NAVAL OPERATING BASE DUTCH HARBOR IN 1942.

NAVAL RADIO STATION APARTMENT BLDG

BUILT IN 1932 AS A SIX-FAMILY APARTMENT BUILDING FOR PERSONNEL AT THE NAVAL RADIO STATION, THE TUDOR REVIVAL STYLISTIC OVERTONES EVIDENT IN THIS STRUCTURE MAKE IT AN UNUSUAL EXAMPLE OF MILITARY ARCHITECTURE PARTICULARLY IN ITS ALEUTIAN SETTING. THE E SHAPED BRICK VENEERED STRUCTURE IS SET ON A CONCRETE FOUNDATION, AND IS REPUTEDLY THE ONLY BRICK BUILDING IN THE ALEUTIAN ISLANDS. THE STRUCTURE SERVED AS CPO QUARTERS. NO 1 FOR THE DURATION OF THE WAR. ALTERATIONS HAVE BEEN MINIMAL AND INCLUDE THE CONVERSION OF THE TWO LAUNDRY ROOMS IN THE BASEMENT INTO A COMBINATION LIBRARY AND LOUNGE, FEATURING A MURAL DEPICTING AQUATIC LIFE, AND A KITCHEN AND DINING ROOM. A GOOD DURING THE JAPANESE AIR ATTACK OF 3 JUNE 1942 SHATTERED ALL THE WINDOWS IN THE BUILDING. THE EXTERIOR WAS SUBSEQUENTLY PAINTED OLIVE DRAB AS A MEASURE OF CAMOUFLAGE.

NAVAL RADIO STATION POWERHOUSE

THE NAVAL RADIO STATION POWERHOUSE, BUILT SOMETIME BETWEEN 1918 AND 1929 GENERATED POWER FOR THE STATION AND HOUSED THE TRANSMITTER. THE UTILITARIAN APPEARANCE OF THE 1 STORY REINFORCED CONCRETE STRUCTURE IS RELIEVED BY FORMWORK ON EXTERIOR AND INTERIOR WALL SURFACES. IN 1942 PORTIONS WERE REMOVED ON THE SOUTHEAST END OF THE BUILDING TO ACCOMODATE LARGER TRANSMITTING EQUIPMENT, AND THE ENTRANCES WERE SHELTERED WITH COVERED CONCRETE PORCHES. ABANDONED SINCE 1947, THE POWERHOUSE HAS FALLEN INTO DISREPAIR.

SITE PLAN

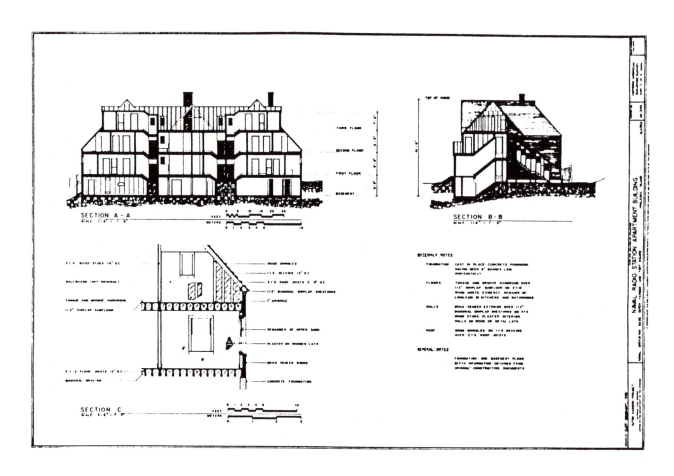

SECTION A - A

SECTION B-B

SECTION C

Radio facilities area, taken from hill behind Chief's Quarters. The Siems Drake electrical and pipe shop is to the right. The large building in the middle is the naval radio station apartment building, which is still standing and is the only brick building in the Aleutians. NA 80-G-32087

Radio Receiving Station, 1942. NA 80-G-70461

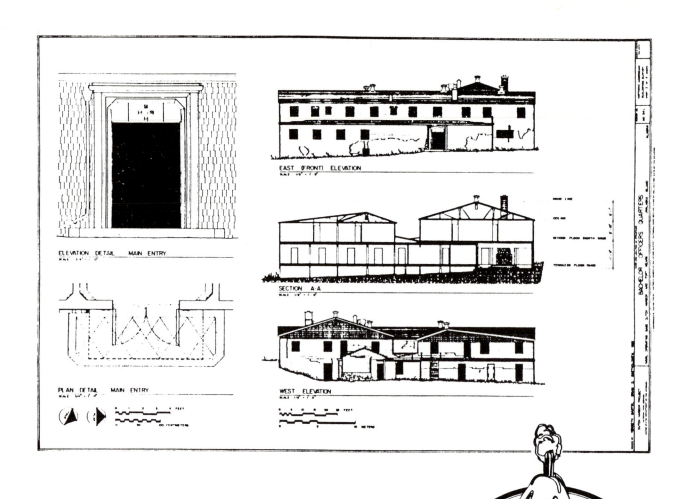

EAST (FRONT) ELEVATION

ELEVATION DETAIL   MAIN ENTRY

SECTION A-A

PLAN DETAIL   MAIN ENTRY

WEST ELEVATION

BACHELOR OFFICERS QUARTERS

The Bachelor Officers' Quarters at the naval station is standing. The terrazzo floor design can still be seen in the building.

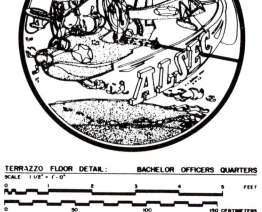

TERRAZZO FLOOR DETAIL: BACHELOR OFFICERS QUARTERS
SCALE: 1 1/2" = 1'-0"

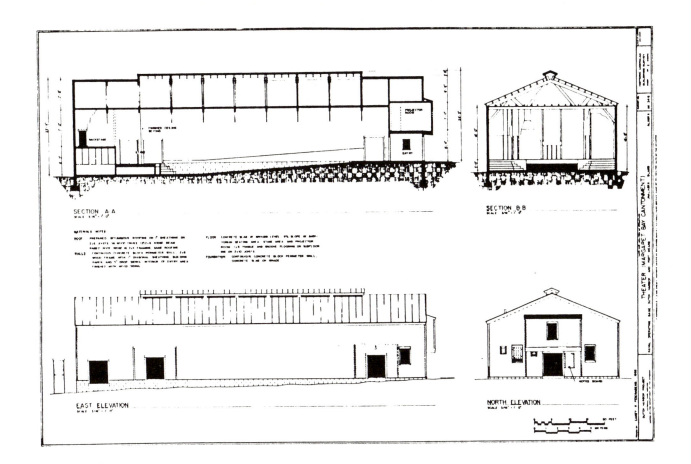

Interior of the Cameo Theater in
Unalaska, 1942.
AP, JESSE DICKERSON COLLECTION

Theater at Fort Mears is now used as a
beer can depository.

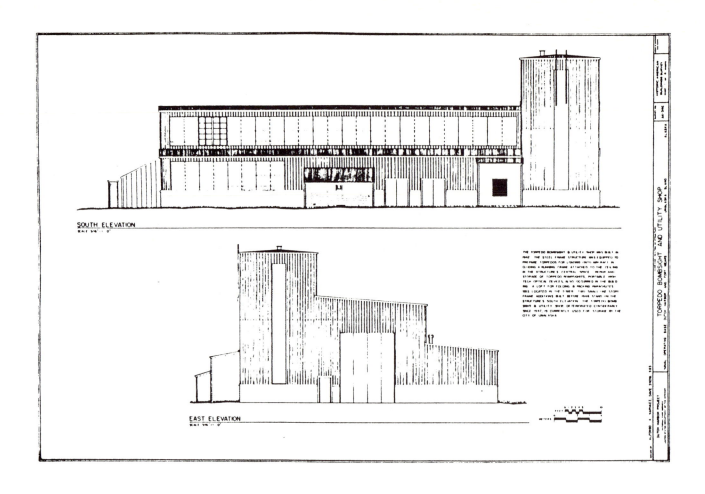

SOUTH ELEVATION
SCALE 1/16"=1'-0"

EAST ELEVATION
SCALE 1/16"=1'-0"

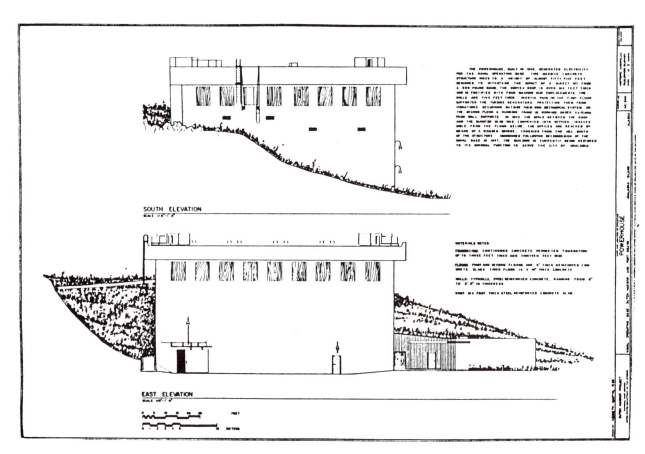

SOUTH ELEVATION
SCALE 1/16"=1'-0"

EAST ELEVATION
SCALE 1/16"=1'-0"

Left: The torpedo, bombsight and utility shop adjacent to the airport is still standing.

Right: The WWII powerhouse and hangar are still in existence. The powerhouse is still being used.

Several pillboxes can still be seen on the roads in the Fort Mears area.

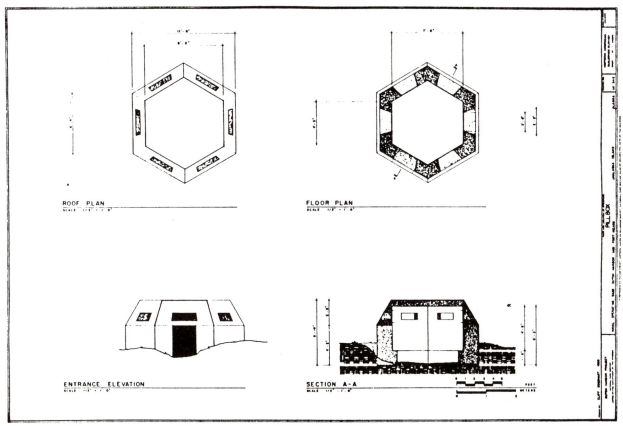

ROOF PLAN
SCALE 1/2" = 1'-0"

FLOOR PLAN
SCALE 1/2" = 1'-0"

ENTRANCE ELEVATION
SCALE 1/2" = 1'-0"

SECTION A-A
SCALE 1/2" = 1'-0"

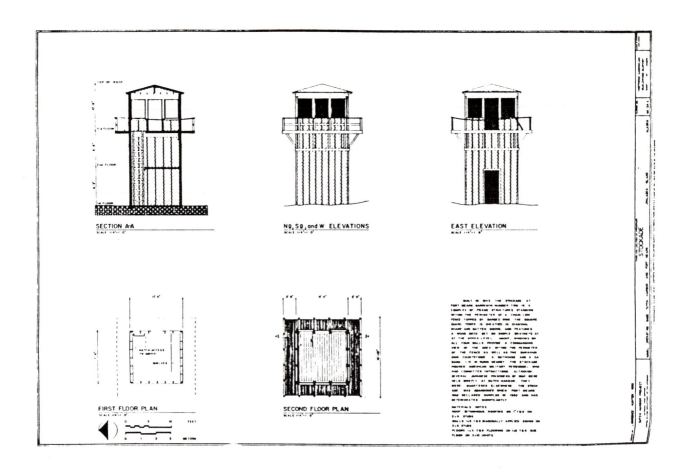

A stockade was built in Unalaska Valley near the Naval Operating Base in 1942 to house expected Japanese prisoners from the occupied islands. However, only 29 prisoners were taken on Attu and all Japanese troops were evacuated from Kiska prior to its occupation in August 1943.

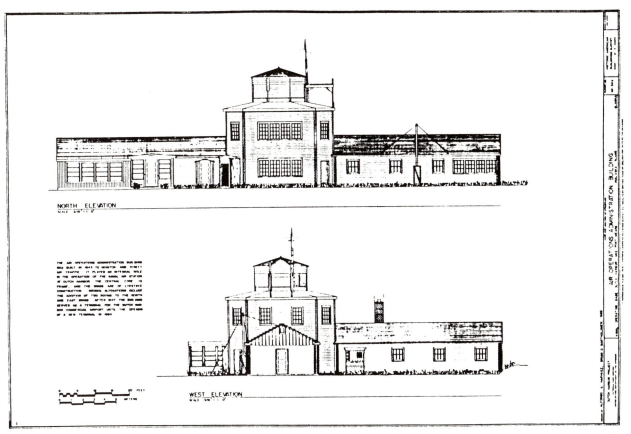

NORTH ELEVATION

WEST ELEVATION

Interior of the Air Operations Building,
June 1943. NA 80-G-73716, 80-G-73715

Back of the Air Operations Building.
This building, still standing, was
formerly the Dutch Harbor airport
terminal. NA 80-G-72723

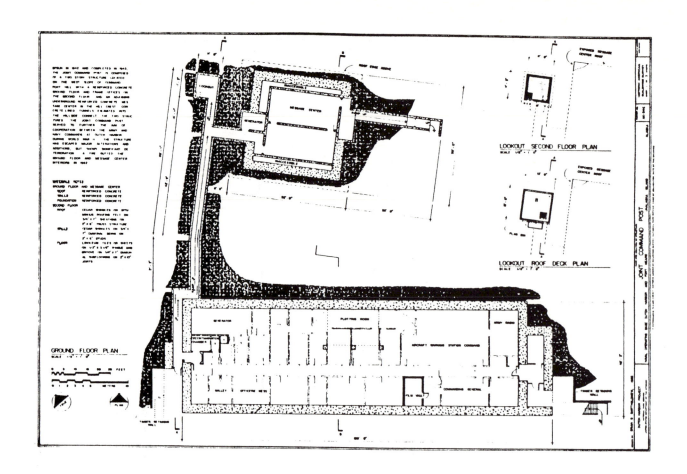

GROUND FLOOR PLAN

LOOKOUT SECOND FLOOR PLAN

LOOKOUT ROOF DECK PLAN

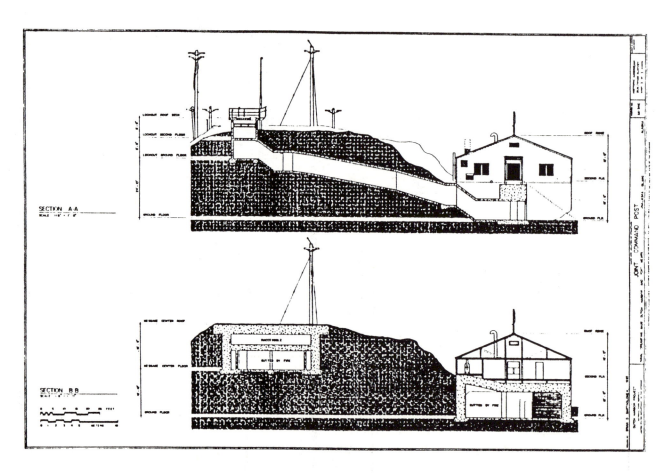

SECTION A-A

SECTION B-B

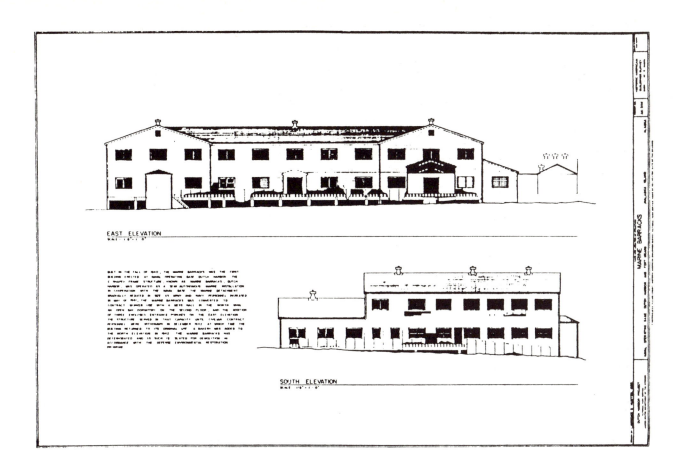

EAST ELEVATION

SOUTH ELEVATION

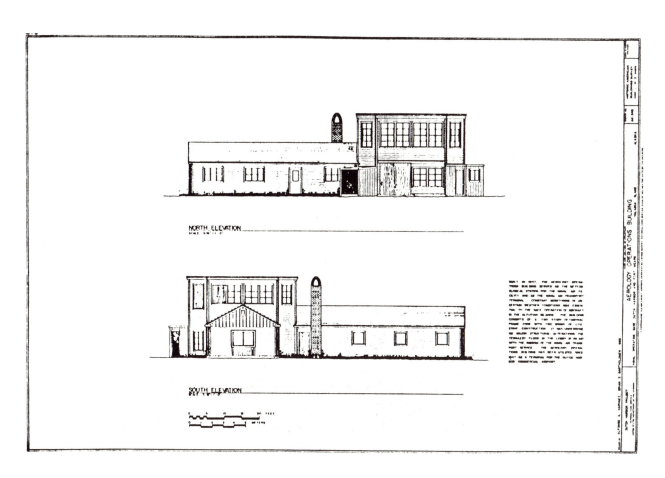

NORTH ELEVATION

SOUTH ELEVATION

Dutch Harbor Album

Lined up for the theater in Unalaska.
COURTESY LAWRENCE WHITE, MINNEAPOLIS, MINNESOTA

Gladys Anderson, left, Marwood
Siverts, center, Ann Christenson, right.
Gladys was one of 12 Army nurses who
came to Dutch Harbor in 1941.
COURTESY MARWOOD SIVERTS,
FRESNO, CALIFORNIA

Troops at Dutch Harbor in front of a
camouflaged building. AMHA

A lookout which was manned around
the clock by L Co 3rd Bn 58th Inf.
during 1942-43. Contact with base camp
was by telephone. The lines were laid on
the ground between the two points.
COURTESY BOB REAL, BANNING,
CALIFORNIA

After the June attacks, troops were dispersed by scattering these huts around Dutch Harbor, eight men to a hut. The tent housed their gear.

PHOTOS COURTESY OF BOB REAL, BANNING, CALIFORNIA

Base camp for L Co 3rd Battalion 58th Inf. Reg. on Unalaska Island.

Winter of 1942. There was a Quonset hut at the end of the tunnel.

This loosely strung bridge was on a trail to a remote outpost. Some of the outposts around Unalaska Island were so isolated that the men and supplies were taken in by sea on converted fishing boats.

Dutch Harbor Revisited

By Admiral James S. Russell (Ret.)

Hostilities of World War II began in the Aleutian Islands with a Japanese aircraft carrier raid against Dutch Harbor on June 3 & 4, 1942. The installation of a granite stone monument to mark the 40th anniversary of that event was planned, organized and effected by Ted Spencer of Anchorage, president of the Alaska Historical Aircraft Society. He invited me to attend and asked me to help him assure the attendance of suitable representation from Japan. Okumiya, air operations officer on the staff of Admiral Kakuta, who commanded the two carrier Japanese raiding force was not available. However, Hiroichi Samejima, who led the "Kate" torpedo bombers from *Ryujo*, was. Samejima, then a commander, came to Washington, D.C., in 1955 as the first naval attache after World War II. Thereafter Samejima rose to the top of their Navy, and went on to become Chairman of the Joint Staff Council, the Number One military post in Japan. Upon receiving his invitation to Alaska he telephoned me from Tokyo. Uncertain as to the attitude of the Aleuts toward the Japanese, he said to me "if you'll go, I'll go." He did attend, and brought along with him Colonel Zenji Abe who commanded the "Val" dive bomber squadron flying from *Junyo*.

Samejima survived World War II because he was assigned test pilot duty during the latter part of the war; Abe because he engaged in the Mariannas "Turkey Shoot." Without enough fuel to return to his carrier, he landed on Rota, a small island between Guam and Saipan, and eventually was taken prisoner.

The highlight of the trip to Dutch Harbor was when Ted Spencer engaged Tom Madsen and his twin Beech airplane to fly us the 60 miles from Dutch Harbor to Otter Point on adjacent Umnak Island. Abe was still hurting from having lost four of his Vals to P-40s based at Otter Point, an airfield unknown to Japanese intelligence. We landed at that abandoned airbase, took a short walk, and were impressed with the size of the base and its present complete disuse. Along with us was B.Gen. Benjamin B. Talley, (Ret.), who, as a colonel, was charged with the construction of our two secret airfields—this one at Otter Point another at Cold Bay near the end of the Alaskan Peninsula. Leaving Otter Point to fly back to Dutch Harbor, and over the southwest tip of Unalaska Island across the channel from Otter Point, we spotted one of the two P-40s shot down 40 years ago still lying on its back on the tundra! As we progressed over the terrain so familiar to me I realized we were not going directly to Dutch Harbor. Sitting in the left front passenger seat I identified Beaver Inlet below us, then it became apparent that Samejima, flying from the copilot's seat was taking us to the south shore of Unalaska Island. From there he turned to take us over the route he flew early in the morning of June 3, 1942, to lead the attack on Dutch Harbor!

The Japanese were regarded by the Aleuts with more curiosity than anything else. During the afternoon banquet in Unalaska village high school gymnasium they were called upon, as were many of us, to make remarks. This they did very well in English. Mr. Philemon "Phil" Tutiakoff, an Aleut and chairman of the Aleutian and Pribilof Islands Association, was Master of Ceremonies. The religious part of the proceedings at the monument was conducted by Father Gromoff, the Russian Orthodox priest in Unalaska, and the service was conducted in Russian. At one point Mr. Tutiakoff announced that a number would be sung by the choir. He then left his post as master of ceremonies and joined the choir. There were four in the choir and they sang in Russian. Six World War II pilots from Patrol Wing 4 were present—among them four from my VP-42 squadron. Raiford Perry, a veteran of the 11th Army Air Force, and a B-26 pilot, was there. Represented also were the U.S. Army, Navy, Air Force and Coast Guard, the Alaska National Guard and the Canadian Forces by active duty personnel. It was truly an impressive occasion—even to the laying of a bottle of saki among the wreaths at the memorial stone by Colonel Abe so that the spirits of the departed might be refreshed.

Honor guard at attention at the commemoration monument ceremony held at Dutch Harbor on June 4, 1982. AP

Former military foes pose at Dutch Harbor on June 5, 1982. Front row from left: Phillman Tutiakoff, Raiford Perry, Adm. James Russell, Hiroichi Samejima, unidentified, Zenji Abe. Top from left: unidentified, Gordon Diamond (Canadian Forces), unidentified, unidentified, Gen. Benjamin B. Talley, Col. Robert Gooney. AP

Japanese World War II commanders, Zenji Abe, bowing, and Hiroichi Samejima, pay their respects to their war dead at the commemorative ceremony on June 4, 1982. A bottle of sake accompanied the wreath they laid down. AP

Unalaska Today

Near the end of World War II, the Aleuts were allowed to return to their island home. The homecoming brought dismay. Military personnel had occupied some of the buildings, property and possessions were damaged or missing, some structures had been razed, and new buildings occupied once-empty lots. Moreover, the military restricted Aleut movement and activities in large parts of the community until the last of the Navy left in 1947. The Army declared its land and structures surplus in 1952. About that time, commercial fishermen discovered Unalaska as a base of operations for the processing of halibut, salmon and king crab. Growth in the king crab industry, especially, was rapid. By 1979, the National Marine Fisheries Service placed Unalaska at the head of the list of fishing ports in terms of money made and poundage taken—$97 million.

The city of Unalaska, which includes all of Amaknak Island as well as the original community, is the most populated of all the communities in Southwest Alaska. The city has a mayor, city manager, fire chief and police chief. Its permanent population is about 600, which triples at the height of the seafood processing season. In 1971, the United States granted the Aleuts lands and money under the Native land-claims settlement. At Unalaska, the Aleuts formed the Ounalashka Native Corporation which holds title to nearly all the private land on the main island and nearly all of Amaknak and its former military structures. The city of Unalaska is the proprietor of the Navy's giant wartime power plant. The Navy's airstrip is now paved and the state of Alaska operates the airport which is served by both commercial and charter air companies. A handsome bridge now joins Amaknak to the main community.

Many of the military structures of World War II have already disappeared. Others, particularly on Amaknak, have deteriorated beyond recovery. Some, however, have been rehabilitated. The Navy's air operations building and aerology building served as airline terminals. Many of the Navy's officers' quarters, now owned by the Ounalashka Corporation, have been refurbished as residences. The submarine base has been converted into an industrial area for the fishing industry. A smart motel and a shopping center now flourish adjacent to the Marine railway. The Army's pier at Chernofski is used for the storage of commercial crab pots. Yet the evidence of World War II is much present. Gun emplacements, command posts, pillboxes, tunnels, trenches, and magazines continue to dot the landscape as reminders of the world at war.

Gun mount and observation post.

Storage tanks. The one on the right still shows bomb damage from the June 1942 attack.

Dutch Harbor dock, powerplant and airport.

General view of the Dutch Harbor area.

Observation post.

Remains of the Naval Operating Base.

This ship in Captain's Bay was thought to be the remains of the *Northwestern*, but it is not.

WWII warehouse.

Monument dedicated in 1982 at the airport.

Akutan Zero

As a result of the Japanese attack on Dutch Harbor on June 4, 1942, an intact Zero airplane was forced down on Akutan Island near Dutch Harbor. The plane flipped over upon landing on the tundra, killing the pilot instantly. The following is a report on the salvage of the aircraft released on July 22, 1942, by the commander of Patrol Squadron 41.

On 10 July 1942 a member of the flight crew with Lieutenant William Thies, A-V(N), U.S.N.R. when returning from a tactical patrol sighted a small crashed Japanese plane on its back on the southwest side of Akutan Island. From its size it was believed to be a zero type Navy fighter. Lieutenant Thies returned, reported his discovery and immediately was placed in charge of a party to investigate and salvage such parts of the plane as were of intelligence value. The party was transported to the nearest beach on Akutan Island by YP-151.

After considerable struggle the plane was found in a high valley about a mile and a half from the beach in a soft marshy land. It is believed that the crash occurred on or about 4 June 1942, the date of the last raid on Dutch Harbor. The pilot apparently attempted to make a normal wheels-down flaps-down stall landing in the soft ground, skidded along for a short distance carrying away the landing struts, damaging flaps, and belly tank and going over on his back, in which position he skidded somewhat farther damaging the wing tips, vertical stabilizer and trailing edge of the rudder. The plane was resting with the fuselage and engine half buried in the knee-deep mud and water. The pilot's head and shoulders were submerged in water.

The pilot's body, in its decayed state, was first removed. This was very difficult owing to the boggy ground and the two safety belts and rudder stirrups which held him in place. With fifteen men assisting, it was possible to raise the tail of the plane only slightly. To release the safety belts it was finally necessary to cut through the side of the fuselage. Each time this was done unexpected equipment was encountered making it necessary to cut again. Eventually the body was removed and carefully examined for insignia markings etc., of intelligence value. The label on the uniform was removed, as also were various other articles of clothing. Nothing was found in the pockets. The local Japanese interpreter believes that the pilot was a Lieutenant Commander, the yellow band around the fuselage of the plane bears out the fact that he was a group leader.* He was buried with simple military honors and Christian ceremony near the scene of the accident.

Flight Petty Officer Tadayoski Koga, INJ, pilot of the Zero that crash landed on Akutan. He was found hanging from the cockpit, so these views were taken some time after the discovery, when his body was removed from the aircraft.
TOP: REEVE ALEUTIAN AIRWAYS. BOTTOM: USN NH 82484

---

*According to Jim Rearden's article on the Zero in the September 1987 issue of *Alaska Magazine*, the pilot's rank and name was Petty Officer Tadayoshi Koga.

In addition to the articles mentioned above, a transparent plastic folder of several leaves was found secured around the pilot's neck. This contained: (a) pictures of the latest U.S. Army and Navy planes, (b) simple Japanese Voice Code, (c) engine power curve, (d) simple graph for drift determination, (e) Jap Panel Code (obscured). All had been submerged in water. The writing had been partially obliterated since the ink and photograph chemicals used in making them were soluble in water, apparently for security purposes. The cards were read by the local Japanese interpreter and forwarded with interpretation to the Office of Naval Intelligence via Commander Patrol Wing Four. It is believed that the plane was assigned to the carrier *Ryujo*.

The 20 mm guns, optical reflector gun sight and certain small articles were removed for immediate attention. It was then found that the condition of the plane warranted attempts to recondition and flight test it. It was also discovered that the wings were integral with the fuselage making the salvage extremely complicated. At this time the press of other operations necessitated recalling the salvage party to Dutch Harbor.

On 12 July 1942 the second salvage party, with Lieutenant R.C. Kirmse, A-V(N), U.S.N.R. in command, equipped with heavy salvage equipment and a heavy tractor started for Akutan Beach. In this second salvage party the Commanding Officer of Naval Air Station, Dutch Harbor arranged for the services of an experienced rigger, Mr. Jerry Lund, attached to the Siems Drake Construction Company. The services of Mr. Lund were invaluable. He was later placed in charge of the third salvage party. While attempting to unload the gear onto the beach, the "Mary Anne" carried away two anchors and was forced to return to Dutch Harbor without having landed the tractor. After working for two days under great difficulties in knee-deep mud and by working on plywood "islands," the salvage party managed to lift the engine of the plane partly out of the mud by means of a suitably placed "high lift." A prefabricated skid made of $6'' \times 6''$ timbers was assembled on the spot, but it was found that the plane was too heavy to get onto the skid without a winch. It was again necessary to return to Dutch Harbor for more suitable equipment.

On 15 July the third party, Mr. Lund in charge, left in YP-72 taking a barge, medium sized bulldozer fitted with a winch, a second and heavier prefabricated sled and with considerable gear and lumber. The "Mary Anne" was determined unsuitable for this use. The plan was to land the bulldozer from the barge thru the surf, bulldoze a sort of road a mile-and-a-half up a small river-bed to the plane's position. All material had to be dragged up to the spot and assembled. With the "high lift" in place the engine was hoisted out of the plane and placed on a sled. The plane was then lifted, still in the upsidedown position, and placed on a similar skid. During these operations the tripods sank three to four feet into the mud. The two sleds were dragged laboriously down to the beach fording two three-foot streams enroute. It was then necessary to drag the skids through the surf and onto the lighter. This difficult feat was accomplished without further damage to the plane.

The Zero after it had been laid on its back by the salvage crew. JRC

On arrival at Dutch Harbor 18 July 1942 the plane was righted and carefully guarded while being cleaned. Certain additional parts were removed for preservation. In spite of special guards and precautions it was found almost impossible to anticipate every whim of souvenir hunters and for that reason the cleaning was kept to the minimum. Crating of the plane and parts was accomplished as rapidly as possible while awaiting suitable Navy transportation.

It was possible, however, to recondition the machine gun's optical reflector, gun sight, the pilot's parachute, most instruments, radio equipment and landing gear aerol struts. The engine and propeller were carefully cleaned and all water removed from the engine cylinders. Several cylinders exposed to water show some rusting, but most are in excellent condition. It was found that the oil scavenger line had been severed by a bullet and considerable oil lost, however, the engine can be turned freely by hand. It is regretted that the pneumatic system used in conjunction with the 20mm guns could not be removed for shipment with the ordnance gear since it would have necessitated considerable disassembly of the plane. This may be done by a better qualified agency.

The plane's construction with wings integral with the fuselage interposed a difficult problem of crating. The resulting crate dimensions are such that rail shipment will probably be impracticable. Accordingly, it is recommended that reconditioning and reassembly be accomplished at the Naval Air Station, Seattle, Wash. Shipping details are given in reference (b).

The essential data concerning this plane has already been forwarded by airmailgram, reference (c), and additional data by enclosure (B). The fuel rating is given as 92 octane, power curves have not been interpreted. No leak proofing, armor protection, destructor devices, IFF or similar equipment was discovered.

The plane will necessitate considerable repair, but it is believed entirely practicable to rebuild and flight test it.

Hoisting the damaged Zero on the dock at Dutch Harbor, July 17, 1942. NA 80-G-206216, 80-G-206213

The Zero on the dock. Note that the wing tips bend up for tighter placement on the aircraft carrier. AMHA

PFC George J. Jarkowski guards the motor of the damaged Zero on the dock at Dutch Harbor to keep souvenir hunters away. USMC #1317-A

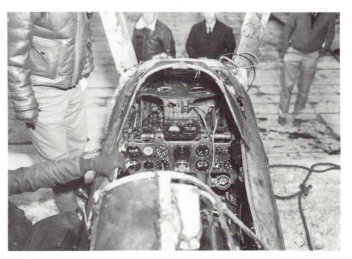

Control panels of the Zero. NA 80-G-206212

The restored Zero in #40 hangar at North Island, San Diego, September 1944. Letters on the tail read ZERO-1 (small) and TAIC (Tactical Air Intelligence Center) where the early evaluations were done in late 1942. The Japanese designations ultimately adopted by the U.S. military was Zero type 21. It had been built in 1942 and bore serial number 4593. By 1944 the paint had been stripped off making it possible to discern patched areas—darker U.S. duraluminum versus bright Japanese metal. The restoration produced a sound and high fidelity Japanese fighter that served for over two years exposing the strengths and weaknesses of enemy technology.
COURTESY ADM. W.M. LEONARD, VIRGINIA BEACH, VIRGINIA

The Zero undergoing restoration at NAS San Diego in late 1942. COURTESY AL MAKIEL, CALUMENT CITY, ILLINOIS

AVIATION INTELLIGENCE BRANCH
NAVY DEPARTMENT
Bureau of Aeronautics
Washington

TECHNICAL AVIATION INTELLIGENCE BRIEF #3
(November 4, 1942)

PERFORMANCE AND CHARACTERISTICS TRIALS
JAPANESE FIGHTER
HISTORY

A Japanese aircraft was sighted, on its back, on Akutan Island, Alaska July 10, 1942. It is believed that the aircraft was forced down about June 4, 1942 as a result of the oil scavenger line having been severed by a bullet. Salvage was successfully accomplished under extremely difficult circumstances. The aircraft arrived at the Naval Air Station, San Diego, August 12th, where it was rebuilt by Naval personnel. Flight tests were conducted under the cognizance of the Test Section of Naval Air Station, Anacostia, and of the Bureau of Aeronautics.

Preliminary tests were conducted at the Naval Air Station, San Diego, between 26 September and 15 October, 1942. During the progress of those tests information was released as it was obtained, for promulgation to the Fleet. The following summary of results is submitted after final analysis of the data obtained, and supersedes the previous informal releases.

Considering the circumstances under which the airplane was recovered and operated, it is obvious that the Zero is a very serviceable and dependable airplane. An excellent job of reconditioning was done by the Naval Air Station, San Diego, and no major difficulties were encountered other than failure of radio and brakes to function. The latter are inherently deficient in design and capacity. The preliminary program was delayed by continuous efforts to improve brake operation, and by discovery that the alternate air intake was partially open which required repeating certain performance tests.

All performance tests were made with the airplane ballasted for its full armament and maximum internal fuel load. The engine power output was determined by a propeller and governor setting which permitted a maximum RPM in take off, climb, and level flight of 2550 to 2575, and an automatic power regulator which limited manifold pressure to 35 in. Hg. The performance results given below are somewhat at variance with preliminary figures due to further tests with improved instruments, reduction to standard conditions, and corrections for compressibility. It is probable that the airplane in the original condition was somewhat faster than is indicated here, due to the lack of a flush fit at wheel well fairings and cabin enclosure in the overhauled plane, and the addition of non-specular paint.

No information was available as to the power characteristics of the engine. It has a piston displacement of 1690 cu.in. and is believed to develop approximately 900 H.P. The settings found on the propeller governor and manifold pressure regulator were retained as being correct for rated power. However, the propeller stops were shifted in order to obtain the maximum RPM at take off and in climb at low altitudes. The pitch range of the propeller is comparatively small, and it is assumed that the Japanese use the higher pitch settings originally found in order to make available a more economical engine speed for cruising. The manifold pressure regulator has an emergency shift which raises its regulating figure from 35" to 38". The latter figure was used only for brief comparisons as the engine appeared to be definitely rough at this power. Further tests will be made at a time when an engine failure will be less critical to the test program. The engine operation was otherwise smooth and satisfactory. Cooling appeared to be unusually good. A critical altitude of 16000 feet is obtained with a single stage, single speed blower. Manual regulation of the mixture was necessary, although it is understood that the carburetor is fitted with an automatic mixture control feature which was not operative.

DESCRIPTION OF AIRCRAFT

DESIGNATION: Translation of the nameplate indicates that the aircraft is a:

Zero Type I   Carrier Fighter   Model 2

MANUFACTURER: Mitsubishi Heavy Industries Corporation, Nagoya works. Date of manufacture February 1942.

GENERAL: All metal low-wing monoplane, flush riveted with clean smooth exterior. Great emphasis has been given to saving weight wherever possible. Wing is integral with the fuselage, no leakproof tanks or armor, and wings fold only at tips. Landing gear, flaps, and brakes are hydraulically operated. Visibility is excellent with no difficulty seeing astern. Cockpit is not much more cramped than a Spitfire, except that the longest pedal position is quite short and knees stick up rather high. Arrester hook retracts into lower part of fuselage. Flotation bag in rear of fuselage - watertight compartments in wings, outboard of cannons.

DIMENSIONS: Span 39'-5" Length 29'-6 5/8", Wing area 248 sq. ft.

WEIGHTS: Empty 3718 lbs., Gross 5555 lbs. (without external tank).

ENGINE: Nakajima "Sakae" NKI, 14 cylinder, twin-row, air-cooled, rated at approximately 900 h.p.. Fuel 92 octane. Diameter 44". Weight approximately 1250 lbs.

PROPELLER: 3 bladed constant speed, all metal.

ARMAMENT: 2 × 7.7 mm guns (500 rounds each) synchronized to fire through propeller, (muzzle velocity 2400 ft. per second; 2 × 20 mm guns (60 rounds each) mounted in wings, muzzle velocity 2000 ft. per second. Electric reflector sight. Provision for two bomb racks on wings. Weight of guns and ammunition 344.5 lbs.

INSTRUMENTS: Completely equipped, including two-way radio (4596 KCS); radio compass (Fairchild); oxygen with altitude regulator.

FUEL CAPACITY (U.S. gallons): Wings 103 gals. Fuselage 38 gals. External 87 gals.

OIL CAPACITY (U.S. gallons): 15 gals.

PERFORMANCE

Maximum speeds and rates of climb are given below.

Maximum speed	Sea level	270 (m.p.h.)
Maximum speed	5000 feet	287
Maximum speed	10,000 feet	305
Maximum speed	16,000 feet*	326
Maximum speed	20,000 feet	321.5
Maximum speed	25,000 feet	315
Maximum speed	30,000 feet	306
Rate of climb	Sea level	2750 (ft/min)
Rate of climb	15,000 feet	2380
Rate of climb	20,000 feet	1810
Rate of climb	30,000 feet	850

*Critical altitude.

SERVICE CEILING: 38,500 feet.

The Zero, after repairs in San Diego, was flown for the first time in October 1942. JRC

The airspeed instrument, left, and manifold pressure instrument, right, from the captured Zero. The airspeed reads in knots, the needle sweeps through two revolutions to get to the 300-knot reading. The manifold pressure gauge has a red sector for + readings. It is graduated in metric measure—centimeters of mercury with 0 equalling sea level pressure. To avoid confusion a standard Army/Navy gauge was installed alongside the original instruments so the test pilot could deal with more familar instruments.

COURTESY ADM. W.M. LEONARD, VIRGINIA BEACH, VIRGINIA

The left wing tip is now in the Navy Museum at the Washington Navy Yard, Washington, D.C. The restoration was done by the Naval Air Repair Facility at North Island, San Diego, California, in the fall of 1942. In the initial crash the lower surface, forward wing ribs and port running light were all damaged. It is hard to see where the restored rib joins the original rib as excellent rivet work was done throughout the restoration.

COURTESY ADM. W.M. LEONARD, VIRGINIA BEACH, VIRGINIA

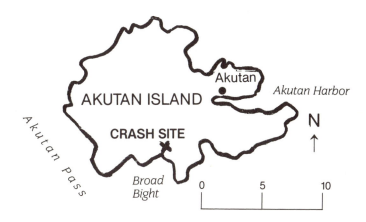

Japanese war art painting in custody of the U.S. Army. Painted by Fujita Teuguji in 1944, showing the final assault by Japanese forces on Attu. USA SC 301118

CHAPTER NINE
ATTU

A pre-war view of the village of Attu. At right is the the
Russian Orthodox Church. USN NH 70063

Japanese commander and staff on Attu.
AUTHOR'S COLLECTION

A Japanese coastal
defense ship leaving
Attu. JRC

Light cruiser *Abukuma*
and destroyer *Asaki*
anchored in Holtz Bay,
Attu. JRC

Anti-aircraft gun and
crew on Attu. JRC

Japanese troops on Attu.
Their living conditions were
sparse and got much worse as
the U.S. Naval blockade
became effective. JRC

This photo of Japanese troops
on Attu was found in a hut
on the island after the battle.
REEVE ALEUTIAN AIRWAYS,
BOB REEVE COLLECTION

Mr. and Mrs. C. Foster Jones on Attu*

In the summer of 1941, Mr. and Mrs. C. Foster Jones took up their duties on the island of Attu. Mrs. Jones was the teacher of the community school, and Mr. Jones acted as special assistant and as weather reporter and radio operator for the Weather Bureau. They had both had long experience in Alaska. Mr. Jones had been there for nearly forty years, fifteen of which were in the Indian Service. His wife, a graduate of the Pennsylvania Hospital Nurses' Training School, was qualified as a teacher, community worker, and nurse. She was first employed in the Indian Service in 1928. Together Mr. and Mrs. Jones made a fine combination, for the Indian Service used married couples at the isolated stations in Alaska where the two were the only white people in the community, and where contact with the outside world was limited to the radio and one or two visits a year from the mail boat. Mr. Jones came from St. Paris, Ohio, and his wife, born Etta Schureman, grew up in Connecticut.

On September 8, 1941, two weeks after their arrival on Attu, Mrs. Jones wrote to Claude Hirst, General Superintendent of the Alaska Native Service, telling him her impressions of the village and its people.

"There are 45 people in the village. They are progressive, intelligent, clean, and friendly. They live and work as a community, making their living from blue fox trapping. They operate as The Native Community of Attu, pooling the season's catch of pelts, and selling them in the name of the community to a fur dealer in New York. The proceeds, after ten dollars for each skin is taken out for the trappers, is divided equally among all members of the village, children included. Thus widows and helpless ones are taken care of. There are no indigents here.

"Their houses are models for construction, neatness, and furnishings. There are nine houses, having from four to seven rooms each, and they are well lighted and beautifully painted, inside and out. All have excellent stoves, good linoleum on the floors, gas lamps, and all but one have running water piped into the house from a spring. The yards are neat, all refuse being carefully disposed of. The American flag, flying from the village flagpole, was one of the first sights which greeted us as we came into the harbor on the Coast Guard cutter Atlanta. They have a beautiful Greek Orthodox church, electrically lighted by means of a small light plant.

"They all speak a little English, much to our astonishment, considering their extreme isolation. People from occasional boats which stop here are the only ones outside the village they see.

"The villagers have used the school room for dances on various occasions but have left everything in good condition. Written on the blackboard we found the chief's orders: 'Pealse dont spate on the Flower and dont brake loking Gleese' (windows). They are cooperative and helpful in all work concerning the school. All want to help without pay when there is building or lifting or special work to be done. They have an abundanace of all kinds of fish and the boys are generous with their gifts of fish. At first we paid them, but the chief asked us not to pay. The boys themselves made that request. They have plenty of fish and they wanted their gifts to be free.

"They are a proud people; proud of the fact that they differ somewhat from the people of Atka and Unalaska. There has been no intermingling with the Japanese. In fact, they dislike and distrust the Japs. They accuse them of stealing their foxes, and even of killing some of their trappers years ago. But for three years they haven't seen a Jap or a Japanese boat."

In late December 1941, Mr. Jones wrote that all was well and that no Japanese had as yet put in an appearance. Further east, on the island of Atka, another Indian Service couple taught the school and ran the radio station. Ralph Magee talked each day with Foster Jones by radio, exchanging weather data and other news. On June 7, 1942, they talked together at the usual time in the morning, but in the afternoon Magee was unable to make any contact with Attu. He surmised correctly that the island had been invaded, and he immediately began to plan for the evacuation of the inhabitants of Atka.

From the morning of that day until August 1945, no word was received concerning the fate of the Joneses and the forty-five natives on Attu. The island was recaptured after a long and bloody campaign. The village had been destroyed, and no trace remained of the inhabitants. Many rumors were circulated, none of which had any foundation in fact. The Indian Service and the Interior Department made every effort to find out what had happened to Mr. and Mrs. Jones and the Aleuts, and although no information was forthcoming, hope was held out that they might have survived. In June 1944, the Board of Suggestions and Awards of the Interior Department cited Mr. and Mrs. Jones for courage and devotion to duty, giving them Awards of Excellence and especially meritorious promotions. Letters from Secretary Ickes, commending them, were sent to the Juneau office to be held for the day of their release.

Early in July 1945, the Swiss representative of the International Red Cross, who had finally been allowed to visit the prisoner-of-war camps, discovered

Mrs. Jones in the small village of Totsuka, in the Tokyo-Yokohoma area. When the Americans landed, a short time later, she was released and flown back across the Pacific.

After landing in California on September 12, Mrs. Jones went to Seattle, where she began to straighten out a three-years' accumulation of business matters, and where she received letters from the Secretary of the Interior and the Commissioner of Indian Affairs. She arrived in Chicago on September 30, 1945, her sixty-sixth birthday, and was met by her sister and her niece, who had come from Muskegon, Michigan, to welcome her.

At the Office of Indian Affairs, Mrs. Jones told of her long imprisonment and her release. On June 7, 1942, some 2,000 Japanese landed on the island and surrounded the village, firing at the inhabitants from every direction. One woman was hit in the leg, but there were no other casualties, and no resistance was offered. Mr. Jones put the radio station out of commission just as the Japanese landed. The invaders handled the inhabitants roughly, separated Mr. and Mrs. Jones, and Mrs. Jones did not see her husband after the second day. The Aleuts told her secretly that he was dead and that they had buried him in the churchyard. The following day a high officer, evidently an aristocrat, landed and imposed order on his command. The Japanese soldiers were forbidden to enter the village and they were obliged to return food which they had stolen from the town. The mayor was appointed liaison officer to handle arrangements between the military and the Aleuts, and from this time on the prisoners were well treated. After a few days Mrs. Jones was told to pack her clothes for the voyage to Japan. She was taken directly to Yokohoma, where she was lodged temporarily in a hotel in company with eighteen Australian nurses who had been captured in New Guinea.

In the Yacht Club to which they were moved and where they lived for two years there was a well-stocked library. The prisoners could read, and they passed some of the time knitting for the Japanese Red Cross. Morale was high among the nurses, and in spite of their predicament they had some hilarious times together. Because of her white hair Mrs. Jones was not allowed to do any work, and she was looked upon with special respect.

The food was not satisfactory. One day the cook said to Mrs. Jones, "In America got plenty fish?"

"Got plenty fish, got plenty rice in America," she answered.

"In America got everything. In Japan got nothing," he replied.

The first Christmas was marked by the arrival of parcels from the British Red Cross. A year later American parcels arrived, and during the latter part of the war these were received every few months. At Christmastime, 1942, each American prisoner received a gift of 90 yen in the name of the Vatican, although there was little to buy with the money.

After two years the women were moved to a Japanese house in the village some miles from Yokohoma, where they were eventually found. There was no heat, and water had to be pumped from the well in the yard. But in the summer they had a garden where they grew tomatoes and other vegetables. They knew that the invasion was coming. They had heard of the liberation of the Philippines and they knew of the fighting on Okinawa. They often heard the bombs falling and saw the fires set by incendiaries. On July 3 the representative of the International Red Cross came to see them and insisted to the Japanese Government that they must be allowed to send cables to their relatives at home—the first word of them to reach the world outside Japan.

The Japanese guards told them about the atomic bomb, and said that one bomb had killed 20,000 people, but they found it difficult to believe. They went on working in the little vegetable garden and waited for the day of liberation.

Mrs. Jones could not say enough about the treatment of the released war prisoners. The Army, the Navy, and the Red Cross did everything possible to help them. A planeload of oranges was flown from California for them. In Manila, where she spent a week on her homeward journey, the Red Cross had, among other morale-building facilities, a beauty parlor and a shop where ready-made dresses or material for sewing were available.

Less than half of the Aleuts returned from imprisonment in Japan. Forced to work digging clay, many died of tuberculosis and malnutrition. Those who came back settled on the island of Atka, where they had friends and relatives.

---

*Excerpted from an Office of Indian Affairs Memorandum in October 1945.

Oleon Prokopeuff: An Aleut native on Attu*

1942 Sunday morning we were captured by the Japanese, they shot come down from the Hill, (this is what I was trying to say).

At that time, the people saw a Japanese plane fly past the village, and it was reported to the teacher and he said that there are American Patrol planes flying the area all the time, at that it was forgotten.

After that the villagers went to the lookout hill and saw the Japanese ships in the bay beyond the village.

After the ships were observed, the Japanese started coming to the village shooting, as a result a woman's foot was shot, the only reason why they stopped shooting was that one of the Japanese soldiers got shot by one of their fellow soldiers.

From there I went to Alfred's wife's house, because they were shooting at my house. I got Lizzie who was just a baby and headed over to Alfred's wife's place. Lizzie was only 3 years old at that time.

Alfred's wife's foot hurted her so I went over there to assist her. Then the Japanese surrounded the house with rifles pointing at the house, so Perescovia and I sat down, because I didn't want to fall with the baby in my arms, if they were to shoot me. The soldiers did not shoot, then an officer got there and was really mad, so the soldiers that were pointing their guns at the house moved away. There was a Japanese that spoke English very well, so we were told to follow him to the school. After we were taken to the school, the Japanese set a fire and I thought that they were going to burn the school down with us in it, but instead, they told us if we were all present and we told them that we weren't all here. There are three younger people hiding some place.

Then the Japanese were looking for them, but did not find them until some of the men from the village was sent out to get them and finally they were brought back by the villagers.

The only time we were sent home was when the three young people came back. And when we were sent to our houses, we were surprised to find almost all our belongings had been searched, things all over the floor, even the Easter eggs, we never could figure out what they were looking for.

We couldn't go anyplace because there were Japanese guards guarding our houses, and they were very scary standing there holding their guns. So we stayed home until dawn, they started shooting flares, we were so scared we hid under our beds, not realizing what they were.

Three days later we were taken by boat away from our village. Our houses were opened and burned, then we were taken out to the boat.

Then there was commotion on the boat with people running and whistling. Then it was said that they saw an American submarine, that was what the commotion was all about, then they, the Japanese, said that they were going to take the short-cut (I don't know which route they took us).

Then we passed the Navy yard. We were kept in this hole on the ship and the hole was stinky, we never saw light until we arrived Japan. When we arrived Japan the Captain bumped into the dock, and threw us off of our seats. And we thought that our ship was shot and we were scared.

We were gathered on the dock and were sprayed, then the Japanese took us in the car to a black house. En route to Japan on the ship we had brought our own food so that was the only food we had until we got to Japan. We were given warm rice, that is the only warm food we ate, since we left home.

The Japanese asked us if we were hungry and we told them we were, so they brought us some food on a tray with chopsticks but we couldn't eat with them. There was a policeman with a partner, whenever he turned to talk we ate with our hands fist-like. We just wasn't used to using chopsticks. There were small birds still with feathers on them, so nobody ate them.

After we ate, they let us go to bed on the floor, and our pillows were hard, but we didn't complain. Then our blankets were thick as a mattress and heavy too, but we used it.

Every morning we mopped the floor in our house. The kitchen was low stairs leading down to it. We kept the stove that we brought in the kitchen.

We used to eat grass like food with rice. When all the food we brought was all gone, the salted fish and dried fish we started eating vegetables. Carrots and potatoes were boiled and eaten. After eating the boiled vegetables I was in pain from having gassed up stomach.

After that they brought in Japanese officials, after that we got a Japanese cook. Then the Japanese cook put wood inside the oven and smoked up the whole house.

Then we were gathered once again and we were asked if we were eating good food, we didn't say anything. Then they asked us to talk, and we told them that we didn't want to talk so after that they started bringing food for us to eat.

Then the men were asked to go to work. So the men started working, then people started going to the hospital. People were getting sick. People were getting sick and I was the only one cooking for the people. Then my husband got sick and was taken to the hospital. Then my children were hungry, so whenever I fetched water I would gather orange peels, and I baked them over the heater and fed them to my children, only then they were not hungry.

Then I was called to the hospital, then I saw all those sick people. I couldn't stand it so I asked them to put me to work so they put me to work on cement. The place we worked was so hot, we worked with pick and shovels, breaking cement. The cement was dried and crushed, and in the winter it was worked on in a factory.

While I was working I got a piece of cement in my right eye and I thought that I was going to lose my eye sight but I came back to Atka without glasses.

The people (Attuans) who were taken home from the hospital were taken back to the hospital again, because they were sick again and I went to the hospital to see them. Then I asked what was done to them and they said that they were given shots, I really don't know what was done to them.

Then there were lots of people who died there. My son and daughter were sick, and they would say scratch me and I didn't know where to scratch, so I would go over and scratch them.

When my husband was ready to die, he called for me so I went to see him and he had kept cigarettes for sometime so he gave them to me. I stayed up with him all night then he told me if I wanted to sleep I could go lay down, but he died while I was sleeping, so I was awakened, then I observed something which is never done to our dead. They were dressed and taken out, but didn't know what was done to them.

Then one day my son Leonty died. They put him in a oven, then they told me to set a fire on the flowers so I did, and I didn't like what I saw. I asked the priest if it was a sin to do that and he told me that they were doing that because there wasn't room for burial.

Lots of the people died here on Japan. Just a few of us were left.

Then we heard a plane fly overhead, and apparently it was an American plane, so the plane dropped food from the plane by parachutes in drums. So we sat up and ate all that night.

After the food was dropped Americans came there in cars, whenever the car was going it was smoky. The cars were cranked until one got tired it got started. Then we saw cars with no noise, then we were gathered once again in a house, and we were asked if we wanted to go home and we said yes! They were American and they said the war was over, and we were going to be taken home. That next day we were taken to the airport. We stayed at the airport 3 nights, maybe they didn't have a plane available or might have been something else I didn't know.

When we left in the plane we were taken to islands and I can't recall any names of those islands.

We were shown the island which was bombed by the Americans, and it looked like kindling wood, from the plane it looked as though everything was crushed.

Whenever the Americans bombed we were taken inland in to fallout shelters on Japan.

I don't remember any names of those three islands, the only island I remember is Okinawa. We stayed at Okinawa for 2 and a half weeks, then we were flown out of Okinawa to Manila. From Manila we were transported to San Francisco.

When we were in Alaskan water it was stormy and I was hoping at least they could drop us off at Unalaska but they didn't. We continued on to San Francisco.

From San Francisco to Seattle we rode on a train.

From Seattle we took a boat to Adak. We stayed in Seattle for a long time and we didn't want to come home because Christmas was near. But we were taken to Adak with lots of military men.

From Adak we were taken to Atka on a small tug and I was scared because I've gotten used to the big boat that we previously rode on.

After the tug made it to Atka, a truck picked us up and brought us to the school, that is where they decided where we were to be kept. So I moved in with Cedar Snigaroff. Before the houses were made for us we were kept in Army quonset huts, then a year later houses were built for us to live in. They have been had as house for a long time and they are old now. Now days I don't trust my house.

*Translator comments:

This article was a literal translation from Aleut. If you discover any irregularities in grammar, it is due to literal translation. Any mistakes are due to the translator.

Moses Dirks

*Author comments:

I didn't really get everthing on what I wanted to say because I didn't have someone from Japan who was with me. But I let it finish.

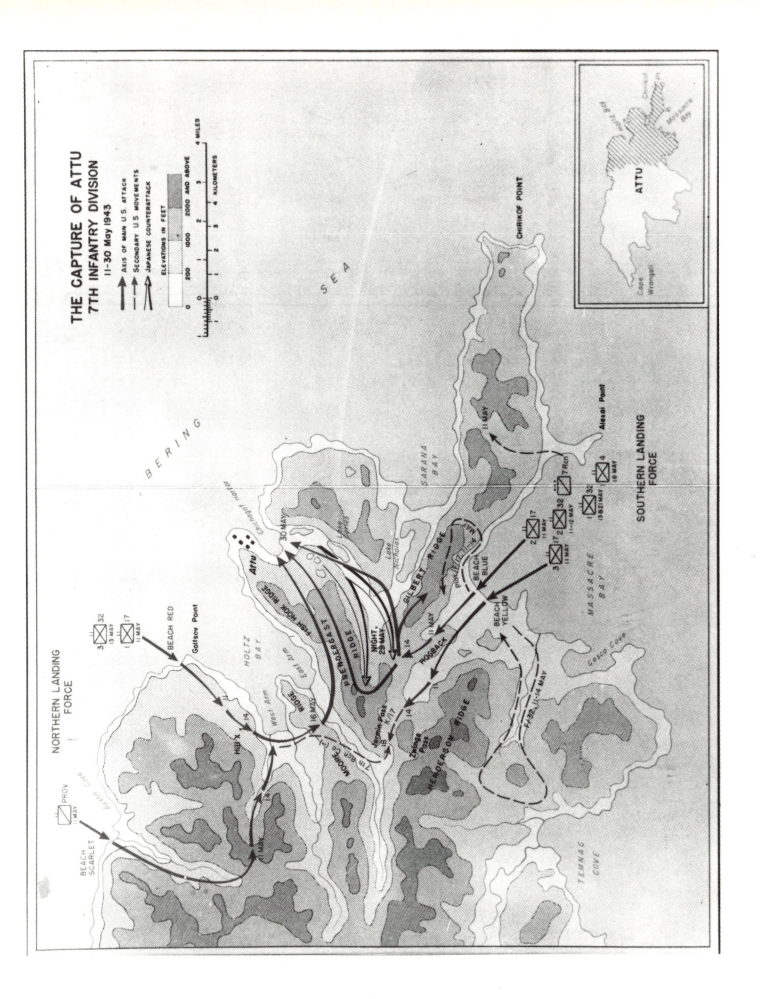

THE CAPTURE OF ATTU
7TH INFANTRY DIVISION
11-30 May 1943

Axis of Main U.S. Attack
Secondary U.S. Movements
Japanese Counterattack

ELEVATIONS IN FEET
0 200 1000 2000 AND ABOVE

MILES

KILOMETERS

ATTU

CHIRIKOF POINT

SEA

BERING

HOLTZ BAY

West Arm

East Arm

Chichagof Harbor

Attu

SARANA BAY

Alexai Point

SOUTHERN LANDING FORCE

BEACH BLUE

BEACH YELLOW

MASSACRE BAY

GASCO COVE

TEMNAC COVE

HENDERSON RIDGE

MOORE RIDGE

FISH HOOK RIDGE

PRENDERGAST RIDGE

GILBERT RIDGE

MOGBACK

BEACH RED

Goltsov Point

NORTHERN LANDING FORCE

BEACH SCARLET

Austin Cove

Hill "X"

Lake Nicholas

Lake Cories

Services for the dead at the conclusion of the battle. AMHA

Most of the supplies had to be carried by hand up the steep slopes in the wet tundra. It was not a pleasant place to visit, much less fight. AAC

Looking north from atop the high ridge overlooking the passes leading into Holtz and Chichagof bays. American forces were attacking enemy-held positions in the pass leading to Holtz Bay. Besides being located in the scar-marked saddle, the enemy had gun positions just above the fogline, which the troops were also attempting to eliminate. In the right foreground are several American gun positions overlooking the area. This saddle was heavily shelled by a 105mm howitzer located on the beach. On the snow in the foreground is earth scattered by an enemy shell which burst nearby. USA SC 174501

Evacuating casualties. AMHA

General Buckner and staff examining the Japanese command post on June 2, 1943. Note the American flag flying over the post. AAC

Dead Japanese soldiers viewed by an American soldier.
REEVE ALEUTIAN AIRWAYS,
BOB REEVE COLLECTION

These gruesome photos show the ferocity of the battle that was very costly to both sides. Of the 2,600 men in Col. Yamazaki's original forces, only 29 survived the battle, 2,350 were counted dead. None of the survivors were officers. Americans suffered nearly 4,000 casualties: 549 dead, 1,148 wounded, 1,800 injured or became sick from the severe weather and terrain conditions and the rest by miscellaneous accidents, drownings or mental breakdowns. This battle, the first to demonstrate the Japanese suicidal banzai attacks and the U.S. Army's first amphibious landing on an enemy occupied island, was only a prelude of many more battles to come.

Extraction of Diary

This is a translated copy of a diary found after the battle for Attu. The officer, Nebsi Tatsuqochi, a 35-year-old doctor attached to the Japanese garrison, died in the last suicide attempt against a U.S. Army artillery position. This diary gives an insight into the thoughts of an enemy soldier under battle conditions.*

---

*This translation is a compilation of several different versions that have survived through the years. The main version is courtesy of Mrs. Gladys Nakken, Minneapolis, Minnesota.

Northern 5216 Detachment
North Sea Defense Field Hospital

MAY 12, 1943

Carrier based planes flew over, fired at it. There is a low fog and the summit is clear. Air raids carried out frequently until 1000. Hear loud noises. It is naval gun firing. Prepared "A" battle equipment. Infantry, American transports, about 41, began landing at Hokkai Misaki. 20 boats landed at Massacre Bay. It seems that they are going to unload heavy equipment. Days activities—air raid, naval gun firings, landing of U.S. troops.

MAY 13, 1943

The U.S. forces landed at Shiba Dai and Massacre Bay. The enemy has advanced to the bottom of Misuma Yama from Shiba Dai. Have engaged them. On the other hand, Massacre Bay is defended by only one platoon. Upon the unexpected attack the A-A Machine Cannon was destroyed and we have withdrawn. In nite attack we have captured 20 enemy rifles. There is a tremendous mountain art. gun firing. Approximately 15 patients came into the field hospital. The field hospital is attached to Arai Eng. Unit.

MAY 14, 1943
BATTLE

Our 2 subs from Kiska assisting us have greatly damaged 2 enemy ships. 1st Lt. Sieyuki died by shot from rifle. Continuous flow of wounded in the hospital. In the evening the U.S. forces used gas, but no damage was done because of strong winds. Took refuge in trenches in the day time and took care of patients during the bombardment. Enemy strength must be a division. Our desperate defense is holding up well.

MAY 15, 1943
BATTLE

Continuous flow of casualties to our field hospital caused by the fierce bombardment of enemy land and naval forces. The enemy has a great number of Negros and Indians. The West Arm units have withdrawn to near Shitagata Dai. In a raid, I was ordered to the West Arm, but it was called off. Just layed down from fatigue in barracks. Facial expressions of soldiers back from West Arm is tense. They all went back to firing line soon.

MAY 16, 1943
BATTLE

If Shitagata Dai is occupied by the enemy the fate of the East Arm is decided, so burn documents and prepare to destroy patients. At that time, there was an order from headquarters of sect. unit. Proceeded to Chisagof Harbor by the way of Umanoso. 0100 in the morning, patients from Ind. Inf. was lost so accompanied the patients. There was an air raid attack so took refuge in the former field hospital cave. The guns of a Lockheed spitted fire and flew past our cave.

MAY 17, 1943
BATTLE

At nite, about 1800, under cover of darkness, left the cave. The strecher went over muddy road, steep hills of no mans land. No matter how far or how much we went, we did not get to the pass. Was rather irritated in the fog by the thought of getting lost. Sat down every 20 or 30 steps. Would sleep, dream, wake up again. Same thing all over again. The patient on the strecher, who does not move is frostbitten. After all the effort, met sector Commander Col. Yamsaki. The pass is a straight line without any width and a steep line towards Chicagof Harbor. Sitting on the butt and lifting the feet, I slide very smoothly and changed directions with the sword. Slid down in about 20 min. After that arrived at Chicagof Harbor after straggling. Time expended was 9 hours for all this, without leaving any patients.

Opened a new hospital. Walking is now extremely difficult from left knee rheumatism which reaccured on the pass.

The result of our navy, the submarine and special under water crafts in vicinity of Chicagof Harbor since the 14th: Battleship, cruiser, 3 destroyers, air borne troops, transport 6. By the favorable turn since the Battle of the East Arm, reserves came back. Off shore at Shiba Dai, 6 destroyers are guarding one transport.

MAY 18
BATTLE

The Yenegewa Det., abandoned East and West Arms and withdrew to Umanose. About 60 wounded came to the field hospital. I had to care for all of them all by myself all through the nite. Heard that the enemy carried out a landing in Chicagof Harbor. Everybody did combat preparation and waited. Had 2 grenades ready. 2nd Lt. Omura left for combat line on Ha Kuchin Tama. Said farewell. At nite a patient came in who engaged a friendly unit by mistake and who received a wound on the wrist. The counter sign is Isshi Hoke.

MAY 19
BATTLE

At nite there was a phone call from section unit headquarters. In some spots of the beach there are some friendly float type planes waiting. Went into Attu village church, felt like some ones home. Some blankets were scattered around. Was told to translate a field order presumed to have been dropped by an enemy officer in Massacre Bay. Was ordered to draw a detail map sketch of Massacre and Holtz Bay which was in the posession of Capt. Robert Edwards, Adj. of Col. Smith. Got tired and went to sleep. 1st Lt. Ujie is also in charge of translation.

MAY 20
BATTLE

The hard fighting of our 303 Bn. in Massacre Bay is fierce and it is to our advantage. Have captured enemy weapon and have used that to fight. Mowed down 10 enemy closing in under fog. Five of our men and one medical N.C.O. died. Heard enemy pilots faces can be seen around Umanose. The enemy naval gun firing near our hospital ward is fierce, drops around 20 meters away.

MAY 21
BATTLE

Patient was strapped when amputating arm. It is the first time since moving over Chicagof Harbor that I went

into our air raid shelter. Enemy plane is a Martin. Nerviceness of our C.O. is severe and he has said his last words to his officers and NCO's that he will die tomorrow and gave all his articles away. Hasty chap this fellow. The officers on the front are doing a fine job. Everyone who heard this became desparate and things became disorderly.

MAY 22
BATTLE

0600 air raid again. Strafing killed one medical man. Okayaki wounded in right thigh and fractured arm. During the nite a mortar shell came awful close.

MAY 23
BATTLE

Friendly naval bomber destroyed an enemy cruiser off shore. By naval gun firing a hit was scored on the pillar pole of tents for patients and the tents gave in and two died insantly. From 0200 in the morning to 1600 stayed in fox hole. Days ration 1 go, 5 shaker (1.5 lbs). Nothing else. Officers and men alike at the front. Everybody looked around for food and stole everything they could find.

MAY 24
BATTLE

It sleeted and was extremely cold, stayed at Hisumi barracks alone. A great amount of shells were dropped by naval gun fire and rocks and mud flew around and the roof falls in. In fox hole about 5 yards away from Hayaska, a medical man died instantly by a penetration of shrapnel through his heart.

MAY 25
BATTLE

Naval gun firing, aerial bombardment, trench warfare. The worst is to come. The enemy is constructing their positions. Bn. Commander died at Umanose. They cannot fully accomadate all the patients. It has been said at Massacre Bay district the road comming to section headquarters unit is isolated. Am suffering from diarrhea and am dizzy.

MAY 26
BATTLE

By naval gun fire, it felt like the Hisumi Barracks had

blown up and everything was shook up tremendously. Consciousness became vague. One tent burned down by hit from incendiary bomb. Strafing planes hit the next room, 2 hits from 50 cal. shells, one stopped on ceiling and the other penetrated. My room looks an awful mess from sand and pebbles that come down from the roof. Hirose, 1st Lt. of Medical Corps is also wounded. There was a ceremony of Grant_____ of Emperial Edict. The last line of Umanose was broken through. No hope for reinforcement. Will die for the cause of Emperial Edict.

MAY 27
BATTLE

Diarrhea continues, pain is severe. Took everything from pills, opium, morphine, then slept pretty well. Strafing by planes, roof broke through. There is less then a 1000 left from more then 2000 troops. Wounded from coast defense unit, field hospital headquarters, field post office, the rest are on the front lines.

MAY 28
BATTLE

The remaining rations is only for two days. Our artillery has been completely destroyed. There is a sound of trench mortar, also of AA guns. The companys on the bottom of Attu Fuji have been completely annihilated, except one. I wonder if Commander Yenegawa and some of the men are still living. Other companies have been completely annihilated except one or two.

303 Bn. has been defeated. Yenegawa Bn. is still holding Umanose. Continuous cases of suicide. Half of sector unit headquarters was blown away. Heard that they gave 400 shots morphine to severely wounded and killed them. Half fried thistle. It is the first time that I had eaten something fresh in six months. It is a delicacy. Order from the unit commander to move the field hospital to the island, but it was called off.

MAY 29
BATTLE

To day at 2000 we assembled in front of headquarters. The field hospital took part too. The last assault is to be carried out. All the patients in the hospital are to commit suicide. Only 33 years of living and I am to die here. I have no regrets. Banzi to the Emperor. I am greatful I have kept the peace in my soul which Ehkist bestowed on me. At 1800 took care of all the patients with grenades. Good-bye, Taeki, my beloved wife, who loved me to the last. Until we meet again, greet you God-speed. Misaka, who just became 4 years old, will grow up unhindered. I feel sorry for you Takiko, born Feb. of this year and gone without seeing your father. Well be good. Matsuo (brother) Kochan, Sakechan, Massachan, Mittichan, Good-bye. The number participating in the attack is a little over 1000 to take enemy artillery positions. It seems that the enemy is expecting an all out attack to morrow.

Personal History of Nebsi Tatsuqochi

■ Translation of captured enemy diary from Headquarters Landing Force, Office of A C/S, G-2. Massacre Valley, Attu Island, June 1, 1943.

■ March 1929 — Graduated from Fraizer English Acadious

■ Sept. 1929 to May 1932 — Pacific Union College, Medical Dept., Agwin, Calif.

■ Sept. 15, 1933 to Jan. 1937 — College of Medical Evanglist

■ Sept. 8, 1938 — Received Calif. medical license

■ Jan. 13, 1941 — Transfered to 1st Imperial Guard Infantry Regt.

■ May 1 — Ordered as officer guard promoted to PFC medical dept.

Captured Japanese photos of troops on Attu.

U.S. sailors of Fleet Air Wing looking over captured Japanese equipment, May 1943.
AAC, LARRY REINEKE COLLECTION

Soldiers and sailors eat a hot breakfast on a makeshift stove on the beach. Note the propped up ski, May 1943.
AAC, LARRY REINEKE COLLECTION

A massive amount of supplies were unloaded on Attu after the battle. This is a supply depot at Massacre Bay, May 31, 1943. AAC, LARRY REINEKE COLLECTION

Wrecked enemy tents, fox holes and a jeep, reminders of the fierce battle just concluded, May 1943. AAC

An enemy coastal gun position.
AAC, BERTRAND HOAH COLLECTION

Float off a Japanese plane. AAC, LARRY REINEKE COLLECTION

On the northwest end of the beach were found several Japanese barracks and supply depots camouflaged against the side of the hill. These were constructed of wood and covered over with tundra and rock. From a short distance they were almost invisible to the naked eye. Around the entrance of the building a wall of rocks and tundra had been constructed. Next to it was a cave, dug into the ground, in which other supplies were stored. This photo shows an interior view of a building of this type in which were stored office and writing materials. After the area was taken over, this building was used by intelligence officers of the Ordnance Corps who were studying the Japanese equipment captured during the battle. West Arm of Holtz Bay, May 26, 1943. USA SC 177681

Soldiers examine crashed Zero at the south end of West Holtz beach, May 1943.
AAC, LARRY REINEKE COLLECTION

This photo was found on Attu after the battle, probably on the body of this soldier.
COURTESY PETER ORNAWKA, HOLLYWOOD, FLORIDA

This Rufe, float-type Zero reconnaissance seaplane was raised from Chicagof Bay and taken to Adak for examination. It had folding wings, a plywood tail, Mitsubishi engine, one free machine gun and its bomb bay held two live bombs when it was lifted from the water. USMC

Gracious Living on Attu Island

I never hear the grumble of a distant bulldozer without being drawn irresistibly back over the rocky roads of memory to Attu, the Rock from which, thank God, I was not hewn. Whether in the golden haze of a late autumn day in mid-September or in the lurid streaming fogs of high summer, life in the war-time Aleutians was attuned to a perpetual reel for winds, played in a minor key against a basso continuo of bulldozers, pianissimo.

It was on one of those lurid high-summer days in 1943 that our party of gentlemen-adventurers went over the side of the Libertyship Moore-Mac-Hawk via landing nets and was ferried by barge across Massacre Bay to Alexai Point, Attu. The immigrants were welcomed ashore with the thinly veiled contempt which the older inhabitants of military installations always display to newcomers. "Crawlers" (caterpillar tractors and trailers in tasteful olive drab) were thoughtfully furnished for the transportation of the gentlemen to their sumptuous living area: a low rise, ankle-deep in tundra, just off the end of the spanking-new steel-matted fighter strip. In perfect July weather (just enough moisture in the air to soak the windward side of everything to the dripping point) pyramidal tents were pitched. The gentlemen-adventurers, having had previous experience at Adak, placed their tent poles on pieces of board to prevent them from sinking slowly out of sight, and the little pot-bellied stoves, no bigger than pony kegs of beer, were rigged with stove-pipes which ran up through special metal tent-caps.

In the ensuing months several schools of thought were to grow up as to the care and feeding of these little soft-coal stoves. It was early determined that turves of tundra would not burn like peat, and frequent trips to the coal pile remained a necessity. The most vexed problem was the frequent choking of the pipes with soot. This challenge was met in several ways, none entirely satisfactory. The pipe-bangers would clang on the stove pipe, usually bringing the whole rig down in a cloud of soot and sections of pipe. The boiler-men preferred to toss half a canteen-cup of water onto the coals, slam the lid and let her blow. This was generally the most effective technique, unless an excess of water also put out the fire. An anti-aircraft artillery liaison man later assigned to us tried a variant of this technique with a little gun powder, which not only brought down all sections of pipe and all the soot, but blew out the fire, cracked the stove and gave the inventor a rather nasty bruise on the foot when the door blew off. My personal preference was the acrobatic technique, which required the would-be chimney sweep to climb up one corner of the tent and drop a hunk of coal down the pipe. (The original inventor used rocks, but soon found that they did not burn very well and so tended to fill up the

stove.) With a brisk fire to kick back the soot on the up-draught the acrobatic technique was very effective. In addition, a good laugh could always be had by sending a greenhorn up the leeward side and watching him grope his way down with a face full of soot.

On that first afternoon, however, our adventurers were concerned only with getting under cover and finding the banquet hall, which was a spacious tent operated by the deft and knowledgeable chefs of our hosts the 42nd Engineers.

On a floor covered with a deep lush wall-to-wall carpet of that black oily mud obtainable only from well trampled tundra, a sumptuous stand-up repast was served. Dinner music, of course, was a susurrus of the ubiquitous caterpillar tractors, sostenuto. After a delicious entree of luke-warm C-ration hash and watery navy beans a la mess kit, the dessert of canned fruit salad was embellished with what were then known as "C-biscuits" with canned butter or "salve" and jam. The recipe for the jam, piece de resistance of our hosts, was later borrowed or stolen by our own mess sergeant and became a tradition on the tables of the 58th Fighter Control Squadron. Military jellies and jams came in cans, and the cans were opened and placed on the tables (when we got tables) on a help-yourself basis. As the strawberry jam got low in the can, grape jelly was poured in on top, and when this mixture was partly gone apricot jam or orange marmalade was added and so on. After the first year, when the implacable advance of civilization brought in those effete handleless white mugs which all World War II people will remember, they replaced the tin cans, but the mixture remained pretty much the same except that rust no longer gathered in the bottom layer.

But to return once more to the beginning: Our first night was comparatively uneventful. Only one of our eight tents subsided slowly into the tundra because someone had forgotten to put a board under the pole. Only one cot tipped over for lack of similar boards. Only one man woke up shouting that he was being bayonetted in his sleeping bag. (Although the battle was long over, there were still a few Japs in the back country, so our dreamer got a less appreciative audience than he deserved).

We awoke to a changed world. Yesterday's rag-bag of low clouds and luminescent mists had been blown clear over the horizon by a boisterous breeze of about 30 knots, leaving a few tattered banners streaming from the higher peaks. The sky was the high hard blue with a high hard sun that one usually associates with the clearing after a winter blizzard, but the temperature must have been up to 50 degrees fahrenheit, and everything was sparkling with dew of sea-spray or whatever it was that could resist evaporation in a 30-knot breeze. Exhilarated by this apparent change in our fortunes, we shouldered our raincoats and digging utensils and set off on foot up the nearest mountain to dig holes in the mud.

We had apparently worn out our welcome at the 42nd,

for the crawlers of yesterday were droning away at other jobs. In those days before roads the caterpillar tread and the human foot were the only things that could move freely in that great land of rock and gunk, though there were places in the valleys where the cats could and did dig themselves almost out of sight. And in a mysterious mechanical evolution reminiscent of the Age of Reptiles, the sea had spawned the so-called "Alligator," a sort of caterpillar amphibian propelled both on land and water by whirling endless treads.

As we dug on our private mountainside, levelling sites for winterized tents and later more permanent structures, we had a magnificent view of Massacre Bay and the churning alligators, each with a white rooster-tail spray as it droned bulldozer-like from Casco Cove to Murder Point or Alexai Point or the Hog Back or West Massacre Valley or wherever. We who had brought raincoats that first day had thought we were reasonably far-sighted when another weather front moved in that afternoon. (Fronts roll along the Aleutians like bowling balls at an industrial league tournament.) But in wet sticky 50-degree weather, cold moisture collects on the inside of an impervious garment, and at that temperature the raincoated fop quickly becomes colder than the proverbial witch's bosom on Boxing Day. As our Texas sergeant, the John Wayne of the 58th, had predicted, the only thing a G.I. raincoat was good for was to "keep the tundra-juice out of the rook-sacks," when we stored them under our cots. Parkas were the only sensible gear, and for the next 27 months we lived in parkas or jersey-lined jackets, adjusting to the temperature by adding or subtracting the inner layers of undershirts, shirts and sweaters. When we finally moved into Pacific huts with oil stoves and plywood floors, we made other arrangements for stowing our gear, and to this day I cannot remember what happened to the raincoats.

Meanwhile, however, we scraped up the tundra (thinner on the mountainsides than on the valley floors) and gnawed away a mixture of crockery-like schist and coarse brown clay to establish revetments for future buildings, and some of us started our real jobs at the control center: another tent on a bare ridge, where we sat with our feet in boxes of shredded paper for warmth and handled a couple of radios and a batch of field phones. And always in the background was the moaning of the bulldozers, scraping a goat-track up along the hillside to our "ay-ree" as the southern Appalachian troops called it.

Those were the days of foolish pleasures and simple triumphs: setting up and winterizing our own mess-tents, the predecessor of the more palatial building to be known as "Willie Joe's Stew and Goat House;" or switching from latrines under canvas to good solid driftwood four-holers which would resist not only the wind but all efforts to tear them down when we finally got a building with running water and all that that implies.

One of our greatest early triumphs was the timber footbridge which we built in a little valley over a ravine 15 feet deep in the middle of our area. With the first snowfall some clown managed to slide under the handrail into the drink, and the C.O. promptly assigned a detail to keep the treads clear of ice and snow at all times. Shortly thereafter the Old Man took off for Command and Staff School and when he returned two months later he found the bridge still clear of ice and snow; but the ravine had long since drifted over, and the foot-boards were now in a ditch dug five feet down into the snowdrifts.

Other simple pleasures: the raisin-jack factory, the moonshine still of Chichagof Harbor, the bare-handed salmon fishery and the like, may only be alluded to here; and by the end of our first autumn, whiskey and many other trappings of civilization were rapidly undermining the good-clean pleasures of frontier days.

Like all old-timers everywhere who quickly learn to regard newcomers with thinly-veiled contempt, we of that advance detachment of the old 58th looked back on our first months at Alexai Point with a certain fond possessiveness. After the weird Kiska campaign the 7th Division pulled out, dragging the 42nd Engineers in their wake like a kid pulling a toy tractor, leaving the advance elements of our fighter group in full possession and with unchallenged seniority, first on Alexai and ultimately on the whole island. It is true that Willie Joe's Stew and Goat House was never listed among the leading cuisines of the Near Islands, and Massacre Valley was eventually crowded with raw recruits who never heard of the 58th F.C. Squadron; but nevertheless preparations for our ultimate departure were widely and appropriately noted.

On a clear calm October day in 1945, when the first snow pellets had made cinnamon cake of the higher peaks and ridges, the Fighter Group switchboard was swamped with calls from as far off as Navytown at Casco Cove, all worriedly inquiring about the great pillars of brown smoke rising from Alexai to soil the gray-blue empyrean.

"Why, that's only the 58th burning their old latrines," the operators would reply. "They're leaving for home on Friday."

Written by Frank Davis, Cincinnati, Ohio.

Attu Album

A possible Japanese ship.

Japanese barracks.

Underground hut.

Landing craft.

ALL PHOTOS COURTESY R.M. WEIKEL,
MISSOULA, MONTANA

The Williwaw post theater.

Tower, 1944.

Status board of the 58th Fighter Control Squadron.

ALL PHOTOS COURTESY R.M. WEIKEL, MISSOULA, MONTANA

Agattu Island.

Little Falls Cemetery on Attu, built in late 1944.
The extent of the development on Attu in 1944
can be seen in the background.
COURTESY TOM KEELY, FLUSHING, MICHIGAN

Monument placed on Attu in 1950. It is dedicated
to Col. Yasuyo Yamazaki, commander of Japanese
troops during the battle in May 1943. He was killed along with most of his command.
REEVE ALEUTIAN AIRWAYS, BOB REEVE COLLECTION

A monument erected by a Japanese delegation to Attu in 1953. It designates the high water mark of the Japanese counterattack, which was stopped by an engineering battalion on May 29, 1943.

USN NH 69570

COURTESY REEVE ALEUTIAN
AIRWAYS

A large naval gun brought to Kiska for the defense by Japanese forces. NA 80-G-80384

CHAPTER TEN
KISKA

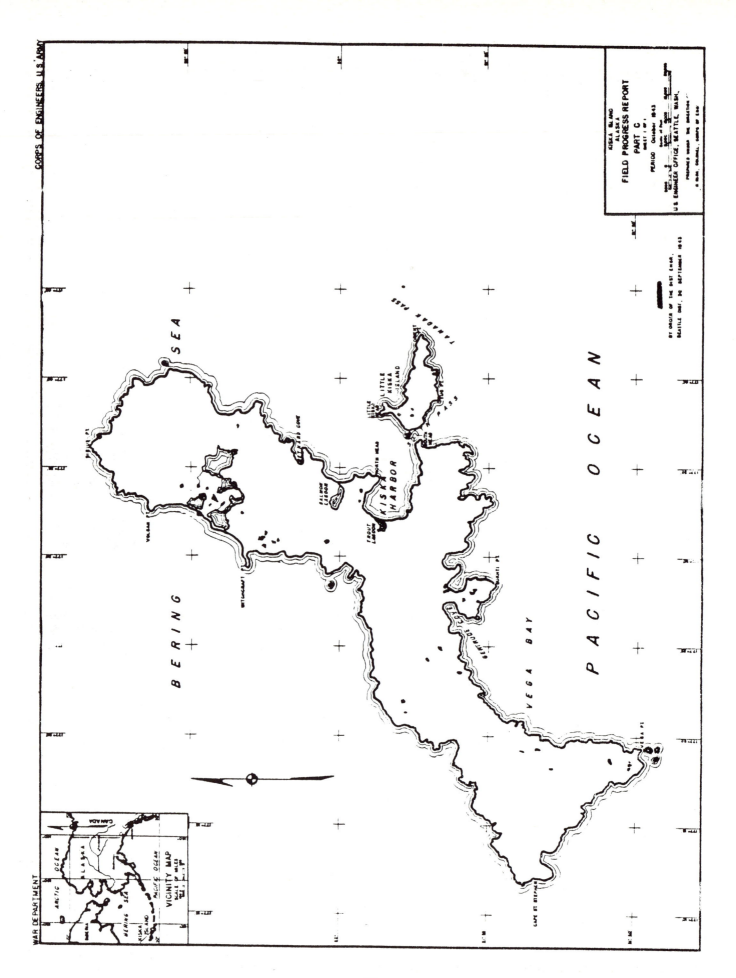

William C. House and the Kiska Weather Station

William C. House was a petty officer in charge of the 10-man Navy weather station which had arrived on Kiska in late 1941. In the early morning hours of June 7, 1942, the Japanese forces occupied the island and the Navy men tried to escape into the fog. House, who was lightly dressed, was separated from his men, and by the next day he had moved higher up into the mountains on the west side of the island and hid in a cave.

He was to spend the next 48 days in this area, hiding from the Japanese occupiers and living on plants and earthworms. His weight went down to 80 pounds, and after fainting on the 48th day, decided he would have to surrender to survive.

The next day he walked up to an enemy gun position. He was treated with some kindness, but after experiencing many dangerous American air raids on the expanding Japanese facilities, he left the island on September 20, 1942.

On the Japanese ship *Nagata Maru* with him were 39 Aleuts taken from Attu. House survived nearly 39 months as a prisoner of war, fighting starvation and disease and dodging bombing raids at Yokahama and Kamaishi, where he was a slave laborer in a steel mill.

All 10 of the captured weather station men were liberated from prison at the end of the war. House received a bronze star in 1946 for burning communication ciphers before the Japanese could capture them. He retired as a full commander from the U.S. Navy in 1959 and now lives in Valley Center, California, where he grows grapes.

Two of the 10-man weather detachment taken captive by the Japanese. USMC 315172

The Navy weather detachment on Kiska on Dec. 26, 1941, six months before they would be captured by the Japanese. Left to right: RM 3/C Christiansen and AERM 3/C Winfry operating radio equipment. USN NH 70058

William "Charles" House at his home in California.

The following captured Japanese photos give the viewer some idea of the occupation of Kiska.

Japanese battle flag being raised on Kiska, June 6, 1942. USMC 315168 & JRC

Rear Adm. Katsuzo Akiyama, commander of Japanese naval forces at Kiska. JRC

Troops exercising. JRC

Japanese troops netting fish. JRC

A Japanese gun crew poses for their moment of history. JRC

Anti-aircraft guns. JRC

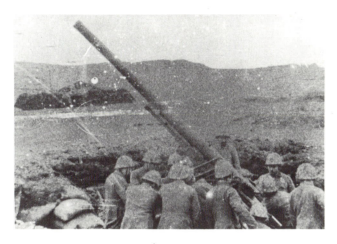
Anti-aircraft gun crew. JRC

One of the large naval guns brought to the island for defense. JRC

The Japanese spent over one year building up their defenses of Kiska, such as these structures and gun emplacements. JRC

Kimikawa Maru, seaplane tender, in Kiska Harbor with a near miss from an aerial attack. JRC

A Japanese transport burning in Kiska Harbor after a B-24 attack. JRC

Two views of a E13A "Jake" Japanese Navy reconnaissance plane in Kiska Harbor. Note the biplane in the background.
JRC & USAF #169793

Float planes in Kiska Harbor. JRC   Unloading a "Jake" at Kiska. AAC

The cruiser *Tama* and destroyer *Akalsuka* off Kiska during the June 1942 occupation of the islands.
NA 73041 & 73049

Conference of U.S. and Canadian Army and Navy chiefs before the Kiska invasion. Sitting left to right: Adm. Francis W. Rockwell, USN, Com. Phib. Pac; Vice Adm. Thomas C. Kinkaid, USN, Com. Northern Pacific Naval Forces; Maj. Gen. Charles H. Corlett, USA, Com. Gen. USA troops on Kiska; Lt. Gen. Simon B. Buckner, USA, Com. Alaska Defense Command. Standing left to right: Cmdr. Robert L. Dennison, USN, Chief of Staff to Adm. Rockwell; Capt. Oswald S. Colclough, USN, Chief of Staff to Adm. Kinkaid; Col. Carl I. Jones, USA, Chief of Staff to Maj. Gen. Corlett; Brig. Gen. J.H. Ready, USA, one of Gen. Corlett's unit Com.; Brig. Gen. E.D. Post, USA, Chief of Staff to Lt. Gen. Buckner.
AMHA

Conference of U.S. and Canadian Army and Navy chiefs before the landings on Kiska.
AMHA

French Canadian troops from Montreal and Quebec that participated in the Kiska operation.
ASL, U.S. ARMY SIGNAL CORPS

A B-24 low-level attack with delayed action bombs against anti-aircraft gun emplacements.
REEVE ALEUTIAN AIRWAYS

Getting ready for the invasion on board one of the many ships of the task force. NA 80-G-103712

Low-level raid by a B-24 on Kiska. In the left background is an airfield under construction. To the right is Salmon Lagoon. The trenches connect gun batteries. The photo shows the impact of bombs bouncing toward Japanese in the foreground gun emplacement.
REEVE ALEUTIAN AIRWAYS

This aerial photo taken by Pat Wing Four on June 18, 1942, shows the extent of the enemy landings just 11 days earlier. Landing barges can be seen in the harbor, along with a build up of supplies and huts apparently already constructed.
NA 80-G-11691

This aerial photo taken sometime later, possibly in 1943, shows the midget sub base and ramp (center), float planes in the harbor and considerable building activity. AAC

Landing on Kiska, August 1943. NA 80-G-78481

Description of "Kiri Leaf."

"The Kiri Leaf Falls" ("Kira Hitcha") is the title of a famous Japanese play by Tsubouchi, foremost Japanese playwright of the Meiji Era. It depicts the downfall of the house of Toyotomi immediately before the establishment of the Tokugawa regime in 1603. At the end of the play a leaf does fall, a symbol of the end of the hopes of the characters who tried to seize power for themselves.

Translation: *In large letters:* The Kiri Leaf Falls. Its fall is the ill omen of the inevitable downfall of militarism. With the fall of one Kiri Leaf comes sadness and bad luck.

Reverse side: Before Fall comes, the raining bombs of America, just like Kiri Leaves fluttering to the ground, will bring sad fate and misfortune.

This leaflet plays on the superstitiousness of the Japanese soldier. Over 60,000 copies of this leaflet were dropped over Attu and Kiska before troops landed on Attu, May 11, 1943.
COURTESY IRVING P. PAYNE

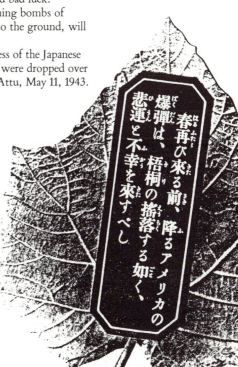

FH-1

8/19/43 at Adv I & I Det. Hq., Kiska Harbor, for Force Hq.

COMPLETE TRANSLATION: Found in vicinity of Kiska Harbor, near Radio Station.

Confidential

AO Defense Unit (BUTAI) Instruction Number One.

July 8, 1943

(Stamped in red): Military Secret

Commanding Officer of the AO Defense Unit - AKIYAMA, Katsuzo

Regarding Operation "K", orders to your subordinates:

According to recent orders this unit will discontinue the defense of Kiska Island, and with the North Sea Garrison Units (SHUBITAI) will transfer its entire force at once to "X" area.

For a period of little over a year, since occupying this Kiska Island in June of last year, you have, under a very difficult situation, delayed the enemy's counter-attack with a small number of troops. You have increasingly strengthened the defense, maintained an unconquerable position and finally succeeded in preventing any enemy interference, and also displayed the power of the Imperial Navy. The success in the duty to secure Kiska Island was due to the bravery, courage, and endurance of all of you under the Emperor.

(A page missing)

It is necessary to prevent disorder and arguments by governing, in an orderly manner and under a strict military discipline, the actions of each individual. The experience you have undergone during the past year on this island, engaging in severe battle day after day and striving to strengthen the defense of the island under severe head-winds and cold, is an honor to the Imperial Navy. It is useless to die recklessly, but the above mentioned material should be used to destroy the enemy in the future. In conclusion I would like to give my deepest regards to those brave men who died gloriously on the field and to the spirit of those who unfortunately died of illnesses.

—-END—-

In Alaska during World War II, I commanded a radio intelligence company, whose mission was then highly classified. We were to intercept all radio transmissions in and out of the Japanese-occupied islands of Attu and Kiska, not only copying all radio traffic, but locating the stations by radio direction finders, breaking their codes and reporting all findings daily to the Chief-of-Staff, G-2, Alaska Command and Commander-in-Chief, North Pacific Fleet.

On June 1, 1942, I reported to G-2 that a large task force of the Japanese 5th Fleet was moving into Alaskan waters. On June 2, enemy carriers were reported less than 400 miles south of Kiska. The following two days, carrier-based enemy bombers attacked Dutch Harbor. June 6, the enemy's N-3 MIZURI Special Task Landing Party, composed of 500 marines and commanded by Lt. Cmdr. Muki Hifumi, occupied Kiska Island.

During August I reported that the enemy had reinforced the Kiska garrison with a second landing party of about 1,000 marines, plus about 500 civilian construction workers. They redesignated Kiska the 51st Naval Base and placed it under the command of Rear Adm. Akiyama.

August 31, 1942, I landed with the U.S. Task Force on Adak Island and set up what was known as the Alaska Intelligence Center (AIC). This center received all intercepted radio traffic and radio direction finder bearings, not only from our Alaska stations, but also from our stations along the west coast of the mainland and from Hawaii. Through traffic analysis, plotting of bearings and the actual breaking of codes, we knew just about every operator by his first name. All intelligence gathered was reported to G-2 and Naval Headquarters on Adak.

On September 21, 1942, I reported that the 301st Independent Infantry Battalion under command of Major Hozumi Matsutoshi had withdrawn from Attu. This was verified the next day by air reconnaissance. The next radio traffic intercepted relative to this unit was on October 1 out of Kiska.

On November 25, intercepted radio traffic out of Paramushiro indicated a convoy was moving towards Attu. In early December, radio traffic out of Kiska indicated that the 302nd Infantry Battalion and the 32nd Independent Antiaircraft Unit were now established on Kiska.

With the American occupation of Amchitka five months after our landing on Adak, aerial reconnaissance and bombing missions over Kiska and Attu picked up and surface vessel radio traffic between the Kurlie Islands and Kiska and Attu was almost nonexistent. Also the construction of the runways on Kiska and Attu was interrupted, and these runways never were completed.

In April of 1943 tactical command of Kiska and Attu was transferred from the Japanese 5th Fleet to Lt. General Higuchi Kiichiro, commanding General, Imperial Northern Army, Sapporo, Hokkaido.

On the morning of July 9, 1943, I reported that an evacuation order, dated July 8, had been intercepted. On July 29, I reported that all radio traffic in and out of Kiska had ceased and it had been evacuated by what appeared to be about seven submarines. Naval Headquarters on Adak received this information with scepticism. Admiral Kinkaid said, "Impossible, we have a ring of steel around the island."

August 13, 1943, I joined the Joint Task Force of 30,000 Americans and 5,000 Canadian military personnel for the invasion of Kiska. We landed on August 15, the Americans in the south sector between Quisling Cove and Lief Cove, and the Canadian troops in the north sector in the area of Wheat and Barley coves.

The plan was a pincer movement, with the allied forces coming in from two directions against the enemy, across the island to the submarine base area in Kiska Harbor. Shortly after landing, enemy contact reports were received, followed by allied casualty reports: The American and Canadian troops mistook each other for the enemy and opened fire.

No enemy troops were encountered. Everything left by the Japanese was booby-trapped, which caused further casualties. The steepness of the Kiska terrain, the limited expanse of good, sand landing areas and the low marshy areas behind the beach bluffs would have made Task Force landings untenable had the enemy held its ground.

Captured documents on Kiska indicated that the enemy evacuated the island by bare or small craft during the night of July 28, to waiting submarines, which in turn took them through the so called "ring of steel" around the island to waiting ships of the Japanese 5th Fleet. They in turn transported the troops to Paramashiro.

Thus ended the 14 months Japanese occupation of the Aleutian Islands, and my eventual return to the "main land."

Based on intercepted radio traffic, and later verified

by captured documents, the following Units were on Kiska:

Navy:
2nd Regiment Special Troops
5th Defense Unit
51st Base Headquarters
5th Medical Unit
Meteorological Unit
26th Submarine Unit

Army:
39th Wireless Unit
51st Communications Unit
302nd and 301st Infantry Battalion
22nd and 32nd Antiaircraft Units
6th Engineer Regiment
301st Engineer Unit
30th Field Hospital
Yasuda Mt. Artillery Unit

Air:
51st Air Base Unit

Much to my disappointment, I found all the communications stations and equipment on the island had been demolished by the Japanese prior to their leaving. Not only was the radio and radar equipment destroyed, so was all mechanized equipment, guns and buildings damaged beyond use.

Kiska was developed far more extensively than Attu. The garrison on Kiska was much different than that on Attu in that Attu was manned almost entirely by the army, while the troops on Kiska were about equal—army & navy. The Navy occupied the Kiska Harbor area, and the army occupied the Gertrude Cove area. All of Kiska's defensive areas were served by a well developed road system. More than 100 vehicles of all types were found on the island. In the harbor area were two machine shops, a foundry and a sawmill. Three complete radio stations, a radar station and an extensive telephone system made up the communications network.

Col. Irving Payne
West Long Branch, New Jersey

AAC

Troops unloading supplies on the beach. AAC

American and Canadian graves. Twenty-nine soldiers were killed accidently by their own comrades. AAC

Interior of the Japanese hospital. NA 80-G-80291

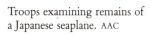

Troops examining remains of a Japanese seaplane. AAC

Japanese shrine at their main camp. NA 80-G-80394

Japanese gun and bunker. The ammunition was left intact due to the hasty evacuation of the island.
NA 80-G-80270

A two-man submarine and pen relatively undamaged from the intense aerial bombing. This sub is still on the island. Several of these were brought to Kiska but never used. AAC

Japanese landing barge.
USA SC 186895

Remains of Japanese facilities on the island. NA 80-G-80754

Interior of a Japanese bunker. Notice the inscription on the wall left by the retreating enemy. AAC

Serving coffee at the first American Red Cross coffee rack on Kiska, August 1943. Task Force Field Director Mat Howard is shown wearing the clothing he came ashore in, days before. The coffee rack was set up alongside a seaplane hangar foundation, which Howard stands on. AUTHOR'S COLLECTION

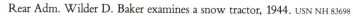

Rear Adm. Wilder D. Baker examines a snow tractor, 1944. USN NH 83698

Kiska Today

Salmon Lagoon.

Kiska Harbor showing the *Nozima Maru*.

Aerial views of Kiska taken by John Cloe, historian of the Alaskan Air Command, 1987.

Remains of the *Borneo Maru* at
Gertrude Cove, 1970.
COURTESY HAROLD WOMBLE,
STOCKTON, CALIFORNIA

The front portion of the
Nozima Maru in Kiska Harbor. After the war a Japanese
salvage company salvaged the
rear section and towed it
toward Japan. On the way a
storm was encountered and
the section sunk.
COURTESY HAROLD WOMBLE,
STOCKTON, CALIFORNIA

Bell of the *Borneo Maru* and Kiska artifacts collected by
Harold Womble, Stockton, California.

One of two 6-inch coastal
artillery pieces still on Kiska.
COURTESY CAPT. N.G. TERRY,
JR., USMC

The first contingent of American troops to land on Shemya were transported with their supplies, ammunition and equipment from Massacre Bay, Attu, by landing barges. In this picture the bulldozer, left of picture, is being used as a "deadman" for holding landing barges next to the beach. Two amphibious tractors, to be used by the engineers, are coming ashore. In the background are some of the tugs and landing barges used in the accomplishment of the movement, June 1, 1943. USA SC-189677

CHAPTER ELEVEN
SHEMYA

Shemya History

During the last days of the battle for Attu, another campaign from Attu was in the making. Brig. Gen. John N. Copeland selected certain of the hardiest troops from the Fourth Infantry Regiment for a landing on tiny Shemya, some 40 miles to the southeast. There were no Japanese on the island at that time. A contingent of Alaska scouts had reconnoitered the island in May and found evidence of a Japanese surveying party which had made tests for an airstrip site. The man in the initial landing party had served in the Aleutians long enough to realize that the perils of natural elements can prove as hazardous as those encountered by engaging the foe. Enemy, or no enemy, the landing was destined to be a difficult one.

Under cover of a thick fog, on May 29, 1943, landing barges loaded with troops from the Fourth Infantry approached the shores of Shemya after six hours of an uncomfortable, sickening voyage over heavy seas.

A dilapidated trappers cabin and two Russian graves were the only signs of former habitation greeting the troops. High waves whipped by lashing winds blew furiously against the jagged shores. The barges tore over partially submerged reefs, ripping open hulls as the craft came to rest atop exposed rocks. Briny ice water flowed between the reaches of the ramps and solid ground. Men waded through the surf burdened with supplies of food and tent material strapped to their backs. The Army had arrived on the island of Shemya. Shelter tents were used to bundle in rather than as shelters until excavations could be dug below the surface as protection against the wind.

A construction program was immediately begun on a 12-hour-per-day schedule. Troops labored, grading the tundra, filling holes with rocks and laying steel mattings for the essential airstrips. After regular duty hours, details were organized involving most of the personnel for the purpose of constructing defense installations. In June 1943, Japan was still a powerful enemy which proved a constant threat.

The first bomber landed on the flat island of Shemya from a mission over the Kuriles on September 11, 1943. It was an unscheduled landing by the B-24 which had taken off from Attu earlier in the day. The plane and crew had been shot up pretty badly, with the pilot losing an arm. Shemya was already beginning to prove its worth.

Work on the airstrip eased up somewhat for the GIs. Civilian construction companies moved crews in to improve on the hurried job initially completed. After that, the soldiers were employed in erecting some substantial living quarters and straightening up defensive installations. The population on this recently deserted stop was swelled by soldiers and civilians. A community began to mushroom from the desolate tundra-covered rock.

Permanent buildings were erected, but like the early tents, they too were constructed in holes as protection against the blowing winds. Pacific huts, prefabricated and shipped in crates, were set up in a day's time. Only the tops of these oval dwellings could be seen above the ground and the protective mounds of dirt. After a few months, a resemblence of civilization grew out of the northern wilds. Recreation facilities kept pace with tactical construction.

Organizational mess halls and recreational huts were constructed as rapidly as possible, until every unit could boast of one in its own area. Roads were improved and electricity and oil stoves were put into the huts. A sewage system was undertaken.

The popular jeep lost its original appearance on Shemya and was turned into a sedan. Because of the weather, these little vehicles were provided with improvised enclosed bodies resembling custom-built automobiles.

Docks were laboriously built and breakwaters installed off what was considered to be the most protected beach on the island. Shortly after the completion of these shipping facilities, a furious storm, lasting from the 11th to the 15th of October 1944, invaded the area. The result of the constant pounding and raging surf, the docks were reduced to kindling and a great part of the breakwater was washed away. This unforeseen happening proved an almost disastrous loss to an island wholly dependent upon shipping for its provisions. Too many men had arrived since the early days of occupation to be supplied by landing craft or parachute, but enough provisions were stored away in warehouses to provide for necessities in case of just such an emergency. To augment these stores, transshipment yards were set up on Attu, 40 miles away, where supplies, bound for Shemya, could be unloaded. Planes and barges shuttled these supplies to the island during the entire winter.

In the meantime, bombers of the 11th Air Force were paying regular visits to the Kuriles. Military and naval installations, along with canneries, furnishing much of Japan's food, were priority targets on these islands.

Shemyaites had heard about Japan's plan to bomb and attack the U.S. with long-range balloons, and pilots in the western Aleutians had been instructed on what to do if they saw one. On January 24, 1945, an unidentified object was spotted at 29,000 feet over Agattu. It proved to be a balloon, presumably sent from Japan. Tracer bullets from the 343rd Fighter Squadron planes sunk the balloon into the sea 25 miles from the southwestern tip of Buldir Island.

On April 13, men of the 343rd on Shemya again had a chance to test their aim. Out of 12 balloons seen over the western Aleutians, nine were shot down.

The most successful raid in the history of the Shemya-based 404th Bombardment Squadron was flown on May 11, 1945. A 12-plane flight, led by Capt. Robert Wichman and Lt. Charles Weniger, found a shipping isle, visible for miles,

Shemya, 1944. Lester H. Best, master sergeant with the 404th Bomb. Squad. and chief photoman, took this aerial photo. He had this to say about it: "Many times we endeavored to make aerial photos of Shemya. Time after time we were unsuccessful, for as we would taxi for takeoff the base would be closed in. After returning from a mission we found this good weather. I luckily had a folding Kodak in my pocket and made this photo." AAC

through a clear sky. Several direct hits were scored on a destroyer escort and much damage was done to shipping in this harbor of Katsoka Naval Base.

On June 19, 1945, Lts. David Long and Paul Clinkenbeard of the 404th flew 2,700 miles over water as far as the island of Urruppu in the Kuriles on a photo reconnaissance mission. They were aloft 15 hours and 30 minutes. This ranked with the longest over-water combat mission flown anywhere in the world.

The enemy knew that the planes attacking them so regularly were Aleutian based, but they couldn't guess what island was their home base.

Shemya was identified merely as APO 729. Its secrecy was well kept despite rumors that Tokyo Rose had referred to the island by name on her radio program a number of times. Japanese submarines patrolled the waters in search of information. One was forced to surface and was sunk just off Shemya's shore. In spite of the vigilance on the part of the enemy, they could still only guess what was going on. Their guess was remarkably inaccurate as is evident by their own action:

1. On a bright moonlit night during the summer of 1943, a flight of Japanese bombers were detected approaching the area of Shemya. It was thought they had gotten wind of the

powerful fortifications on the island, but they dropped their bombs in the waters around Attu. Again they guessed wrong.

2. Toward the end of the war in July 1945, propaganda broadcasts from Tokyo reported that American mountain troops were being trained on Aggatu for an invasion of the northern Kuriles. The Japanese sensed considerable activity in the western Aleutians.

As the island built up, men had more leisure time to spend weaving yarns about their experiences in civilian life and the hardships of Aleutian service. They spoke in the colloquialism of the island. Sudden flurries of snow and wind, reaching velocities in excess of 100 miles an hour, were referred to as "Williwaws." Cots were spoken of as "sacks" and what passed as soil in the Aleutians was called "tundra." Every hut had a pot. In letters written home, Shemya was referred to as "Our Island Paradise." Life on Shemya was a stoic existence from beginning to end. There were bright spots though, such as the time the ground forces had a laugh on the Air Corps when a submarine was spotted by a patrol plane and reported sunk. A dead whale was found in the vicinity a few hours later.

Few who were on the island of Shemya on Sunday, August 12, 1945, will forget what happened that day. Dedication services were being held in the Chapel. Japan was on her last legs. Hirohito and his Premier even then conferred on surrendering. It was a sunny pleasant day and men who'd been on Shemya two years were happier, and yet more serious, than usual as the chaplain prayed; the congregation with bowed heads. Staff officers were tapped quietly on the shoulder and rushed to Post Headquarters. In clipped words, they were told by Brig. Gen. Goodman, island commander, that Shemya had been alerted against Kamikaze attacks as a last desperate gesture by the beaten enemy. Unidentified planes had been picked up by a ship's radar 500 miles southwest of Shemya that morning. Throughout the afternoon and night the Army and the Navy's ships and planes from Adak patrolled the waters of the western Aleutians and toward the Kuriles. The enemy were discouraged by the quantity of our patrol planes or for some other reason never showed up.

The next day, August 13, men of the 404th Bombardment Squadron climbed into their flying suits and took off in their planes to bomb the Kashiwabara staging area on northern Paramushiro. They knew the end of the war was near and hoped against hope that this mission would be their last and that they would never again have to face enemy forces in this war. It was their last mission flown from the Aleutians. The six planes on the flight used airborne radar equipment to bomb the island. Major General Brooks, commander of the 11th Air Force, lead the mission.

One day later, August 14, 1945, the Japanese officially gave in. The sirens on the usually dignified Post Headquarters building blared for 10 minutes. Extra beer rations were given to all soldiers. The next two days were official holidays. Peace came to Shemya.

Among the faces going home for retirement to civilian life in December 1945 was that of Brig. Gen. John B. Goodman, airbase commander. Winter came to Shemya with a raging fury of wind and snow which hit hardest in January to March 1946. Although installations were by this time well prepared for the rigors of weather in the Aleutians, heavy snow was not expected. It started to snow in January and even the 75- to 100-mile-an-hour winds didn't blow it all away. For the next two months a minimum of traffic moved on the island. Engineers battled desperately, working around the clock. Men driving in the storm could see only traces of the road.

Winds blowing at 75 miles an hour for a whole week can make life miserable in many ways. Going to sleep to the tune of a rattling stovepipe and waking up to that same sound isn't very soothing. However, many will remember with pleasure some of the meals prepared in the well under a space heater designed to warm the billets. Sacking in all day was an occupation during that weather.

Constellations began flying from Tokyo to the U.S. via the "Great Circle Route," which passes very near Shemya.

Attu became a sub-base of Shemya. The Air Transport Command put Shemya and Adak on its Great Circle Route to the Far East.

In May 1946 the first woman dependent of a Shemyanite arrived in the person of Mrs. Eleanor Burcky, wife of Maj. Claude Burcky. Quarters were set up for dependents of enlisted men and officers. All who signed to stay overseas became eligible to have their dependents join them. During the ensuing three months the influx continued, even to babies.

From a strictly military point of view, why was Shemya so important? What was its part in winning the war?

1. It provided the major base of operations against the Kuriles, where considerable damage was done by the Air Force bombers.

2. It offered a landing strip to planes flying lend-lease and other strategic materials to our Russian ally.

3. It denied the Japanese:

a. Bases for offensive operation against the United States.

b. Easy access to a prolific fishing area.

c. Freedom of naval movement in the northern Pacific Ocean.

d. Use of numerous troops that were tied up against a possible thrust by the United States from the Aleutians.

4. It provided weather stations for the U.S. Army and U.S. Navy, thereby enabling forecasts of favorable and unfavorable bombing weather for planes operating from bases far south of the Aleutians.

5. It provided a testing ground for various types of clothing, equipment and weapons.

Just how much damage was done in the Kuriles by the 11th Air Force operating from bases in the Aleutians and in conjunction with the Navy can be determined from the following figures: "Reviewing two years of offensive operations, approximately 270 combat missions have been flown, resulting in an incalculable amount of damage to ground targets by bombs, rockets and heavy- caliber machinegun fire, without assistance from friendly fighters, sharpshooting bomber gunners have taken a toll of 109 Japanese aircraft destroyed or damaged in aerial duels. Most of these fighters, and 57 of them were definitely or probably shot down.

"Eighty-seven enemy vessels of all types, by the most conservative estimate, were sunk or damaged severely in Kurile waters. Aleutian-based bombers and search planes accounted for a destroyer escort and a transport, at least three sizeable cargo ships, 22 coastal freighters and numerous picket boats and fishing craft. Light naval units sent a medium freighter, a smaller cargo ship and a sea going tug to the bottom of Okhotsk Sea, probably sunk another small freighter and heavily damaged a fourth. In 12 surface bombardments, naval task forces destroyed or damaged hangars, warehouses, radio stations and ammunition and gasoline dumps at Matsuwa and Paramushiro airstrips."

During the period of January 1, 1945, to August 1945, there was a total of 393 tons of bombs dropped by the 404th Bombardment Squadron. Of this amount, 56.3 percent was dropped by planes using the airborne radar system.

The months of May and June shared the credit for being the busiest months of the year with approximately 88 tons being dropped. The primary target for this period was the Katsoka Naval Base on the island of Shimishu.

These results were achieved despite incredible hazards and handicaps of weather and distances unequalled in other combat zones, at a cost of 16 medium and seven heavy bombers lost in combat to enemy fighters and anti-aircraft fire. The normal complement of these 23 aircraft was 143 officers and men. No damage was inflicted, nor a single casualty suffered, on any of our naval vessels by enemy action in Kurile operations.

World War I ace Eddie Rickenbacker visited Shemya on his inspection tour of the Aleutian area. AAC

Outfits Serving on Shemya During WWII

Compiled by the Shemya WWII Veterans Association

1st Photo Flight
8th Signal Radio Maintenance Team
Advance Command Post, 11th Air Force
11th Fighter Squadron
11th Weather Squadron
18th Engineers (Combat) Regiment
24th Base Headquarters & Air Base Squadron
32nd Service Squadron
54th Fighter Squadron
65th Anti-Aircraft, Battery B
71st Infantry
119th Army Alaskan Communication System
122nd Army Anti-Aircraft Battery
128th Infantry
174th MP Company
177th Engineers Construction Battalion
344th Fighter Squadron
372nd Service Squadron
397th Base Headquarters & Air Base Squadron
400th Base Headquarters & Air Base Squadron
404th Bomb Squadron
408th Signal Company Service Group
464th Base Headquarters & Air Base Squadron
1018th Signal Company Service Group
1128th Quartermaster Company
1910th Quartermaster Truck Company
9427th TSU Signal Corp
Alaskan Transportation Service
Army Air Base Service Unit
Battery E, 40th CA (Harbor Defense)
329th Station Hospital
Navy Port Battalion

VPB-122 Navy
2nd Photo Charting Squadron
11th Air Force Finance Detachment
11th Bomber Command, Headquarters and Headquarters Squadron
11th Flight Control Squadron
15th Tow Target Squadron
21st Bombardment Squadron
23rd Service Group
28th Bombardment Group, Headquarters and Headquarters Squadron
122th Army Ground Forces Band
260th Port Battalion (TC)
279th Coast Artillery
364th Infantry
444th Signal Heavy Construction Battalion (AVN)
478th Truck Company
641st Anti-Aircraft Artillery (Automatic Weapons) Battalion
713th Air Raid Warning Squadron
861st Signal Service Company (AVN)
877th Port Company—ATS
880th Port Battalion
890th Chemical Company (Air Operation)
1084th Signal Service Company (AVN)
1740th Ordnance Supply and Maintenance Company (AVN)
2055th Ordnance Company (AVN)
Naval Construction Battalion
Provisinoal Infantry Regiment, including elements of 37th, 53rd, 153rd and 198th Infantry

"Mission" to the Soviet Union

BY JOHN R. SMITH

It all began with a neutrality pact between Japan and the USSR, signed April 13, 1941, which made the USSR a neutral nation to the United States and Japan in the Far East and came into effect when Japan attacked Pearl Harbor. The agreement remained in effect for exactly four years until April 13, 1945. By the rules of the Geneva Convention and international law, the USSR was to intern American flyers if they were forced down in Soviet territory.

These were not planned or scheduled missions. They happened for various reasons, such as battle damage, fuel shortage and dead and wounded on board.

The first to be affected by this condition was Major Edward J. York and his crew on a B-25 from Doolittle's Raiders on April 18, 1942. They were forced to land at Vladivostok, USSR, due to lack of fuel. The last was Captain Raymond D. Livingston, also on a B-25 on July 16, 1945, from the 77th Bomb. Squadron out of Attu. In the meantime, 34 other planes and crews repeated the journey. Thirty of these came from the 77th Bomb. Squadron from Attu, 404th Bomb. Squadron from Shemya and from the Navy Fleet Air Wing 4, based on Attu. The other four were B-29s from the South Pacific.

The two main landing areas were Vladivostok (B-29s) and Petropovlosk on the Kamchatkan Peninsula, Siberia, located 7½ miles north of Japan's northern Kurile Islands. The men involved in this can tell some stories of how and why they ended up in the Soviet Union.

This is the story of one crew, that of Lt. Donald Taylor of the 404th Bomb. Squadron, Shemya on November 17, 1944. I was the radar operator on that crew.

The targets were Karabuzaki and Suribachi Air Fields on the southern tip of Paramushiro, the Japanese "Gibraltor of the North," some 800 miles from Shemya.

Six planes were in the initial formation. Three led by Captain William Beale and three by Lt. Corbin Terry. Some time out of our base, Lt. William Salzman's plane developed engine trouble. Captain Beale, Mission Leader, told him to return to the base. The remaining five planes flew in a dense pea-soup fog the rest of the way. I kept our plane (Lt. Taylor's) in visual contact with the formation by radar to avoid running into a plane or vice-versa.

Landfall was made on the Southern tip of Kamchatka. A swing was made to the south along the east shore of Paramushiro. We continued to climb with a 5 plane "V" formation. South of Karabu, a turn was made to start the bomb run heading north. Midway through the banking turn, Taylor's plane was hit by fighters that attacked the formation out of the sun. An exploding 20 mm. shell hit Lt. Taylor in the arch of his left foot and continued down and hit the navigator in the left hand. The navigator had just been hit by a 7.7 mm. shell in his left thigh.

Lt. Taylor headed for cloud cover. Co-pilot Lt. Ray Yelland took control of the plane while Lt. Taylor was being treated. Lt. Taylor took over controls again and headed for "Petro" (Petropavlock). At the northern end of Paramushiro, 2 fighters were waiting. One pass was pressed, with the only damage done being more holes in the wing and some circuits shot out.

A fast moving weather front from the north stopped any further attacks. The front developed into a blizzard. I turned on the radar with no luck. It had been shot out. We had no way to keep contact with land. We were lost. With two engines out we couldn't climb to get above the storm.

Lt. Taylor, with a silver dollar size hole in his left foot, stayed at the controls for an hour and a half. He found a hole in the storm which he descended through to find us over a long flat coastal beach area. One pass was made to look over the terrain. We bellied in on the second pass, to a nice soft landing. We were still carrying 30 100-lb. bombs since the bomb-bay doors were jammed shut with only a six inch opening.

We all piled out of the plane, and removed the pilot through a waist window. Now it was really snowing. We looked the plane over. It was fine, we had a home; for how long we didn't know.

No attempt was made to contact our base as the plane was full of gas fumes; a spark from the radio operator's key could cause an explosion.

Little sleep was to be had that night. The storm raged all night. In the morning, the first job was to clean 16 inches of snow off the wings and the fuselage, for identification from the air. We found at least 75 holes in the plane. Radio contact was tried but the signal was weak. It was discovered in the attempt to remove Lt. Taylor, a toggle switch was pushed to the "on" position, which drained the battery. Corporal Ben Bendorovich, the radio operator, said it would recharge a little on its own so Lt. Taylor said to wait.

We had no food and a small amount of medical supplies. The survival chest contained but two hatchets. Lt. Taylor asked for three men to go north the next day to look for civilization. Flight Officer Leo Lodahl, Corporal Tex Burnett and I volunteered. We took off at day break. It was tough going because of the deep snow. We made 25 miles and were stopped by a swift mountain stream and decided to return to the plane. We were stopped by another storm, this time freezing rain.

We had passed a pile of stacked telephone poles earlier. We decided to wait out the storm there. It was a make-shift shelter from the rain but with leakage. With a hatchet we were able to cut wood from the poles to build a fire.

It had turned dark by now and Tex got sick. Leo and I stayed awake that night and kept up a good fire to keep us warm and somewhat dry, as well as to serve as a signal fire.

By daybreak the rain stopped and we started back to the plane. Upon arriving we learned Bendorovich had made contact with the home base and a radio bearing was shot on us. Our people knew we were alive, and had an idea as to our location. Lodahl and I rested that day and took off again this time with Corporal Martin Lakin, who also spoke Russian. This time we were equipped with a rubber raft. We found the stream was too swift to cross, so back to the plane we went. Leo and I had already walked 100 miles in two days.

The next day four more men of our crew went south with the raft, only to be turned back by a 200 ft. cliff.

While our latest recon party was gone, Captain Beale, on orders from home base, had departed on a rescue/supply mission with a 404th B-24. He was successful in locating us and in dropping food, medical supplies, sleeping equipment, blankets plus other survival equipment.

I was in the flight deck area sending out "SOS" on the "Gibson Girl." A cold chill came over me and I looked up to the north and saw Captain Beale's plane coming down the beach at 200 ft. altitude. I notified the rest of the men. Captain Beale made four passes over us, dropping supplies by parachute. One chute hit the water and was lost. Another with a 24-volt battery was dropped 1200 yards north and was never found. A walky-talky was dropped to contact Captain Beale, which proved unsuccessful. But the food and medical and survival equipment did reach us and probably, as we hoped, saved our lives.

Captain Beale circled 4 miles off the beach for 1½ hours waiting for contact, then returned to base; needless to say we ate that night and slept in sleeping bags.

With no battery, it was necessary to dig out the buried auxiliary generator, which was located on the underside of the plane. This was done only to discover the insulator on the spark plug had been hit. By using a plug from one of the engines, adjusting the gap, and a day of cranking, it started. Benny hooked it up to the radio and contacted base. With contact with base and plenty of food and medicine we decided to sit and wait, knowing contact had been made with "Petro" and a rescue party was in the making. Our morale rose 110%. Taylor, for the first time in five days, smiled, but was still in severe pain.

We waited and waited, while Benny kept in contact with base. On the 13th day, a Russian ship was sighted off shore. They were attempting to launch a life boat but the seas were too rough. So they turned and headed north. Later that afternoon a small Russian plane flew over us, dropped a No. 10 can of "Spam" and a note to watch to the north for three flares and to answer with two of our own. At dusk they came and we responded.

We started to bundle up supplies, food, cigarettes, etc., to take with us. At nine p.m. they arrived, six Russian soldiers with machine guns and two horses, with a Soviet Lt. in charge. Corporals Martin Lakin and Bendorovich, both of whom spoke Russian, did the talking. Lt. Taylor was loaded with morphine. He and Flight Officer Ed Wheeler were put on the horses, which were slightly larger than Shetland Ponies. We also dragged along the rubber raft. After 12 hours and 50 miles we came to an outpost, where we were given a bowl of watered down soup and were allowed to rest for half an hour. Then we were off again. This time Lt. Taylor was on a stretcher. Wheeler, one hour from the plane said, "Hell, I'm no cowboy, I'm from Pennsylvania," and got off his horse and walked.

This time it was only 15 miles to a cove where a ship (apparently a mine-sweeper) was waiting. It was difficult boarding as the seas were still very rough. But we made it, although very wet. Our bundles of supplies were taken for inspection, supposedly to be returned later. They weren't, and years later I found out this was normal procedure with internees that landed at "Petro."

The wounded were taken to the ship's dispensary. The rest of us went below deck to be fed more watered down stew. Then four or five hours of interrogation, with the Soviets demanding to know the whole operation in the Aleutians and the Kuriles. They got nothing. This irked them and they left only to return an hour later with the same song. This went on for hours, what they ended up with was name, rank and serial number. They said as allies our government wanted them to know everything. They weren't, of course, an ally of the U.S. in the Pacific area. They protested to our embassy in Moscow every time a plane went to "Petro" or flew over Russian air space. Some of our bomb runs began over the southern tip of Kamchatka. They fired flak at our planes heading to "Petro" as well as on many planes near Kamchatka. One B-25 was even shot down with the entire crew killed.

At midnight we were given bunks to sleep in. Some men removed their high altitude flying boots only to find them gone in the morning. They were left with only boot liners for footwear.

We docked at "Petro" December 1, 1944. We were taken to a meeting hall where a breakfast was set up. Good, according to their standards; then to a wooden building with bunks and wooden springs. This was home for 1½ months. We had bed bugs for company. Food was scarce and awful, all very starchy. We washed in the snow, sanitary facilities consisted of an outside "one holer" with no toilet tissue. We had nothing to do but look at each other; we were all talked out.

December 6, 1944, we were joined by another 404th crew, headed by Lt. Robert Weiss. Now there were 25 of us, minus the two in the hospital. This gave us some new faces to talk to.

On January 13, 1945, we left our "home," picked Taylor

and Wheeler up at the hospital, boarded a C-47 with skis for landing gear and headed for Magadan on the northeast shore of the Sea of Okhotsk. When we landed the temperature was −74 degrees F. We were taken to a building with a large room set up with beds. After a few hours we were led to a dining room set up with four foot square tables. At each table was a Russian officer, no doubt Intelligence, who spoke English. We watched our tongues.

The meal was seven courses with Vodka between each course. Some men got real "loaded." When we went to bed the bed bugs came out in force. The dinner for a change was tasty. They eat caviar like we eat potatoes.

The stay at Magadan was two days, then it was off for Khabarovsk, north of Vladivostok. We were housed at a rest resort for Russian officers from the "Eastern Front." Conditions here were well above par compared to earlier experiences. Food was good and plentiful. We saw movies and had our first real recreation in three months. Sledding and skiing. It was only −40 degrees F. now!

We stayed here until January 24, 1945, when we boarded a train for a 12 day trip on the Trans-Siberian Railway. The cars were crude, the seats served as bunks at night. Upper bunk was nothing but a normal passage door in a home (2′8″ × 6′8″) held level by chains, with no ladder to climb up. Here the bed bugs reappeared. On the whole it was an interesting trip, and educational.

It took us through the poorest area of the Soviet Union. Poverty was common. Russian people dressed in rags from head to toe were everywhere. At railroad depots they begged for food and sold hot water for tea. Many of them were minus a leg or arm, sometimes both. Yet this area was the center of the USSR industrial might, with steel mills and factories everywhere, going full blast. Planes, tanks and military hardware could be seen for miles. Several times our train was put on a siding so supply trains could pass heading to the far east. Russia was preparing for a long war with Japan. The A-bomb was not known of at this time.

Russia's weakest point was on this route also. The southern tip of Lake Baikal, the largest fresh water lake in the world, contained more water than our Great Lakes combined. The route around the southern shore was a mass of tunnels, carved out of the mountains. A Japanese air strike that could have closed two or three tunnels, would cut eastern Siberia off from the rest of the country as it was the only way of transportation across the country to the Far East. It no doubt would have been Japan's first move in the event of a war with Russia. Needless to say, it was heavily fortified.

Our destination on this leg was Tashkent, 600 miles north of the Soviet-Iranian border, the main internment camp.

We arrived at Tashkent February 5, 1945. This is when my anxiety rose to a fever pitch. At last I was going to see old friends from the 77th Bomb. Squadron and Navy crews from Attu. I knew close to 200 men should have been there

through my knowledge during my eight months with the 77th.

When we arrived at the camp, it was empty. I asked the same question at all stops across Siberia: "Where are the others?" and got the same answer: "The next camp." Then I asked myself, "How long are we going to be in this God-forsaken country?"

Our first meal was breakfast, two fried eggs; we all said, "This is great!" Not so! Meals resumed as terrible, goat meat, rice laced with goat grease, starchy dough-balls, with no milk or vegetables.

On our arrival, the key to the supply room was given to Lt. Weiss, the senior officer in charge, and supplies were very low. There wasn't enough toothpaste to last a month, no brushes, no toilet tissue to go around. Efforts were made to contact our embassy in Moscow to get more supplies. Russia's NKVD turned this down.

The housing was adequate, but we were still plagued with bed bugs. (I should mention here that throughout our stays and travels, most of us developed dysentery and diarrhea, which plagued us and made life additionally miserable. These persisted until after we reached Iran.) We found homemade softballs and bats, which gave us some recreation. But armed guards were always around, which made our men very uneasy.

In eastern Siberia the Red Army was in charge; at Tashkent the NKVD was. It was like two different worlds—from so-so to bad.

Three of our men were placed in solitary for violating camp rules and restrictions. These we were never told about.

In April of 1945 we were joined by Lt. Kenneth Elliot and crew, another 404th crew. Lt. Taylor was still in the hospital. He finally joined us in late April. It was a blessing to have him back. He engineered some changes in American command that were needed. Lt. Edward Miller, a weatherman, was given command by virtue of outranking Lt. Weiss. Interior things ran smoother.

In early May 1945 we were joined by Naval Lt. John W. Powers and crew. There were 43 men in camp now. Lt. Powers took command and things remained the same. Officers removed rank insignias; we were family on a first name basis.

A strange incident happened at Tashkent that has kept me wondering for 40 years. When we arrived at the camp we were greeted by a woman interpreter in her forties. She was known as "Mama" by the internees. She had been a mother to over 200 of us.

At our first meal, she sat at the table with our three top officers. They talked in low tones. They did this for two days. The third day "Mama" disappeared. All that remained was her small white poodle. She was replaced by another woman. We asked where "Mama" was and got a silent answer. And the poodle turned up missing by the end of the week.

Our officers informed us that "Mama" had discussed an escape plan with them, in case anybody wanted to try it. It was then that we assumed they had been overheard, and that is why "Mama" came up missing. What happened to her is anybody's guess. I have mine.

May 23, 1945 started out like a normal day. We went to breakfast of rice and goat grease, and on leaving the dining room you could feel a change. No guards, gates were open. We all stayed outside the U-shaped 20 room building. Something was in the air, what we didn't know, but it was there.

Then we saw a figure walking up the road and into the camp. As he came closer we saw the gold oak leaves of a U.S. Army major. We saluted him and he introduced himself as Major Paul Hall. The first thing he did was break out a carton of Chesterfields, his brand, but we didn't care. They were American cigarettes! Then a jeep drove up with two sacks of mail for us, our first in months. The mail was just for Taylor's and Weiss's crews; Elliott's and Powers' crews were not allowed to write until they arrived in Tashkent, which didn't allow time for mail and return.

The rest of the day was spent reading letters from home and learning of brothers missing in action and killed in action, parents who had passed away and the ever present "Dear John" letters.

At supper Major Hall told us we were moving to a new camp, but not saying where. We had mixed feelings about it but we were going to move and that was the main thing.

On May 24, 1945 after a late supper and under the cover of darkness we got aboard Studebaker trucks and left the camp. We arrived at a railroad depot outside of Tashkent and got aboard a train car like at Khabarovsk, in eastern Russia. This took us to Ashkabad near the Iran border. It was a two-day trip. It was then that Major Hall told us of our destination, Tehran, Iran. We all gave a sigh of relief; some cried.

Upon reaching Ashkabad and under the cover of darkness again we boarded trucks. It was a "hairy" night, crossing the border, hair-pin turns that had to be made in forward and reverse movements to within four or five inches of the road's edge. From there it was straight down for 2000 ft. This went on all night.

In the morning we roared out onto the desert floor. Freedom was not in sight yet, due to the border of Iran being moved further south for military reasons. We still had border check points that had to be reached at a certain time for clearance by the NKVD. We made them all on time. Stops were made to give all a chance to sleep, mainly the drivers. We had one more race to an oasis that had fresh water. Our water was low as the trucks became overheated and needed a drink too. If we missed a time deadline the water supply would have been gone. We maintained our schedule and GI cans were filled as were canteens.

This is when a humorous aspect happened. At Tashkent we were blessed with the birth of two pups, by a camp dog. By the time we left they were a month or two old, two bundles of fur. We asked Major Hall if we could take them along, the answer was a **flat no**! We didn't hear him and smuggled them out. The Major never found out until we were in the middle of the desert in Iran. He was furious, but said we can't leave them here. They safely rode with us all the way to Tehran. We couldn't see them ending up in a Russian stew.

On the desert floor it was hot like 120 degrees F., even worse inside. The trucks were enclosed in canvas, some of which ended up as shorts.

On the fifth day out of Tashkent we ground to a halt. Major Hall told us all to get out. We were on a small hill outside of Camp Amirabad, Tehran headquarters of the Persian Gulf command. We saw the American flag flying. Ahead was freedom; Russia was behind us and for the first time we rode without canvas cover into the camp.

We were driven to the base hospital where we were deloused with DDT, then to a shower for the first time for our crew in 7½ months. The two pups got the same treatment and were turned over to a hospital orderly who took them to the mess hall where no doubt they became mess hall mascots.

Major Hall turned us over to two American intelligence officers, and then left. We never saw him again.

After showering, our old clothes were taken and burned after a search for anything that would identify where we had been. We were issued clean khakis and shoes that fit and then came ice cold Coke and beer, and briefing on security measures. Then a brief medical exam, showing we all had lost an average of 35 pounds. Then came the chow: roast chicken, roast beef, baked ham, vegetables, fresh salad and gallons of milk. What a feast! We were locked into a wing of the hospital. We could care less, we were free. A movie was shown. A food cabinet was left for us to munch on; then to bed for the first real night's sleep in months. This was just short of Heaven.

In the morning, it was bacon and eggs, donuts, sweet rolls and coffee and more milk. Then more briefing on security, with signing of security affidavits. This was jammed down our throats, because the group ahead of us was turned back at the Russian border because of a security leak. That Mr. Stalin didn't like.

At dinner, it was steak, mashed potatoes, etc. We got the "Red Carpet" treatment.

During the next afternoon we were bused to the air base where two C-54s were waiting. On board each plane were one intelligence officer, one doctor, a flight nurse and an FBI agent. We were "Top Secret" all the way.

The C-54s were to take us to the States with a few stops on the way. The first was Cairo, in north Africa. It ended up as a sight-seeing tour, over the Holy Land, the Dead Sea, Mecca, around the pyramids and over the Nile. Upon landing at Cairo, to eat and refuel, the "Red Carpet" came out again. For different reasons, a radio message was sent from Tehran with "Top Secret Orders" for meals and refueling for crews and personnel. The General at Persian Gulf Command apparently looked at this as a way toward promotion. We were met with staff cars and taken to the officers' club, where a meal fit for a king was laid out. Nobody of importance was present. After eating, the staff cars were gone, and in their place were convoy trucks to return us to the planes. The General said, "Major, if you come this way again, I want to know who is on board." The Major said, "You run your base your way, I'll run Intelligence my way!"

Our next main stop was Casablanca with refueling and food, after stops at Tripoli and Algiers.

At Casablanca they met us with staff cars and took us to the Anfa Hotel, site of the Casablanca conference between Franklin D. Roosevelt and Winston Churchill. This was housing for Colonels and above in the area. They were moved out for two days. The "Red Carpet" came out again. Here there were more security briefings. This was getting to be "old crow." We were given a partial pay here. Food and lodging overnight, then it was the USA the next day with stops for food and fuel in the Azores and Bermuda. June 1, 1945 we touched down at Andrews AFB in Washington, D.C. where we received coffee and donuts and Red Cross kits.

We were taken to Fort Meade, Maryland where a comedy of errors developed. Due to security we couldn't say one word as to where we had been. The local officials were hard pressed to handle incoming personnel who "didn't exist" according to regulations! In time, a Colonel stepped in and "waived" the problems aside, clearing the way.

The Colonel told us to go to the PX and get what we needed as we had to be off the base by 5:00 p.m. This is where we all split up for various bases to have furlough papers cut. Five of us went to Fort Sheridan. There we ran into one of the FBI agents we picked up at Tehran. He got lost in a hurry.

We were given 60 day relay in route. June 3, 1945 I was home in Minnesota.

It was a memorable experience, one never to be forgotten. Of the 291 men and two dogs involved only about ½ remain alive at this writing, August 2, 1985.

Four men from Taylor's crew are known to be alive. I see Lt. Taylor every winter as he has a winter home 15 miles south of me. We are in constant touch all year. Not enough can be said about radioman Benny Bendorovich. He was a lifesaver while on the beach. The rest of the crew, though young, were a great bunch of troupers. It was only their 3rd mission. Captain William Beale deserves a lot of credit, along with his crew, for finding us and dropping supplies. His plane could have been shot down by Russian or Japanese fighters, as his presence there violated Russia's air space and neutrality, as well as being close to Japanese territory.

My thanks also to Major General Davenport Johnson and Major Jack T. Loney for their help. And last but not least to my pilot and closest friend for 40+ years, Don Taylor. His flying skill saved the lives of 12 men. He was born to fly then and still is today, in his own private twin engine jet.

This is my story.

Kurile Islands

CHAPTER TWELVE
LEGACY OF THE WAR

The Alaska Veterans Memorial is in place at Milepost 147.5 of the George Parks Highway between Anchorage and Fairbanks, south of Denali National Park. Five upright concrete slabs honor Alaskans of all wars who served with the Army, Marine Corps, Navy, Air Force and Coast Guard.

Fort Richardson Cemetery

ALL PHOTOS COURTESY LYMAN WOODMAN, ANCHORAGE, ALASKA

During a training cruise in July 1967, officers and men of the Japanese Maritime Self-Defense Force participated in a memorial service at the Japanese grave site.

JAPANESE SOLDIERS

TERABAYASHI CHICKAYASHI	TAKEHARU FUKUDA
TAKAHASHI GOICHI	ICHIRO HASHIMOTO
KUBO HISAHARU	EDA JINICHI
SEKIKAWA KICHIO	TATEMATSU KOKI
HATANAKA MANZO	MORI SHIGEAHARU
MORITA SHINZO	KIMIZUKA SHOJI
GENTARO TOKUNAGA	OKONOGI TOSHIANU
HIRABASHI TUSKASA	MURAKAMI TUSTOMU
ODAGAWA USHIZO	EIKICHI YAMADA

TWO HUNDRED AND SEVENTEEN UNKNOWN

ALL PHOTOS COURTESY LYMAN WOODMAN
ANCHORAGE, ALASKA

JOHN
WHITEFORD
TOMLINSON
PILOT OFFICER
ROYAL CANADIAN
AIR FORCE
DECEMBER 20 1921
MARCH 28 1943

PETER
POSHTAR
PVT
WINNIPEG
GRENADIERS
CANADIAN ARMY
FEBRUARY 12 1920
AUGUST 22 1943

KERMIT
ROOSEVELT
NEW YORK
MAJOR HQ ALASKAN
DEFENSE COMD
WORLD WAR II
OCTOBER 10 1889
JUNE 4 1943

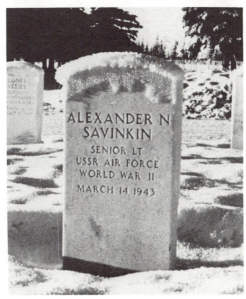

ALEXANDER N
SAVINKIN
SENIOR LT
USSR AIR FORCE
WORLD WAR II
MARCH 14 1943

Atka Remains

The village of Atka as it looks today.

The dock constructed by the Army in 1943.

Submarine net floats.

Airfield strip remains.

Fuel barrel dump.

Great Sitkin Island in 1983. The Sand Bay area was a fuel and ammunition depot. Numerous bunkers were built into the sides of the valley running approximately one mile north into the Fox Creek Valley. The two adjacent valleys to the southeast hold about 37 fuel storage tanks. A large pier, now mostly destroyed, provided berths for the tankers to off-load fuel.

ALL PHOTOS COURTESY CAPT. N.G. TERRY, JR.

P-40 remains at Dutch Harbor.

World War II Army barracks at Skagway, Alaska.
COURTESY KERMIT EDMONDS, MISSOULA, MONTANA

There are no wartime remains on St. Paul Island in the Pribilof Island group except these depressions in the tundra from old hut or tent sites that housed the few soldiers on the island for a short time.

Fort Richardson soldiers celebrate V-J Day in Anchorage.
ASL

1981 (top) and 1983 (bottom) reunions of O Company, 37th Infantry at Astoria, Oregon.
COURTESY LAWRENCE WHITE, MINNEAPOLIS, MINNESOTA

1987 reunion of the 341st Engineers in Champaign, Illinois. The 341st worked on the Alcan Highway.
COURTESY CARL LINDLEY, DANVILLE, ILLINOIS

The Algonquin

The *Algonquin*, a steam and sailing ship, was built in 1898 and used for years in Bering Sea patrol work. During the war it was converted to the U.S. Navy ship YAG29. It was used to supply military outposts up and down the Aleutian chain and to Seward, Cordova and Kodiak. Up until the time it had radar installed, its biggest problem was keeping itself from being beached due to poor charts and extreme weather conditions. These weather conditions are evident in these icy photographs.

ALL PHOTOS COURTESY ART JONES, SEQUIM, WASHINGTON

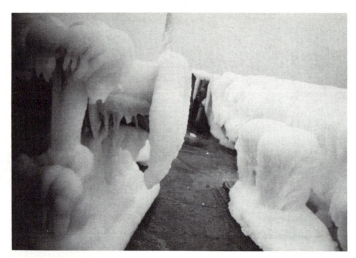

The Princeton Hall

The *Princeton Hall* was built in 1941 by the Presbyterian Church at its Sheldon Jackson School in Sitka. She replaced the earlier mission boat, the *Princeton*, which was lost on a reef in 1938. A family named Hall contributed to the construction of the boat, which began in 1940, and was honored in the name of *Princeton Hall*. Shortly after she was launched in December 1941, the Navy appropriated the *Princeton Hall*. During the war, the boat was painted gray and a "P1" was painted on her bow. There are varying reports that she was used as a minesweeper to lead boats through the minefields in Icy Straits, that she carried prisoners to Excursion Inlet, and that she was run aground and taken to Seattle for repairs. In 1944 the *Princeton Hall* was returned to the Presbyterian Church and operated as a mission boat for 15 years, ferrying people from village to village in Southeast. She carried ministers, choirs and basketball teams. In 1958, the church purchased the *Anna Jackman* for its village ministry, and the *Princeton Hall* passed into private ownership. She is now being operated as a charter boat for week-long trips around Admiralty Island. COURTESY BILL AND KATHY RUDDY, JUNEAU, ALASKA

In naval service as P1 Patrol
1942-44. COURTESY LESLIE YAW

The *Princeton Hall* as a charter boat.

UNITED STATES AND CANADIAN AERIAL VICTORIES, ALEUTIAN CAMPAIGN

DATE	NAME	UNIT	CR	A/C FLOWN	A/C DESTROYED	REMARKS
3 Jun 42	2Lt Jacob W. Dixon	11FS	1/2	P-40	Dave	1
3 Jun 42	1Lt John B. Murphy	11FS	1/2	P-40	Dave	1
4 Jun 42	2Lt John J. Cape, Jr.	11FS	1	P-40	Zero	2
4 Jun 42	2Lt Lester M. Chancellor	11FS	1	P-40	Val	3
4 Jun 42	2Lt James A. Dale	11FS	1	P-40	Val	
4 Jun 42	2Lt Herbert C. White, Jr.	11FS	1	P-40	Val	
4 Aug 42	2Lt Kenneth W. Ambrose	54FS	1	P-38	Mavis	4
4 Aug 42	2Lt Stanley A. Long	54FS	1	P-38	Mavis	
13 Sep 42	1Lt Frederick E. McCoy	54FS	1	P-38	Rufe	
14 Sep 42	1Lt Gene L. Arth	42FS	1	P-39	Jake	
14 Sep 42	2Lt Wintow E. Matthews	42FS	1	P-39	Rufe	
25 Sep 42	Lt Col John S. Chennault	11FS	1	P-40	Rufe	
25 Sep 42	Sq Ldr Kenneth A. Boomer	11FS	1	P-40	Rufe	5
28 Sep 42	Maj Milton H. Ashkins	54FS	1	P-38	Rufe	
28 Sep 42	Capt Arthur T. Rice	57FS	2	P-39	Rufe	
2 Oct 42	1Lt James R. Burgett III	56FS	1	P-39	Rufe	6
2 Oct 42	Capt Kenneth E. George	42FS	1	P-39	Rufe	
2 Oct 42	1Lt Cecil A. Thomas	42FS	1	P-39	Rufe	
3 Oct 42	2Lt George Laven, Jr.	54FS	1/2	P-38	Jake	
3 Oct 42	1Lt Victor E. Walton	54FS	1/2	P-38	Jake	
3 Oct 42	Capt Louis H. Bowman	42FS	1	P-39	Jake	
3 Oct 42	Capt Pat M. Deberry	42FS	1	P-39	Jake	
3 Oct 42	Capt Robert L. McDonald	54FS	1	P-38	Rufe	
3 Oct 42	1Lt Frank A. Beagle	57FS	1	P-39	Jake	7
13 Feb 43	Capt Morgan A. Giffin	54FS	1	P-38	Jake	
13 Feb 43	1Lt Francis A. Evans	54FS	1-1/2	P-38	Rufe	
13 Feb 43	Capt George Laven, Jr.	54FS	1-1/2	P-38	Rufe	
18 Feb 43	Maj Clayton J. Larson	18FS	1	P-40	Rufe	
18 Feb 43	1Lt Elmer J. Stone	18FS	1	P-40	Rufe	
23 May 43	2Lt Harry C. Higgins	54FS	1	P-38	Betty	
23 May 43	1Lt Frederick Moore, Jr.	54FS	3	P-38	Betty	
23 May 43	Lt Col James R. Watt	343FG	1	P-38	Betty	8

REMARKS:

1. The aircraft shot down, according to one U.S. source, was a type 95 bi-plane (Dave). Probably Dave or Alf. The Japanese had both types during the Dutch Harbor attack.

2. Lt Cape was given credit for a Zero. He in turn was shot down and killed by another Zero. Cape AAF at Umnak was named after him.

3. U.S. sources claim that three "Stuka type dive bombers" were shot down by three other lieutenants. Commander Kesatake Okumiya, air officer on the aircraft carrier Ryujo during the Dutch Harbor attack, claims the Japanese lost two Zeros and two Vals.

4. First P-38 aerial victory of World War II.

5. Squadron Leader Boomer, Commander Number 111 Fighter Squadron, RCAF and other Canadian pilots were attached to the 11FS for operations during the period. He was also credited with aerial victories over German, Japanese and Italian aircraft.

6. On detached duty with 42FS from 56FS.

7. On detached duty with 42FS from 57FS.

8. Colonel More, commander, 343FS, was killed in the engagement.

Commanders of the Eleventh Air Force

Lt. Col. Everett S. Davis*	15 Jan 42-16 Feb 42
Col. Lionel H. Dunlap*	17 Feb 42-7 Mar 42
Maj. Gen. William O. Butler	8 Mar 42-10 Sep 43
Brig. Gen. Robert V. Ignico*	11 Sep 43-12 Sep 43
Maj. Gen. Davenport Johnson	13 Sep 43-3 May 45
Brig. Gen. Isaiah Davies*	4 May 45-21 Jun 45
Maj. Gen. John B. Brook	22 Jun 45-17 Dec 45

*Interim commander.

INDEX

Bibliography

Cloe, John Haile, *The Air Force in Alaska, Part I, Early Flights and Strategic Importance, 1920-1940*, Alaskan Air Command, Elmendorf AFB, Alaska, 1983.

_____, *The Air Force in Alaska, Part II, Buildup to Dutch Harbor, June 1940-June 1942*, Alaskan Air Command, Elmendorf AFB, Alaska. 1986.

_____, *Top Cover for America, The Air Force in Alaska 1920-1983*, Pictorial Histories Publishing Co., Missoula, Montana, 1984.

Coates, Kenneth, *The Alaska Highway, Papers of the 40th Anniversary Symposium*, University of British Columbia Press, Vancouver, 1985.

Garfield, Brian, *The Thousand Mile War, World War II in Alaska and the Aleutians*, Ballantine Books, New York, 1969.

The Infantry Journal, *The Capture of Attu, As Told by the Men Who Fought There*, The War Department, Washington, 1944.

Jordan, George Racey, *Major Jordan's Diaries*, Harcourt Brace Jovanovich Co., New York, 1952.

McDonald, Lucile, *Alaska Steam, A Pictorial History of the Alaska Steamship Company*, Vol. II, No. 4, Alaska Geographic Society, Anchorage, 1984.

Mills, Stephan, *Arctic War Planes, Alaska Aviation of WWII*, Bonanza Books, New York, 1978.

Morgan, Lael, *The Aleutians*, Alaska Northwest Publishing Co., Edmonds, Washington, 1980.

Prince, Bernadine, *The Alaska Railroad, Vols. I & II*, Ken Wray Printing, Anchorage, 1964.

Remley, David, *Crooked Road, The Story of the Alaska Highway*, McGraw-Hill Co., New York, 1976.

Scrivner, Charles L., *The Empire Express*, Historical Aviation Album, Temple City, California, 1976.

Torrey, Barbara Boyle, *Slaves of the Harvest*, TDX Corporation, St. Paul Island, Alaska, 1978.

Unalaska High School Students, *The Aleutian Invasion, World War Two in the Aleutian Islands*, Unalaska City School District, Alaska, 1981.

_____, *The Unknown Islands, Life and Tales of Henry Swanson*, Unalaska City School District, Alaska, 1982.

About the Author

The Forgotten War, Volume II was written by Stan Cohen, who in the last eight years has been deeply involved in the study of World War II history in Alaska and Canada. He is a native of West Virginia and a graduate geologist from West Virginia University with two summers of geologic work in Alaska in the early 1960s. From this brief work period, he became fascinated with the history of Alaska. Since entering the publishing business in 1976, he has written or published 14 history books on Alaska and the Yukon. He maintains offices in Missoula, Montana and Charleston, West Virginia and has written 35 books and published a total of 100. He is now at work on Volume III of *The Forgotten War* plus other Alaska/Yukon history books.